Business Finance

Business Finance

B K R Watts

Principal Lecturer, Thames Valley University

Seventh Edition

THE M & E HANDBOOK SERIES

Pitman Publishing
128 Long Acre, London WC2E 9AN

A Division of Longman Group UK Limited

First published as *Industry and Finance* 1971
Second edition published as *Business and Financial Management* 1975
Third edition 1978
Fourth edition 1981
Fifth edition 1984
Sixth edition 1988
Seventh edition published as *Business Finance* 1994

© Macdonald & Evans Ltd 1994
© Longman Group UK Ltd 1994

British Library Cataloguing in Publication Data
A CIP catalogue record for this book can be obtained from the British Library.

ISBN 0 7121 1050 X

Founding Editor: P W D Redmond

Typeset by ROM-Data Corporation Ltd, Falmouth, Cornwall
Printed and bound in Singapore

Contents

Preface to the seventh edition

This book under its new title (it was formerly *Business and Financial Management*) is intended for students preparing for the Diploma in Management Studies examinations and those Institute of Chartered Accountants, Association of Chartered and Certified Accountants and Chartered Institute of Management Accountants' examinations which require a detailed knowledge of a wide range of subjects relating to business and financial management. In addition, it will certainly be of value to students taking other examinations at intermediate or final level, in particular those of the Chartered Institute of Bankers, Institute of Chartered Secretaries and Administrators, Higher National Certificates and Diplomas, Institute of Administrative Management, CNAA degrees in Business Studies, as well as for practising managers who wish further to develop their understanding of finance. Furthermore it has proved to be valuable as a working text and supplementary reading on in-company finance courses for middle and senior managers.

This *Handbook* is derived from the author's lecturing and consultancy experience, and the material is selected to help students studying for financial and accounting examinations and for the non-financial managers who need to understand the terminology of accountancy to break down the mystique that tends to surround the subject.

For the seventh edition the chapters have been rewritten to incorporate the many developments since 1987. Effective business planning, monitoring and control have proved to be of crucial importance to so many businesses during the recession years of the 1990s. For these reasons, a range of practical budgeting techniques and handy commercial formulae for managers is covered, which will help the decision maker who needs to consider the options available to secure desired targets and identify the key performance indicators in the areas for which he/she is responsible.

Methods of study
This *Handbook* will be of value to students for revision purposes since

the essentials of business and financial management are here combined under one cover. However, it is not intended to be an exhaustive textbook, for no single book can cover the demanding requirements of the final professional examination syllabuses in adequate scope and depth.

Students are advised to read quickly through the Chapter and section headings and the numbered paragraph headings to get an overall picture of the contents. Then they should read through each section in sequence. The Progress Tests at the end of each chapter are for self-examination and revision.

Keeping up to date

No textbook can tell final-level students all they need to know or replace the students' own judgment; if they find it difficult to master any section they should not hesitate to refer to other books on the subject, particularly those on the recommended reading list. Students must keep up to date with current developments and, in particular, they are advised to read *The Financial Times*, *The Times Business Supplement*, *The Economist* and, of course, the appropriate professional magazines. It is also a good idea for students to collect relevant press cuttings for future reference. Students will find that by diligent reading, by keeping up to date, by drawing from their own professional and business experience and by working through these study notes, they will build up a considerable fund of knowledge and should have no difficulty in meeting examination requirements.

Part one
The structure of industry

1
The firm and industry

The concept of industry

1. The establishment or plant
This is the business premises at a particular address. Since it is readily identifiable, it serves as a basis for official statistics.

2. The firm
The accountant regards the firm as an unincorporated business whereas the economist, recognising this legal distinction, regards a firm as the 'planning unit' where economic decisions are taken, e.g. what is to be produced, in what quantities and qualities and how. Frequently the firm coincides with the plant; however, large-scale industry is made up of multi-plant firms in a variety of organizational structures.

The firm, in carrying out its day-to-day activities, requires an organizational support appropriate to the scale and range of its operations. Capital must be raised, personnel employed and trained, equipment purchased and serviced, and these must be organized to ensure that they are available in the correct combinations at the right time and the right place.

An insight into the complex nature of the operation may be gained by considering an input–output model which assumes the firm to be a converter of resources, i.e. it receives a variety of resources which it converts into outputs. The respective resources and their suppliers are shown in Figure 1.1.

Figure 1.2 illustrates the concept that the firm is a converter of

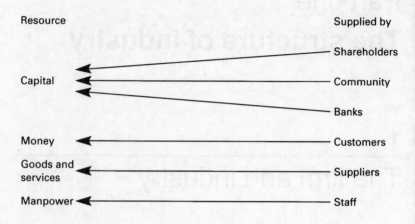

Figure 1.1 *Resources and their suppliers*

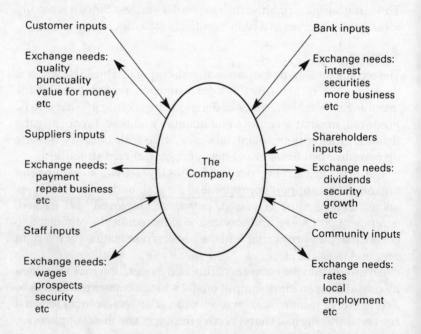

Figure 1.2 *The firm as a converter of resources*

resources; it receives resources, and coordinates and converts them into end products, but at a cost, which may or may not be monetary.

Thus the business unit is a complex organization: it is continuously using resources contributed by a variety of parties, whose interests and exchange needs may be divergent. Management, of course, is charged with the task of pursuing corporate objectives, but in doing so must recognise that it is dealing with a coalition of interests. It should consider the respective contributions and costs of the resources, and coordinate them to keep inputs and outputs in balance for the mutual benefit of all. If it fails in the task then the firm will not survive.

Much more than money is involved in this exchange process – job satisfaction, esteem, etc. – but most of the need requirements we have considered involve financial costs: product quality for the customer and a pollution-free environment for the community incur costs, less easily quantifiable, but monetary costs nevertheless. Consequently, management should pay particular attention to the financial aspects of the resource conversion process, measuring and comparing the values of inputs and outputs, substituting for more cost effective inputs where possible.

3. The industrial group
This occurs where a single firm exercises financial and policy control over other firms, e.g. GEC, the UK industrial group. In 1993 it employed 138 000 workers and had a group turnover of £9.41bn.

The principal group activities are Electronic Systems, Power Systems, Telecoms, Consumer Goods, Electronic Metrology, Office Equipment, and Medical Equipment. These activities are carried out by divisions of the GEC company and its many subsidiary and associated companies. Each one is run by a director, but ultimate authority rests with the GEC board consisting of executive and non-executive directors who formulate overall objectives and strategies for the group. The Annual Report states: 'We will continue to exercise the style of management which has been proven over many years.'

4. The financial group
This exists where a parent company exercises financial control over a number of otherwise autonomous subsidiaries. A frequently cited example is Hanson Trust which was created in 1964 when Wiles Group Ltd obtained a quotation on the London Stock Exchange and changed its name to Hanson Trust in 1969. Hanson is a conglomerate well known for its acquisitions, with widespread interests in construction, brick making, animal feedstuff, machinery, etc. Such

extensive diversification makes intervention by the parent company in the day-to-day management in its subsidiaries impracticable. It applies close financial control with the emphasis on positive cash flow and strict control of capital employed whilst allowing operational and local management a free hand.

5. The joint venture

This is where two or more companies co-operate to overcome a common problem or exploit a market opportunity. They may establish a jointly owned company, as, for example, when ICI and DuPont took equal shares in a new company to tackle the European car paint market.

6. The cartel

This is a defensive arrangement where companies agree to limit individual freedom regarding output, price and capacity. The cartel tends, however, to be short-lived as success depends on the loyalty of its members and this cannot be guaranteed for ever. Ambitious members may find the restrictions frustrating, while any success in maintaining high prices will induce members to exceed their quotas. Since 1945 monopoly and restrictive-practice legislation has in any case limited the scope for collusion.

7. The need for industrial classification

Firms and plants need to be classified for the following variety of reasons:

(a) Similar firms wish to associate because they:
  (*i*) produce similar goods;
  (*ii*) employ similar techniques;
  (*iii*) employ similar types of labour; or
  (*iv*) have common interests.

Through their trade association, an interchange of information helps them overcome their common problems and advance their interests in negotiations with unions and the Government.
(b) Economists require information to advance theories and examine industrial problems.
(c) The State needs information for control and economic planning, e.g.:
  (*i*) the National Plan set targets and outlined the main problems facing specific industries;

(*ii*) The Regional Employment Premium was based on industrial classifications.

8. Methods of classifying industries
The task of classifying industry is made difficult by its diversity and its tendency to change. Ideally, an industry consists of a group of firms producing identical products, which they sell in the same market, all with a common technology and labour types. However, the immense variety within industry makes this criterion impracticable and a more sophisticated classification in terms of products, resources and activities may be thought necessary. Thus an industrial group may be demarcated by:

(a) products (e.g. vehicle and aircraft industries);
(b) raw materials (e.g. rubber and chemical industries); or
(c) processes (e.g. spinning and weaving industries).

9. Indicators to industrial groupings
The various trade associations provide a guide to industrial groups (e.g. the Society of British Aircraft Manufacturers), although many vertical amalgamations (e.g. the Society of Motor Manufacturers and Traders) and lateral mergers of product associations make trade association membership a less meaningful indicator of narrow industrial classes.

10. Standard Industrial Classification
By using the Standard Industrial Classification (SIC), produced in 1948, the Government secures uniformity and comparability in official statistics on production, distribution and employment, etc.

The SIC consists of 'establishments', classified into industries according to their principal activities or products, so that if the Government requires statistics on production or employment in a particular industry it can survey the establishments of that classification. Clearly the 'firm' is too imprecise to be the unit of industrial analysis because a firm may own or control many establishments specialising in different trades.

It consists of seventeen major industrial groups (A to Q). These are divided into subsections (each denoted by the addition of a second letter). Then these are broken down into divisions (denoted by two digits), which are further broken down into groups (three digits). Further subsections are classes (four digits) and subclasses (five digits).

Example _____

Group Section D
Manufacturing (comprising divisions 15 to 37).

Subsection DB
Manufacture of textiles and textile products (divisions 17, 18)

Division 17   Manufacture of textiles
Group 17.4   Manufacture of made-up textile articles, except apparel
Class 17.40   Manufacture of made-up textile articles, except apparel
Subclass
     17.40/1 This includes:
               Manufacture of soft finished articles of any textile material
               including of knitted or crocheted fabrics e.g. cushions,
               pouffes, pillows.

The size of firms

11. Criteria for measuring size of firm
Several criteria are available for measuring the size of firms:

(a) *Output*. If statistics of output volumes are available, they provide a satisfactory guide to the size of firms, but only when firms are producing similar goods.

Value-of-output figures (quantity produced multiplied by price) permit comparisons between firms whose products are more dissimilar, but they are less satisfactory for comparisons between industries, where values are certain to reflect differences in costs and market forces.

(b) *Raw materials*. The consumption of raw materials in real or money terms indicates the relative sizes of firms, but the same limitations apply as for **(a)**.

(c) *Employees*. The numbers on the payroll are commonly used, although it should be noted that not all companies publish details and this method neglects other factors, particularly capital, which is more important in capital-intensive industries (e.g. petroleum and chemicals). Nor does it distinguish between types of workers and skills.

(d) *Capital*. This standard is widely used for inter-firm comparisons. Capital employed is the most useful measure since it is supplied by all companies. It may be either:

    (*i*) gross capital employed (i.e. the value of fixed and current assets); or

Table 1A *Large British companies ranked by size (various criteria) 1991*

Company	Activity	Sales £m	Rank	Assets £m	Rank	Employees	Rank
Shell	Oil	74 435	1	56 435	1	133 000	2
BP	Oil	41 267	2	28 955	2	115 250	4
Unilever	Food	23 163	3	13 484	4	298 000	1
ICI	Chemicals	12 488	4	10 830	5	128 600	3
BAT	Tobacco	13 817	5	27 652	3	105 855	5

Source: Handbook of Market Leaders

(*ii*) net capital employed (i.e. the value of fixed and current assets less current liabilities). Even so, this method may understate the relative importance of a highly labour-intensive firm.

(e) *Profits.* Profit figures are provided by all companies but are less suitable as a consistent yardstick because of their volatile nature.

(f) *Market capitalization.* This is a possible method of judging, although it is impracticable for consistent comparisons between firms because it is volatile and eliminates the several large private companies and British subsidiaries of foreign companies.

The relative size of a firm will depend on the criteria adopted, so that a firm highly ranked on one basis may be lower ranked and seemingly less important on another. However, any disparity is un-important, for a firm is certain to be either large, medium, or small whatever basis is used.

12. What is a small firm?

Although definition is necessarily arbitrary, the small firm may be indicated by turnover, the number of employees and balance sheet totals.

For example, the Companies Act 1989 defines small and medium-sized companies in the following ways.

	Small company	Medium-sized company
(a) Turnover not exceeding	£2m	£8m
(b) Balance sheet total not exceeding	£975 000	£3.9m
(c) Average number of employees not exceeding	50	250

A private company which satisfies two of these three conditions is exempt from the full legal requirements for published accounts. A qualifying small company need file with the Registrar of Companies only an abridged balance-sheet; a medium-sized company need not supply details of turnover and gross profit margins in its returns to the Registrar. However, companies must still present unmodified accounts to shareholders.

It is interesting to note that a small company as defined by the Companies Act 1989 is large by comparison with other standards. For example CoSIRA (Council for Small Industries in Rural Areas) provides assistance to businesses employing not more than twenty skilled people.

It has been estimated that enterprises employing less than 20 people accounted for 35 per cent of non-Government employment, up from 27 per cent in 1979. (Small firms in Britain report 1992.)

13. Reasons for the survival of the small firm
Although the mortality rate is high for small firms, they survive in large numbers as a group for the following reasons:

(a) The optimum size of firm (i.e. the best or most efficient firm which has lowest production costs per unit of output), may be small in an industry because:

(*i*) technical process may favour small scale, e.g. power looms in weaving.

(*ii*) the market may be small if customers prefer personal services and variety, rather than impersonal, large-scale organizations and standardized products.

(b) There may be the following obstacles to further growth:

(*i*) Difficulties of raising finance for expansion.

(*ii*) Active competition or restrictive practices or monopoly legislation.

(*iii*) The lack of ambition, self-interest or managerial ambition of the original entrepreneur.

(*iv*) Many small firms are content with the non-monetary advantages of independence and prestige.

(*v*) Risks increase with growth; further growth may become unacceptable to the management.

(*vi*) Administration may become less efficient because of inertia and low morale.

(c) Industry is not static and a small size is a transitory stage between 'birth', large-scale success and 'death'.

(*i*) There seems to be an unlimited supply of would-be entrepreneurs possessing experience and capital who are prepared to start in business on a modest scale. Many eventually succeed to a large extent.

(*ii*) Unsuccessful firms decline and are eventually wound up.

The age of the company seems to be an important factor in survival. This can be seen from the following breakdown.

	Percentage of new companies that fail		
	0–1 year	1–3 years	0–10 years
Percentage	10	30	60

This shows that only 40 per cent of new businesses are still trading after ten years.

14. Are small firms needed?
Small firms may be defended on the following grounds:

(a) They are frequent sources of new products and processes (i.e. they are inventive).
(b) New firms have initiative and ambition and stimulate industry.
(c) They are more flexible than larger firms and react quickly and less violently to the activities of the market and Governments, with less effect on, say, employment, or production.
(d) They perform tasks unsuited to large-scale industry often more efficiently.

15. Problems facing small firms
The main areas where assistance is needed are as follows:

(a) Management and accounting techniques for staff and consultancy services.
(b) Sources and methods of finance.
(c) Marketing assistance in modern techniques, and assistance in exporting, purchasing and stock control techniques.
(d) General information, e.g. interpretation of statistics and legislation in non-technical language.
(e) Introduction of positive discrimination towards small companies in public-procurement policies to benefit small businesses.

16. Advice agencies for small businesses
Successful lobbying by small businesses throughout the 1970s, for greater Government help to overcome the 'knowledge gap', created a more favourable climate of support for small businesses, as follows:

(a) The Department of Trade and Industry's Small Firms Service was established to provide free information on a wide range of subjects from sources of supply to Government legislation through its Small Firm Centre shops located in most major cities. They also operated as forwarding agents, putting people in touch with experienced business people who may have faced similar problems, or directing enquiries to the appropriate institutions.

(*i*) In Scotland the Small Firms Service is provided by the Scottish Development Agency.

(*ii*) In Wales the Welsh Office provide an information service: counselling is administered by the Welsh Development Agency.

(*iii*) In Northern Ireland an information service is provided by the Local Enterprise Development Unit.

(b) Local Enterprise Agencies (LEAs) were established in 1981 to complement the work of the Small Firms Service. The 300 LEAs are usually run by business people, bankers and other professionals seconded for a few years by the companies or local authorities sponsoring the local scheme. In addition to providing advice, an LEA can assess the viability of schemes submitted to it and bring together individuals who are looking for companies to invest in and companies looking for finance.

(c) The Rural Development Commission was created in 1988 by bringing together into a single agency the Development Commission and the Council for Small Industries in Rural Areas (CoSIRA). Its role is to provide advice, training and finance to firms and so to help regenerate rural areas. Similar services to rural businesses are offered elsewhere in the United Kingdom: in Wales by the Welsh Development Agency; in Scotland by the Scottish Development Agency; in Northern Ireland by the Local Enterprise Development Unit.

(d) The Training Commission provides a comprehensive range of training programmes for small businesses. The main courses are:

(*i*) The Business Enterprise Programme – a free training course which covers business structure, sources of finance and sales forecasting.

(*ii*) The Private Enterprise Programme – free for new businesses and covers finding new products, marketing and managing growth.

(*iii*) Firmstart – designed for existing but growing businesses.

(*iv*) The Graduate Gateway Programme – gives new graduates 15 weeks' experience in small firms.

17. Sources of capital for small businesses
Small businesses have always found difficulty in raising capital for start-up and expansion purposes. The basic reason for this is that the

provider of capital realises the very high risks associated with investing in small businesses (30 per cent fail in the first two years), and so demands a very high return on an equity investment, or sufficient collateral to safeguard a loan, to compensate for those risks.

This risk-return relationship is shown in Fig. 1.3.

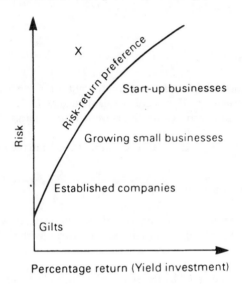

Figure 1.3 *Risk-return relationship*

This shows that investors are generally prepared to accept the lowest return for a riskless investment in government gilts and a higher return for riskier investments in established companies, but demand progressively higher returns for growing and start-up business investments. A start-up company whose risk-return is indicated at point X would fail to attract funds since the risk exceeds the investors' perceived risk-return preference.

However, in 1993 there are literally hundreds of sources of capital for small businesses. The principal sources are:

(a) The Business Expansion Scheme.
(b) Loan Guarantee Schemes.
(c) Banks.
(d) The Unlisted Securities Market. (See Chapter 5 and 6.)

18. Tax allowances and grants to small businesses
The government helps small businesses as follows:

(a) Corporation tax. The rate of tax is reduced for small companies.
(b) The Enterprise Allowance Scheme. This scheme pays £40 per week to unemployed individuals who start up in business.
(c) The Small Engineering Firms Industrial Scheme. Under this scheme companies can claim up to one third of the cost of advanced capital equipment.

Progress test 1

1. 'Large-scale industry is made up of multi-plant firms in a variety of organizational structures.' Comment on this statement. **(1–6)**
(a) Discuss ways in which a cartel differs from a joint venture. **(5–6)**

2. For what reasons are industrial classifications useful to the following?
(a) Firms.
(b) Economists.
(c) Governments. **(7)**

3. Discuss the problems of defining 'an industry' and suggest various criteria which may be used to indicate some industries with which you are familiar. **(8)**

4. What do you understand by the Standard Industrial Classification and what problems does such a classification overcome? **(10)**

5. Compare and contrast the various criteria for measuring the size of firms. **(11–12)**
(a) What do you consider the most pertinent criteria for measuring the size of firms? **(11–12)**

6. How do you account for the survival of the small firm? **(13)**

7. Outline the main problem areas and difficulties facing the small firm. **(15)**
(a) Of the factors for small firm survival discussed in 15, which do you think were the most crucial to the record-breaking number of company insolvencies in Great Britain in the 1990s? **(15)**

8. Outline the role of advice agencies for small businesses. **(16–18)**

2

Economies of scale

1. Sources of economies of scale

The pattern of industrial concentration and the continuing trend towards larger plant capacities and firms may be explained by the following factors:

(a) *Internal economies of scale*:

(*i*) Economies of large-scale plant or economies of large outputs, i.e. technical economies which reduce unit costs of production at high levels of output (*see* **2–7**).

(*ii*) Economies of large-scale organizations, i.e. general economies which reduce unit costs of goods in large-sized organizations (*see* **8–12**).

(b) *External economies of scale*. These are economies enjoyed by large and small firms that arise from the large size, growth or concentration of the industry (*see* **13** and **14**).

Economies of large-scale plant

2. Introduction

If factors of production (i.e. materials, labour and capital) are increased by, say, x per cent, then total output in a large-capacity plant may increase by more than x per cent. The extent of these economies depends on the technological nature of individual industries. The processing industries, for example, employ methods of production which realise considerable savings in unit costs of production when large outputs are handled, while other industries (e.g. the textile and clothing industries) necessarily employ different technologies which cannot effect such savings. However, a technological principle can be identified in all productive operations. Larger plants tend to be more efficient than smaller plants up to a certain level of output.

It is possible to identify the factors responsible for these savings, as follows:

(a) Certain processes require proportionally fewer factors of production for a given output (*see* **3**).

(b) Other processes involve factors of production which are less than perfectly subdivisible (*see* **6**).

3. Non-proportional inputs and outputs

Certain processes require proportionally less inputs for a given output.

(a) Economies of scale operate when demand is random. For example, a small-scale TV rental firm employing a maintenance electrician may discover that he or she is working below capacity, but because TV sets break down at random, his or her services will be demanded more frequently and eventually continuously as the firm's scale of operation increases. Evidently, the cost of maintenance does not increase in proportion to the number of installations.

(b) A firm may be using a process which benefits from the mathematical relationships between length, area and volume.

Example _____

	Building A	Building B
Perimeter	120 m	240 m
	(i.e. length and breadth	(i.e. dimensions are
	is 30 m)	doubled)
Area	900 m^2	3600 m^2
		(i.e. area is quadrupled)

Apparently construction costs per square metre are reduced, as total costs are unlikely to increase in proportion to area. However, in practice builders quote a standard price per square metre, perhaps to subsidize smaller, less economic projects and to insure against contingencies of idle time, wastage, etc.

4. Economies of scale

Economies of scale exist when larger-scale plant results in lower unit costs. An example is found in Watford Refrigeration's brochure *Watford Portable Cold Stores*. The brochure gives the price of single-compartment cold stores designed to operate at $-20°C$.

Model number	724	730	1 134	1 130
Cubic capacity				
(cubic metres)	25	32	44	57

Price	£9 585	£10 064	£12 836	£13 624
Operating costs:				
kW/day				
(estimated)	6.7	6.9	9.2	12.0
Calculations:				
Capital cost/				
cubic metre	£383.4	£314.5	£291.7	£239.0
Operating cost/	0.27 kW/	0.21 kW/	0.21 kW/	0.21 kW/
cubic metre	day	day	day	day

The table shows that for an additional £479 a purchaser of a 730 unit obtains an additional 7 cubic metres of storage capacity compared with a 724 unit; consequently, the cost per cubic metre falls from £383.4 to £314.5, a significant economy of scale which operates throughout the range of units.

5. Economies in operating costs
In addition, the larger-scale units provide savings in running costs. Thus the 730 unit saves 0.06 kW-day over the 724 model and results from the fact that larger-scale plant requires a less than proportionate amount of electrical power to operate.

6. Indivisibility of factors of production
Production may be more efficient on a large scale because some factors of production cannot be varied in proportion to output, as follows:

(a) The principal factor in the production process may not be subdivisible. This is particularly true of heavy plant, which some industries require in large units for efficient operation. For example, a manufacturer incurs a considerable yet non-repeating expense when he installs a press which will later realize economies in the form of reducing fixed costs per unit of output over long production runs, thus:

Fixed cost – one press machine	£100 000
Fixed cost per pressing if 1 produced	£100 000
Fixed cost per pressing if 100 produced	£1 000
Fixed cost per pressing if 1000 produced	£100

(b) There may be several plants of different capacities which are not subdivisible. In these cases, production is most efficient when all plants are fully utilized, i.e. when the optimum rate of throughput is equal to the lowest common multiple of their capacities. Imagine a production process which consists of three activities:

(*i*)	(*ii*)	(*iii*)	(*iv*)
	Capacity	*No. of*	*Total outputs per*
Operation	*per hour*	*factors*	*hour (LCM)*
Pressing	20	20 presses	400
Machining	16	25 lathes	400
Packing	25	16 packers	400

Here the optimum rate of production is 400 units per hour, with no idle time for machinery or packers, so that, ideally, the number of machines and packers indicated in column (*iii*) should be employed. However, in practice some other combination may be employed for the following reason:

(*i*) Reserve machinery is necessary in the event of breakdowns and extra personnel in case of absenteeism. But the choice and number of reserves will depend on the anticipated workload, their comparative costs and their versatility. Usually, occupational mobility varies inversely with specialization; general-purpose equipment can usually perform a number of operations, unlike specialized equipment. On the other hand, efficiency usually increases with specialization, so that a firm is forced to compromise between the conflicting objectives of flexibility and efficiency when dealing with the problem of factor combinations and reserves.

(*ii*) Firms may be unable to afford the optimum number of machines. Instead, they may concentrate on one process, buying semi-finished goods outside and selling or subcontracting their output to specialists.

(c) Specialist employees are not subdivisible, as they each have work capacities. For instance, designers and accountants may be under-employed initially when the scale of activity is low, but, as the firm expands, workloads increase to realize economies in the form of lower salary costs per unit of output.

This is true also of any team of specialists. A design group is to some extent an indivisible unit, so that if one member leaves a team of three then the firm may well lose more than 33 per cent of its results.

7. Limitations of economies of scale
However, 'bigness is not always best'. There are circumstances where companies hold back on expenditure for larger-scale plant or equipment and where small companies manage to survive. Examples are as follows.

(a) Large-scale plant takes longer to build and frequently raises technological problems. However, a number of smaller-capacity plants, although eventually less efficient, satisfy demand and realise profits in the short term.

(b) If the large-scale plant breaks down, then a big proportion of total capacity is out of commission. Once orders are lost it is difficult to restore goodwill.

(c) Large-scale plant requires a large market for efficient operation. However, although exporting offers a solution, it is the most uncertain and competitive market, especially when there is excess world capacity.

(d) A technically inefficient firm may be protected in its local market by transport costs which will be high for certain products, e.g. bricks.

(e) It may protect itself in the market by appointing exclusive dealers (e.g. tied public-houses) so as to ensure adequate outlets.

(f) Small firms may specialize in one aspect of production, but they may buy knowhow and designs instead of pursuing all the benefits which large-scale organization offers.

Economies of large firms

8. Advantages of large firms
The large organization possesses several advantages over the small firm, e.g. a better calibre of management and staff, power and finance, all of which realize economies.

(a) *Management.* Good managers, who can make correct decisions, delegate responsibility, communicate effectively, select suitable staff and provide leadership, are rare. That this is recognized is shown by the emphasis placed on training in management skills in colleges, business schools and industry.

Large organizations, by the nature of their special problems, need good managers and they are probably better placed to attract them with their offers of superior prospects, salaries, working conditions and fringe benefits (e.g. non-contributory pensions, a company car, etc.). Thus, they can be more selective than small firms in their choice of managers.

The larger organization may also be more conducive to the development of management performance. There are many different departments and subsidiaries which can provide all-round experience and which can enable them to exploit the opportunities offered by inter-group comparisons, to bring the efficiency of the whole up to that of the most efficient unit and thereby to extend the size and market share of the organization.

(b) *Staff*. There are four advantages claimed for the large firm in this respect:

(*i*) Often there is a better chance of success in terms of career prospects and salary in a large organization. A large firm thus has a wide choice of candidates.

(*ii*) Internal appointments avoid the friction and resentment which external appointments often cause.

(*iii*) Company staff records provide useful and perhaps more reliable information than application forms from outsiders.

(*iv*) It may be less costly in terms of salary to promote staff internally. Outsiders generally demand considerable financial compensation for losing their present security and to make up for the difficulties in settling into a strange job.

9. Finance
The large firm has the opportunity of economizing in financial matters, as follows.

(a) *Internal*. Large organizations, whose capital requirements are more stable, have an advantage over smaller ones whose requirements are likely to exceed retained profits.

(b) *External*. Although the minimum charges of issuing houses are high, administration costs do not increase in proportion to the size of issues, so there may be considerable economies for a large issue. Furthermore, an established public company may draw upon existing market goodwill for a successful issue of securities. Smaller firms, on the other hand, may be forced to offer more generous (and expensive terms) to secure the investors' approval.

(c) *Working capital*. Compared with smaller firms, large firms need smaller amounts of working capital in proportion to turnover (although they are larger, of course, in absolute terms).

10. Benefits accruing from finance
The large firm probably has a large cash flow as well, which secures for it the following powerful advantages:

(a) *Risk-spreading*. Large firms have finance available to spread the risks of the market by diversifying their interests. Rather than depending on one product and the vagaries of the market, they may enter new industries possessing ideally counter-cyclical characteristics, e.g. Imperial Tobacco Ltd have interests in the food and cosmetic trades.

(b) *Research.* The large firm is more able to afford expenditure for research. This often leads to new materials, products and processes.

(c) *Development and innovation.* It can also better afford:

(*i*) to develop discoveries for commercial production;

(*ii*) to introduce more efficient methods of production.

Consequently, patent rights and royalties are secured and the firm's overall competitiveness is improved.

(d) *Advertising.* The large firm can better afford expenditure for advertising its products, to build up its market share.

11. Power

It has been suggested that very large companies have 'advantages of power' over the following groups:

(a) *Local Government.*

(b) *The Press.* Large companies are sometimes able to secure sympathetic or preferential treatment.

(c) *Suppliers.* Large firms may be able to secure attractive terms from suppliers, because:

(*i*) lower prices may in part be due to economies in production;

(*ii*) suppliers may be tempted to quote lower prices to keep important customers; or

(*iii*) large-scale customers may use their strong bargaining power to demand lower terms.

(d) *Customers.* After the Second World War, manufacturers' restrictive agreements effectively reduced consumer choice. However, the Restrictive Practices Act 1956 outlawed collective action and, although it permitted resale price maintenance by individual manufacturers, the position changed radically with the Resale Prices Act 1964. Today, RPM has disappeared in the high street. Nevertheless, there is some concern that the present trend towards concentration places greater power in the hands of manufacturers and reduces consumer sovereignty, e.g. the investigation by MPs in 1993 into CD pricing by record companies.

(e) *Employees.* In theory, a monopolist employer can force down wages. However, it is doubtful that this would happen in practice, for there are unlikely to be many monopolist employers within one locality. Abuse of power is unlikely for other reasons, as follows:

(*i*) Trade unions would use their collective power to resist such action.

(*ii*) Such a policy is certain to fail in conditions of high employment. Workers will move elsewhere.

(*iii*) Large firms are anxious to uphold their reputations as good employers. Many have been wage pace-setters for industry and have voluntarily provided additional facilities by way of canteens, social clubs, etc.

12. Disadvantages of large-scale firms
The main problems arising from large organizations are due to:

(a) inertia;
(b) low morale;
(c) poor co-ordination; or
(d) reduced flexibility.

There is a danger within a large organization that workers lose their identity, that conflicts of interest arise between workers or between sections of the firm, that delays in communication increase, and co-ordination deteriorates.

However, it would be a very weak firm which suffered from all these problems at once. Moreover, most large organizations only suffer from them because they use procedural rules which are certain to introduce some inflexibility into their operations. Future policy becomes less flexible since these firms are committed by past decisions (e.g. the location of specific plant will necessarily limit the scope of future company policy).

For this reason, since the Second World War many large British firms have followed the example set by General Motors and have become decentralised. They have been split into virtually independent divisions, each with responsibility for trading and investment policy. Each division is responsible to the main board for general policy only. In this way, decentralisation of authority has helped to overcome the problem of inflexibility in large organizations.

External economies of scale

13. Geographical integration
In areas of localised industrial concentration firms tend to specialise. They concentrate on a limited number of standardised products, processes and services on a larger scale than would be possible outside the localised area. This is due to *external economies of scale*. Firms benefit from limited activities in much the same way that

large integrated firms benefit from internal economies of scale. They operate large-capacity plant, meeting orders from numerous other firms who individually cannot afford to use such plant efficiently. Also, close contact improves production planning and reduces uncertainty and the burden on management, while realising economies in communications and transport. Thus in such areas the tendency is towards localised disintegration by small, efficient specialists.

14. Sources of external economies
Firms making up the Lancashire cotton industry benefit from the proximity of the following:

(a) Local specialist cotton markets.
(b) The skilled labour force.
(c) Specialist machinery manufacturers.
(d) Specialized services.
(e) Research facilities.

Progress test 2

1. Distinguish between internal and external economies of scale and indicate the main economies of large-scale production. **(1)**

2. 'In all types of productive operations, larger plants are always more efficient than smaller plants up to a certain level of output.' Identify and explain the factors responsible for these economies. **(2)**

3. Explain the term 'internal economies of scale' and describe its operation in any one industry with which you are familiar. **(4–5)**

4. Explain with examples what is meant by 'indivisibility' of factors of production and its relevance to the concept of economies of scale. **(6)**

5. A manufacturer employs several machines of different capacities:

Machine A	16 units per hour
Machine B	8 units per hour
Machine C	25 units per hour

What advice can you give him on the optimum rate of throughput and the number of machines of each type? **(6)**

6. For what reasons may a firm be smaller than the optimum size of firm that is indicated by the economies-of-scale principle? **(7)**

7. 'The bigger the better.' Under what conditions is this true of industrial undertakings? **(8–11)**

(a) Describe three sectors of the service industry which you feel offer very few possibilities of economies of scale. **(8–12)**

8. Discuss the advantages and disadvantages of large-scale organizations. **(8–12)**

9. Explain how it is that geographical disintegration realises external economies of scale. **(13)**

(a) Comment on the external economies of scale enjoyed by an organization with which you are familiar. **(13–14)**

3

The integration of economic activities

Integration by administration

1. Types of integration

The various stages of the complete production process (raw material, manufacture and distribution), may be linked by markets or by administration, as follows:

(a) A firm which bridges these markets by controlling the necessary factors (materials, labour, plant and premises) at different stages of production is said to integrate its operations *vertically*:

    (*i*) *backwards*, if it expands to the raw material stage;

    (*ii*) *forwards*, if it expands towards the consumer.

(b) If the firm expands by amalgamating with firms at the same stage of production it integrates *horizontally* (*see* **2**).

(c) If it diversifies into other trades, it integrates laterally (*see* **5** and **6**).

These forms of integration may be visualized as in Fig. 3.1.

2. Horizontal integration

A firm may expand by horizontal integration for offensive motives for the following reasons:

(a) It may desire to absorb its competitors' share of the market and profits.

(b) It may wish to realise the advantages of large-scale plant and organization. It is unlikely that a firm wishing to double its output will need to double its labour force, fixed and working capital, administration, purchasing and selling departments. In this way administration and manufacturing costs per unit of output may be reduced. Efficiencies may be further realized by the employment of specialists in management manpower and equipment and from using maintenance and repair services to capacity.

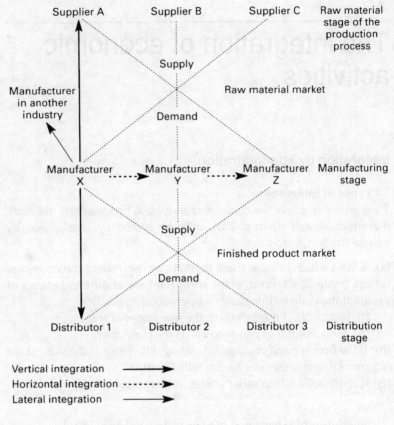

Figure 3.1 *Forms of economic integration*

The optimum size of the firm's technical unit is probably larger than its administrative unit so that economies may be less marked at higher levels of output because of problems of co-ordination and communication in administration and management. Nevertheless, the technical economies are often considerable and are usually sufficient to outweigh uneconomical tendencies elsewhere, especially in process industries and manufacturing industries employing flow-production techniques.

The typical relationship of costs to the size of plant is illustrated in Fig. 3.2. by the curve AC. This shows that economies of scale cause unit costs to decrease until the curve reaches the minimum optimal scale, A, where AC is lowest. If constant returns to scale are then experienced the firm may employ multiples of this scale to secure these minimum unit costs until the maximum optimal scale, B, after which expansion causes diseconomies to set in so that AC rises.

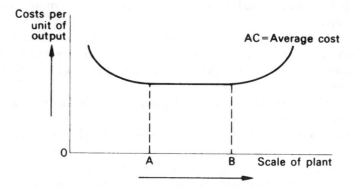

Figure 3.2 *Typical relationship of costs to size of plant*

3. Vertical integration (1)
A firm may expand its operations vertically if it has offensive motives, as follows:

(a) A firm may desire to eliminate the profits of enterprises operating forwards or backwards in the production process.
(b) It may wish to secure economies of scale of non-manufacturing processes. For example, research and development units, production planning, marketing, purchasing and management organizations are less than perfectly divisible and probably have different capacities. But as the principle of multiples shows, common costs of these activities at different stages in the production process are reduced when used to capacity, i.e. they are spread over a larger range of activity, as follows:

(*i*) *Research and development*. The minimum size of unit necessary for significant contributions to knowhow is generally large and expensive, so that R & D are usually the prerogative of large firms who can finance them and utilize them to capacity.
(*ii*) *Production planning*. Efficient production demands efficient production planning. However, difficulties may arise in assembly industries where independent suppliers are linked by the market. Obviously, close liaison between the specialist component producers is essential to decide on job specifications, prices, deliveries

and future development. However, breakdowns in communication do occur, and these may induce firms to bypass the market. They may integrate these operations by administration and build up a team of specialists who collectively can work more effectively.

(*iii*) *Purchasing*. A centralised buying department for a group will realise economies if used to capacity. It may also secure large-order discounts. However, stock-control problems may be aggravated.

(*iv*) *Marketing*. A single selling department will reduce the duplication of effort and costs.

(c) It may wish to secure technical economies of scale. For example, in an integrated steelworks, heat from the blast furnace, which would be otherwise wasted, is used to work the metal into tubes and sheets.

(d) It may wish to control the demands for its product more directly and hence more effectively by bypassing the wholesaler. Large-scale breweries and petrol companies with their tied outlets are examples of this.

4. Vertical integration (2)
A firm which is expanding its operations vertically may be motivated by defensive objectives, as follows:

(a) It may desire to reduce risk by bridging the uncertainty of the raw-material market. The manufacturer who integrates backwards is assured of supplies which may be scarce and costly when demand is high, or they may be controlled by a monopolist.

(b) It may desire to secure adequate outlets for its products.

In summary, there is no general rule that vertical integration realises economies. It may in certain cases but in others it may be uneconomic (e.g. detergent manufacturers do not integrate forward into retailing since their sales would be below the minimum optimal scale necessary for efficient retailing). Alternatively, vertical integration may have a neutral effect on costs, although it may be attempted if some other advantage outlined above is anticipated.

5. Lateral integration (1)
A firm which is expanding its operations laterally may have offensive motives, as follows:

(a) It may desire to benefit from existing goodwill by transferring the firm's brand name or image to new products.

(b) It may wish to expand turnover by entering new industries while employing common techniques, skills, raw materials or by-products from other activities. However, strong competition from specialists is to be expected.

(c) To employ spare capacity profitably.

(d) To exploit a profitable opportunity.

6. Lateral integration (2)

A firm which is expanding laterally may have defensive motives, as follows:

(a) It may wish to secure stability of profits, especially in those trades which are prone to cyclical fluctuations. Profits may be maintained if more stable 'bread and butter trades' or 'counter-cyclical' industries are entered.

(b) It may wish to maintain its share of the market by offering distributors and customers a choice from a comprehensive range of goods.

Integration *v.* standardization

7. Problem of inflexibility

A manufacturer's attitude to vertical integration depends partly on the present and expected state of the market.

Where supply exceeds demand and where this buyer's market is expected to last for some time, vertical disintegration can be expected because of low returns on capital in the depressed supply industry. However, the decision to disintegrate will be influenced by the likely capital loss from the sale of these investments and by considerations of group loyalty and pride.

However, in the long run the issue is determined by the comparative merits of integration and standardization.

8. Integration and standardization

The more a firm of given resources is integrated, the smaller is its scale of operations and efficiency in each activity. Thus integration may militate against scale, thereby encouraging disintegration, although large firms possessing sufficient resources can integrate several activities, performing them on the optimum scale if the market allows.

The smaller firm seems to have a choice between two courses of action, as follows:

(a) The firm can integrate and use small-scale plant. This is less efficient and will produce lower returns than for specialists, but this course may be preferred for the following reasons:

(*i*) It may overcome monopoly situations.

(*ii*) Integration of the complete production process, as compared with market integration, reduces uncertainties.

(*iii*) The firm may already have spare capacity suitable for the integrated activity.

(*iv*) It may be larger than the specialist and perhaps more credit-worthy, which with (*ii*) might make capital issues cheaper.

(b) It can perform fewer activities, each on a larger scale.

9. Limitations of standardization

Firms may be prevented from exploiting the maximum economies from the large-scale standardization of products, even though it is technically feasible, because of the following constraints:

(a) The market for the product may be limited. This is influenced by the following factors:

(*i*) The level of disposable incomes.

(*ii*) The propensity to save.

(*iii*) The size of population.

(*iv*) The age distribution of the population.

(*v*) Tastes, habits and fashions.

(*vi*) The success of competitors.

(*vii*) Advertising.

(b) The high costs of distribution.

(c) The shortage of capital.

(d) The risks associated with standardization may be unacceptable to the management; they may feel they are putting 'all their eggs in one basket'.

For these reasons firms and plants may not necessarily be organized for the largest possible scale of production which their resources or technology permit.

Integration by the market mechanism

10. Reasons for market integration

We have seen that vertical integration may offset scale, inducing firms to specialize in one process, while using the market to obtain other necessary goods and services. Other firms might prefer to administer consecutive processes but may be forced to use the market if they lack the necessary knowhow, expertise or finance. Firms may find it advantageous to use the market in the following circumstances:

(a) *Infrequent purchases.* They may occasionally buy items of specialized plant, equipment and buildings rather than make them themselves. It is probably more reliable and cheaper to use the services of specialist suppliers, who possess knowhow and experience and whose prices may reflect economies of large-scale output.

(b) *Frequent purchases.* Firms often find it preferable to buy regular supplies of raw materials, components and semi-finished goods and services from specialist suppliers rather than attempt to make them themselves. They do this for the following reasons:

(*i*) Specialist suppliers usually offer the trade a range of goods.

(*ii*) Goods may be produced on a scale large enough to secure economies of production.

(*iii*) Suppliers' prices may reflect other economies which may accrue through specialization in management, laboratories or equipment.

(*iv*) They economize in working capital from lower stock levels.

(*v*) Historical reasons, as in the building and shoe trades.

11. Limitations of market integration
Despite the obvious benefits of wider choice, high standards of product design and quality, general flexibility in purchasing and pecuniary advantages, there are circumstances when on balance the market as an integrating device is unsatisfactory, as follows:

(a) Firms are ultimately responsible for the performance, price and delivery of the end-product and they may be unprepared to share this responsibility with suppliers, who may let them down by delivering late, or wrong or poor-quality goods. Obviously, firms who fail once in these respects will not be used again, but the risk always exists, although it can be reduced by late delivery penalty clauses and stock-holding.

(b) Firms may wish to perform the work themselves for security reasons.

Integration by co-operation

12. Objectives of co-operative arrangements
An important feature of British industry is the co-operative or

collective organization, where firms work together to forward their economic activities. They do this:

(a) to combine the financial strength of several companies for large-scale investment projects;
(b) to share a project's risks or its benefits;
(c) to avoid unnecessary duplication of resources; or
(d) to exploit an opportunity more quickly and effectively than by market or administrative means.

13. Co-operative arrangements
These arrangements usually take the form of cartels and consortia. Some may be established temporarily for large-scale investment projects, or for sharing the costs of sales exhibitions. An example is the collaborative venture between aircraft manufacturers in the UK, Germany and Italy (involving the cooperation of hundreds of system and component suppliers) to build the European Fighter Aircraft.

14. Trade associations
There are hundreds of regional and national trade associations representing employers. They are organized on a single product, process and industry basis which are represented nationally by federations. Most of these federations were members of the British Employers' Confederation (BEC), which was concerned with general labour matters, until 1965 when it merged with the Federation of British Industries (FBI), which negotiated for industry on economic and commercial matters, and the smaller National Association of British Manufacturers (NABM), to form a single national organisation, the Confederation of British Industry (CBI).

The main aims of employers' organizations may be summarized under the following headings.

(a) The general protection and advancement of members' interests.
(b) The collection and dissemination of information on taxation, patents, raw materials, demand and other statistics useful to members.
(c) The promotion of legislation favourable to the interest of members.
(d) The standardization of contracts for the trade.
(e) The organization of trade fairs.
(f) Negotiation with the Government.
(g) Negotiation with trade unions.
(h) Formulation of price and output policies.

Progress test 3

1. Explain the term 'integration of economic activities' and the possible ways this integration may be accomplished. **(1)**

2. Discuss the possible motives of a firm which decides to expand its activities by horizontal integration. **(2)**

3. Discuss the possible motives of a firm which decides to expand its activities by vertical integration. **(3–4)**

4. Discuss the possible motives of a firm which decides to expand its activities by lateral integration. **(5–6)**

5. 'A manufacturer's attitude towards vertical integration or disintegration depends on the present and expected state of the market.' Discuss this statement. **(7–9)**

6. A manufacturer of limited resources asks you whether she should specialize in production or use them to integrate vertically. What is your advice? **(8)**

7. Discuss the various factors which may prevent firms from exploiting the maximum economies of large-scale standardization although they may be technically feasible. **(9)**

8. Explain why manufacturers use the market mechanism to integrate their economic activities. Illustrate your answer with two industries which are characterized by 'market integration'. **(10)**

9. Discuss the advantages and disadvantages of 'integration by the market mechanism'. **(10–11)**

10. Discuss the possible ways in which firms may co-operate to integrate their economic activities. For what reasons is this co-operative arrangement preferable to administrative and market solutions? **(12–14)**

11. Discuss the nature and purpose of trade associations. **(14)**

12. In the light of this chapter discuss the statement that business confidence is the main instigator to any type of integration. **(1–14)**

4

Industrial concentration

Nature of industrial concentration

1. Evidence of concentration

Concentration is indicated by the concentration ratio. This measures the percentage share of output or of employees in one industry accounted for by the biggest firms, usually three.

The following evidence suggests that concentration has steadily increased in British industry:

(a) There have been several studies to measure the extent of concentration in particular industries. These include the following works:

(*i*) Leak and Maizels, *The Structure of British Industry* (Journal of the Royal Statistical Society, 1945). Leak and Maizels used the *1935 Census of Production* figures to calculate the extent to which output was concentrated in the hands of the three biggest firms in a number of industries. They also compared these concentration ratios (CR) with those for similar American industries and discovered that the patterns were alike. Also, size of industry and degree of concentration in both countries generally varied inversely and the highest and lowest CR values were in similar industries.

(*ii*) Little and Evely, *Concentration in British Industry* (CUP, 1960). This book compared industrial concentration ratios for 1935 and 1951. This showed that while a number of industries were not directly comparable because technological changes and diversification had altered their character, concentration had increased in those industries highly concentrated in 1935. However, there was little evidence to suggest that concentration had increased throughout British industry generally.

(*iii*) Armstrong and Silverston, *Size of Plant, Size of Enterprise and Concentration in British Manufacturing Industry 1935–58* (Journal of the Royal Statistical Society, 1965). The authors concluded that in terms of employment, the average size of the largest plants had increased since 1935 and in 1958 accounted for a higher proportion of total employment in nearly all manufacturing trades.

Table 4A provides information that is at variance with these earlier findings. It shows changes in employment between 1986 and 1992. The small units (1–19 staff) still account for nearly 80 per cent of the total numbers, and they are more numerous. But the very largest have reduced in numbers and have halved the number they employ and are now clearly less significant as employers compared with the middle-sized units, although part of this can be explained by the recession of the 1990s.

Table 4A *Distribution of manufacturing units by number of employees*

| | No. of units | | | | No. employed | | | |
| | 1986 | 1992 | Percentage | | 1986 | 1992 | Percentage | |
No. employed	(000)	(000)	1986	1992	(000)	(000)	1986	1992
1–9	102.0	99.8	69.8	65.3	323	325	6.6	7.0
10–19	17.3	19.0	11.9	12.4	241	260	4.9	5.6
20–49	12.6	17.4	8.6	11.4	400	536	8.2	11.6
50–99	5.9	7.6	4.1	4.9	417	526	8.5	11.4
100–199	3.8	4.7	2.6	3.1	532	651	10.9	14.1
200–499	2.9	3.2	2.0	2.1	875	958	17.9	20.7
500–999	0.9	0.9	0.6	0.6	643	591	13.2	12.8
1000+	0.6	0.4	0.4	0.3	1447	771	29.7	16.7
	146.0	152.8	100.0	100.0	4878	4618	100.0	100.0

Source: Census of Production

Table 4B *Size distribution of acquisitions and mergers within the UK*

| | | | >£100m | | £10m–£100m | | £1m–10m | | >£1m | |
	No.	Value (£m)	No.	Value	No.	Value	No.	Value	No.	Value
1990	779	8 004	18	4249	89	2542	306	1105	366	106
1991	506	10 354	17	7335	63	2150	205	808	221	60
1992	426	5 725	7	3332	64	1710	182	627	173	53

Source: Central Statistical Office 1993

(b) An analysis of acquisitions and mergers of industrial and commercial companies shows that the number of, and expenditure on, large scale acquisitions has increased.

Moreover, the concentration has increased in specific industries. For example, Nestlé's acquisition of Rowntrees and other recent large takeovers were concentrated in the food, drink and tobacco manufacturing and retailing sectors.

2. Factors causing concentration

(a) Industry has moved towards more capital-intensive production methods, a process which has consolidated the position of large firms in industry. Smaller firms find such methods an obstacle to growth, while newcomers find them an effective barrier to entry.

(b) State activity has contributed as follows:

(*i*) Direct participation in developing certain industries, e.g. aircraft.

(*ii*) Financial assistance in 'rationalization schemes', e.g. cotton and shipbuilding.

(*iii*) High import tariffs of the 1930s insulated British industry from overseas competition. Consequently several giant foreign companies located factories in the UK, e.g. Proctor & Gamble. Also the threat of trade barriers to non-Economic Community companies in the 1990s has led to what some have called the 'trojan horse', i.e. Japanese multinationals locating in European countries, e.g. Nissan.

(*iv*) Nationalization Acts.

(*v*) The Industrial Reorganization Corporation facilitated amalgamations both directly (e.g. GEC and AEI) and indirectly through the 'educational effect' of making industry more aware of the advantages of amalgamations.

(c) Changes in the pattern of demand, as follows:

(*i*) In a stagnant, declining industry, only the strongest firms survive.

(*ii*) Innovators may secure a larger share of an expanding market despite the tendency of new firms to reduce concentration.

(*iii*) Successful advertising and sales promotion, e.g. detergent and petrol 'giants'.

(d) Major technological changes or technical improvements may influence the degree of concentration within a trade and certainly the innovator's share of the market, e.g. Pilkington's flow-glass technique and Wilkinson's introduction of the stainless-steel razor blade.

(e) Industry's attitudes towards mergers and takeovers.

(f) The optimum technical size of firms may have increased.

(g) Highly concentrated industries may have grown more rapidly than the rest.

(h) Restrictive-practice legislation may have encouraged mergers and concentration as an alternative to collusion.

3. International comparisons of concentration

An authoritative source of information is the Fortune Directory of the largest industrial companies outside the USA, which is published annually. Among other things it indicates their nationalities and their industrial diversification (*see* Table 4C).

One possible interpretation of these figures is that, except for the combined food and drink industries, in which Britain has eleven companies specializing (more than all the other countries combined), British industry is generally diffused, especially when compared with the limited industrial spread of other industrial nations. Japan and Germany both have particularly large concentrations in various engineering-, electrical- and chemical-based sectors.

Table 4C *Industrial concentration (by country)*

	Number of non US companies ranked 1–200		Industrial spread	
	1986	*1991*	*1986*	*1991*
Britain	34	27	14	11
France	18	20	9	12
Germany	28	24	9	10
Italy	6	3	5	3
Japan	53	66	10	18
South Korea	7	9	5	6

4. Implications

(a) Diversification militates against economies of scale. Industrial concentrations, alternatively, help to produce such benefits.

(b) However, a diffused economy is less susceptible to structural change and its consequences, e.g. structural unemployment.

(c) The growth rates of those sectors in which Britain is to a degree concentrated compare unfavourably with technically advanced industries in which her competitors specialize. The poor performance of these highly concentrated industries naturally affects the rate of overall economic growth. This is shown in Table 4D which compares the percentage annual increase in production.

Table 4D *Annual change in output of UK industries*

Industry	(1985 average is 100)						
	1986	*1987*	*1988*	*1989*	*1990*	*1991*	*1992*
Chemicals	101.8	109	114.2	119.3	118.3	121.6	123.6
Food & drink	100.8	103.2	104.8	105.7	106.4	106.2	107.4

Source: Central Statistical Office

5. Advantages of rationalization

(a) It is claimed that enlarged corporate groups will yield economies, as follows:

(*i*) They may benefit from synergic advantages, with economies in management, finance, purchasing, marketing, design and, in particular, economies resulting from the use of modern plant for long production-runs. Lower unit-costs should improve competitiveness, which is especially important if Britain is to secure a permanent equilibrium in its balance of trade. The limited size of the domestic market, which may be less than the minimum optimal level of production of modern large-scale manufacturing plant, further underlines the need for success in international markets.

(*ii*) Corporate groups may more easily afford the R & D funds which are vital in technology-intensive industries. This is borne out by evidence from the USA and Britain where a handful of giant firms are responsible for the bulk of private R & D expenditure.

(*iii*) They can better afford to exploit discoveries.

(*iv*) There are savings in scarce R & D resources, as duplication of competitive research is avoided.

(*v*) There are savings of scarce factors of production as wasteful competition is avoided. Stacey (see *Mergers in Modern Britain*, Hutchinson, 1966) stated that at one time in the UK there were 169 manufacturers of electric fires producing 1113 different models, an average of seven models per manufacturer with annual sales of only £1211 each! Fortunately the situation has since improved.

(b) Concentration in industry centralises decision-making and thereby facilitates Government planning and control of the economy.

6. Acquisitions

The estimated number and value of acquisitions in the UK between 1972 and 1992 were as shown in Table 4E.

The high level of acquisition activity in 1972–3 may be attributable to the following factors:

(a) The role of the Industrial Reorganization Corporation.

(*i*) The IRC actively encouraged mergers e.g. the creation of British Leyland, in pursuit of the advantages of rationalization.

(*ii*) It has an 'educational effect', in that it increased industry's awareness of the advantages of mergers.

(b) The merger and takeover boom affected the attitude of potential

Table 4E *Number and value of acquisitions in UK 1972–92*

	Number acquired	Value (£m)
1972	1 210	2 531
1973	1 205	1 304
1974	504	508
1975	315	290
1976	353	448
1977	481	824
1978	567	1 140
1979	534	1 656
1980	469	1 475
1981	452	1 144
1982	463	2 206
1983	447	2 343
1984	568	5 474
1985	474	7 090
1986	696	14 935
1987	1 125	15 363
1988	1 499	22 839
1989	1 337	27 250
1990	799	8 329
1991	506	10 434
1992	426	5 850

Source: Trade & Industry

bidders and the underlying sentiment of the market (i.e. one bid generated others).

(c) The bull stock market in 1970–2 accorded growth companies high P/E ratios, which made low-P/E-ratio companies attractive victims.

Acquisition activity declined sharply after 1973 due to the impact of inflation, extreme economic problems facing industry, the severe bear market and the change in official attitude to acquisitions. In 1965–72 eighteen proposed mergers were referred to the Monopolies Commission compared with thirteen in 1973–4, indicating a now suspicious attitude towards acquisitions.

After 1985 the number of acquisitions and the expenditure on acquisitions increased dramatically. The number increased because the increase in stock market values enabled growth companies to acquire companies through the issue of high value ordinary shares. The value of total expenditure increased because of the acquisition of very large companies. In fact, in 1987 the number of acquisitions of over £10m was 203, some 88 per cent of total expenditure.

The sharp decline after 1990 was due to the extreme economic and financial problems facing companies that resulted from the recession.

The regulation of takeover activity

7. Criticism of takeover activity

Increased takeover activity in the 1950s and the development of questionable tactics revealed the inadequacy of the financial authorities to control events. The chief criticisms were as follows:

(a) The shareholders of offeree companies were not always kept fully informed, so as to enable them to make an independent judgment.

(b) Occasionally there were leakages of information regarding imminent bids which unsettled the market for the company's shares.

(c) Some defensive tactics were of doubtful merit and not always in the interest of shareholders and employees.

8. The Takeover Code

As a result of this criticism, a working party, representative of the City, was established in 1958 to regularize takeovers and mergers. It published the City Code on Takeovers and Mergers which defined general principles of conduct to be observed in bid situations and set up a panel to supervize the operation of the Code.

At the outset the Code proved ineffectual because it lacked disciplinary powers, relying instead on professional bodies and financial authorities in the City to censure or discipline offenders, which in reality they rarely did. However, with time its authority and effectiveness were improved as a result of the following:

(a) The membership of the City Working Party, on whose authority the Code is issued, was extended to embrace all major financial bodies concerned with mergers and takeovers, i.e. the Accepting Houses Committee, the Association of Investment Trust Companies, the British Insurance Association, the Committee of London Clearing Bankers, the Confederation of British Industry, the Issuing Houses Association, the National Association of Pension Funds, the Stock Exchange and the Unit Trust Association.

(b) Amendments and revisions to the code were introduced in the light of experience, e.g. to tighten the wording of the code, to close loopholes that had allowed the code to be breached or to forestall situations which might affect shareholders unfairly.

(c) The Panel showed that it was prepared to use sanctions, e.g. suspension of dealings in company shares.

9. Regulatory powers of the UK system
In order to afford adequate protection for investors, there is:

(a) *Company law*. Companies Acts are introduced as a result of investigations by Royal Commissions or Committees that recommend legislation to bring current law into line with best accounting practice and to plug loopholes in current legislation.

   (*i*) Shareholders and debenture holders are provided with financial details prescribed by the Acts in the company's annual reports which are subject to independent audit.

   (*ii*) Prospective shareholders are similarly supplied with financial information signed by the auditor or independent accountant in all company prospectuses and similar documents.

(b) *Financial Services Act 1986*. This Act attempts to deal comprehensively with the regulation of the investment industry especially with regard to share issues, insider dealings and takeovers.

(c) *The Stock Exchange*. The Stock Exchange requires compliance with its rules on disclosure as a condition for quotation.

(d) *The City Panel on Takeovers and Mergers*.

(e) *The Bank of England* has powers over banks under the Nationalization Act 1946.

(f) *The Treasury and Bank of England* have powers over foreign exchange transactions and therefore takeovers involving foreign companies.

(g) *The Department of Trade* has wide powers to investigate any company's affairs, usually by appointing inspectors.

(h) *The Serious Fraud Office 1988*. This is staffed by lawyers and accountants who investigate major cases of fraud.

(i) *Customs and Excise*.

(j) *European Community (EC) Directives*. In its attempts to achieve harmonisation of company law across member states, the EC issues Directives which have to be incorporated into members' national laws. The three most important to financial accounting, and incorporated into the UK's Company Acts, were the Fourth: dealing with the format and rules of accounting, the Seventh: dealing with consolidated accounts and the Eighth: dealing with the qualification and work of auditors.

10. Regulatory powers of the US system

The Securities Exchange Commission (SEC) was set up in 1934, empowered by the Securities Act 1933 and Securities Exchange Act 1934 to 'protect the interests of the public and investors against malpractices in the securities and financial markets'.

The SEC members, backed by a large permanent staff, are appointed by the President and exercise executive, judicial and legislative powers to police the securities and financial markets. Clearly, their powers are far-reaching.

(a) All companies selling new securities, or whose securities are publicly traded, must file registration documents and periodic reports disclosing financial and trading details demanded by the Securities Acts.

(b) Financial statements certified by independent public accountants that they conform to the accepted professional accounting standards are reviewed by the SEC.

(c) To improve disclosure, the SEC is empowered to formulate rules stipulating the content and basis of valuation of data in financial statements and procedures for their presentation.

(d) It uses its legislative authority to speed up the introduction of new practices. For instance in 1976 it demanded that large companies disclose financial information and the effects of inflation on the figures. Normally, this would be the province of the Financial Accounting Standards Board, but the effect of the SEC's action was to spur on the FASB towards the introduction of an accounting standard on current cost accounting. And in 1978 it overruled the FASB's standard for oil and gas accounting.

(e) It can act instantly:

    (*i*) To make rules that apply to everyone including private individuals.

    (*ii*) To hold investigations with judicial powers of subpoena of individuals and documents.

    (*iii*) To threaten and institute civil and criminal proceedings.

    (*iv*) To suspend quotations and suspend dealers.

Clearly, the American statutory system is in direct contrast with the self-regulatory system of the UK and it is a subject of endless debate whether a similar agency with executive, judicial and legislative powers should be established in the UK to police the financial markets.

11. An SEC for the UK?

The SEC cannot be effectively transplanted into the UK financial system. Indeed, it is unique to the American system where some fifty varied systems of state laws and a Federal legal system, numerous stock exchanges and over-the-counter dealings operate. In addition to the geographical, legal and administrative problems were the excesses, abuses and trauma of the free-for-all system that culminated in the Wall Street crash: it is certainly not surprising that America should adopt a statutory system which concentrates on the prevention of fraud and proper disclosure.

It is argued that the UK already possesses adequate regulatory powers (*see* **9**). The system is essentially one of self-regulation with the various agencies watching over the various disciplines under the overall supervision of the Bank of England. It is argued that the system is flexible: it can accommodate any shifts of emphasis that might be needed: rules can be framed to meet changing circumstances: offenders can be expelled from their professional bodies. However, self-regulation did break down and in 1987 the Serious Fraud Office was set up to investigate when serious fraud was suspected. Yet for all its professional staff, and its powers to demand disclosure, critics say that its record in Guinness, Blue Arrow etc. is poor.

A theoretical framework which might explain the US and UK approach to regulation is provided by Puxty *et al.* (1987). See Fig. 4.1. It is argued that there are three ways financial information can be regulated.

(a) The market. Here a company would provide the information as it pleased.
(b) The state. Here disclosure is demanded.
(c) The community. Here rules are developed that reflect the wishes of the community.

Within these three extremes Puxty has identified four modes of regulation.

   (*i*) Liberalism, where regulation is provided by rules of market principles.
   (*ii*) Legalism, where regulation is imposed by law.
   (*iii*) Associationism, which is between the two extremes of Liberalism and Legalism. Here regulation is provided by bodies that are set up to represent and promote the interests of the members and to some extent is influenced by the interests of the wider community of which they are part.

(*iv*) Corporatism, which is also between the two extremes. Here the state recognises self-interest organisations and incorporates them into its own system of regulation to achieve state goals.

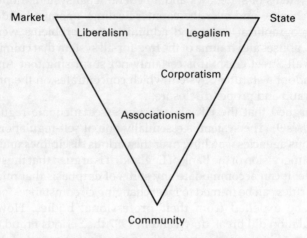

Figure 4.1 *Degrees of regulation*

Puxty applied the framework to several countries and concluded that:

US: elements of Legalism and Associationism with the latter subordinated to the former.

UK: principally Associationism.

Monopoly legislation

12. Background to legislation

The United Kingdom was a free-trading nation prior to 1931 but with the spread of 'economic nationalism' in the depression it was forced to follow the rest of the world and impose tariffs to safeguard employment levels. This transformed the economy into a highly protective one, and in this defensive environment restrictive agreements and monopolies appeared. After the war, however, Government attitudes towards monopolies hardened for the following reasons:

(a) Public attention was focused on the 'harmful abuses of monopoly power'.

(b) The Government had restructured industry through its rationalization schemes in the 1930s and redirected it between 1939 and 1945. It reconsidered Britain's role in the post-war period and realized that an offensive attitude was needed to succeed in developing overseas trade. Consequently the Government took positive action to make British industry more competitive.

13. Monopoly powers
The dangers inherent in monopoly power may be summarized under the following headings:

(a) The exploitation of customers (in the form of higher prices) to earn excessive profits.
(b) Unfair competition to prevent competitors from entering the industry.
(c) The suppression of innovation.
(d) Reduction in choice.

14. The Monopolies Commission 1948
The Monopolies Commission was established to investigate and report on matters referred to it by the Board of Trade, i.e. to find out whether a firm or group responsible for supplying, processing or buying more than one-third of an industry's trade was in the national interest. Its findings suggested that this was best served when competition is encouraged. Occasionally, however, the Commission allowed oligopoly situations to develop to balance the power of monopoly buyers.

15. Criticisms of the Monopolies Commission
The Monopolies Commission has been criticized for the following reasons:

(a) It was originally too small and this delayed its operation, e.g. the report on the supply of electrical equipment for motor vehicles took six years to complete.
(b) It had no powers to implement decisions but relied on Government action. However, only in the case of dental goods and imported timber were 'cease and desist' orders made. The Government preferred to negotiate changes and hoped that 'publicity will operate to cause a monopoly to change its habits'.
(c) Because it lacked authority, its findings did not always command the respect of industry. Some industries even published pamphlets defending their actions, presumably in order to influence public opinion prior to possible Government action.

(d) Its findings set no judicial precedents to deter others, as each case was decided on its facts.

(e) It was not always completely consistent. The absence of judicial procedure has allowed Government economic policies to influence its findings.

16. An important recommendation
In 1955, the Commission published its most important report: 'A Report on exclusive dealings, collective boycotts, aggregated rebates and other discriminatory trade practices.' This drew on information from its investigations and from the reports of various Government departments. Its recommendation for legislation to deal with these practices was accepted and the Restrictive Practices Act was passed in 1956.

17. Restrictive Practices Act 1956
This changed the method of control of restrictive practices from investigation and recommendation by an administrative tribunal to control by statute law and the Restrictive Practices Court. The Monopolies Commission was left to deal with straightforward monopolies.

It was now necessary to register restrictive agreements and they were then submitted by the registrar to the Court for decision.

This law differed from the other law in that the burden of proof was on the defendant. There was a presumption that the agreement was against the public interest and therefore void and the onus was on the defendant to show the court otherwise. This might be done by successfully passing through one of the seven 'gateways' and the 'tailpiece'.

18. The seven gateways and tailpiece
The defendant had to prove to the court that the agreement produced one or more of the following beneficial effects (or 'gateways'):

(a) The restriction was necessary to protect users of the goods from physical injury. This was argued unsuccessfully in the chemists', vehicle distributors' and tyre-makers' agreements because the court held that either the chance of public injury was only slight or, if it was likely, the public should be protected by Government legislation, and not by private agreements.

(b) The removal of the restriction would deny the public specific and substantial advantages. Black bolts and nuts, cement, magnets, books and other agreements were allowed as they resulted in substantial benefits by way of lower prices, standardisation, convenience and co-operation in research and development.

(c) The restriction was necessary to counter the action of a group which restricts competition.

(d) It was needed to enable parties to negotiate fair terms with monopolists. Gateways **(c)** and **(d)** are obviously linked and have not been used outside the boilermakers', transformers' and sulphuric acid cases.

(e) Its removal would cause serious and persistent unemployment. This was successfully pleaded by the yarn spinners in 1959 but the court held that this benefit was outweighed by the harm caused to the public, particularly as prices were higher than they might have been in a free market.

(f) Its removal would cause a loss of export revenue. This was successful in the boilermakers' case.

(g) The restriction was needed to maintain other restrictive agreements already passed by the court. This then allowed it to support a restriction which was essential for the maintenance of another which was in the public interest.

However, it was not enough to prove one or more of these benefits to the satisfaction of the court. The court had to be satisfied that the benefits resulting from the restriction on balance outweighed the detriment its operation might cause in other respects (i.e. the 'tailpiece').

In 1968 the practice of formally exchanging information about prices, conditions of sale, etc., was considered a registrable restrictive practice, and an eighth gateway was added, i.e., 'that the agreement neither restricts nor deters competition'. In addition, in 1973 The Fair Trading Act extended the restrictive practices to cover services as well as goods.

In 1976 The Restrictive Practices Act was passed to consolidate all the previous legislation. Now the Director of Fair Trading would be responsible for referring practices to the Restrictive Practices Court.

By careful selection of cases for referral to the court the majority of practices were abandoned because of the precedents set in the court decisions.

Monopolies and mergers

19. Monopolies and Mergers Act 1965
A Royal Commission investigating the Press in 1961 recommended

public scrutiny of all future concentrations. In 1965 the Monopolies and Mergers Act subjected concentrations in other fields to scrutiny in order to safeguard the 'national interest'. This Act empowered the Board of Trade to refer to an enlarged Monopolies Commission for investigating mergers which would create or strengthen a monopoly situation or where the total taken-over assets exceed £5m. It was also empowered under such references to hold up and dissolve mergers if recommended.

The Act also strengthened Government control over monopolies. The Department of Trade became able to regulate prices, demand price lists and prohibit or impose conditions on monopolists and oligopolists.

20. Criteria for referment
The Department of Trade's criteria for deciding whether to refer an agreement are as follows:

(a) Does the merger come within the scope of the 1956 Act?
(b) If satisfied, the Department seeks factual information on:
    (*i*) the companies involved (e.g. labour force, ownership);
    (*ii*) the industry or market (e.g. products, degree of competition); and
    (*iii*) the merger proposals (e.g. motives, methods, implications).
'The task is to identify possible detriments to the public interest, which may arise from the merger and to assess whether the expected benefits from larger scale and rationalization are likely to outweigh these detriments. The crucial questions therefore relate to the facts of the individual case.' (*Merger, A Guide to Board of Trade Practice*. HMSO, 1969.)

21. Broad considerations
The Board (Department) of Trade booklet mentioned above classified mergers as horizontal, vertical or conglomerate, and examined in detail a merger's possible implications for each type, as follows:

(a) A horizontal merger's possible impact in the short and long run on:
    (*i*) market power;
    (*ii*) efficiency;
    (*iii*) the balance of payments; and
    (*iv*) regional policy and redundancy.
(b) A vertical merger's possible impact on the same factors, plus :
    (*i*) competition;
    (*ii*) efficiency in production and distribution.

(c) A conglomerate merger's possible impact on the same factors, plus:
(*i*) motives;
(*ii*) benefits;
(*iii*) efficiency in the different sectors within the conglomerate's sphere of activities;
(*iv*) the effect on monopolies within these sectors;
(*v*) the effect on the industrial structure of each sector;
(*vi*) in addition, separate accounting information for the different sectors is required.

22. Disadvantages of system of automatic reference

The present discretionary system is preferable to a system of automatic reference since this would have the following disadvantages:

(a) Problems of definition and interpretation. For example, how are the relevant geographical and industrial markets to be defined and what is to be the precise market share or taken-over value of assets that qualify for reference?
(b) Forgoing the flexibility which discretion under the 1965 Act allows, e.g. assurances from the firms, effect on export or import trade, effect on regional development.
(c) An increased workload for the Monopolies Commission. More delay, uncertainty and expense.
(d) Major legislation, which would overthrow the whole basis of post-war legislation.

23. Recent Legislation

In 1973 Government extended legislation in the area of consumer protection when it established the Office of Fair Trading (OFT) under a Director General under the power of the Fair Trading Act 1973. The effects were far reaching.

The Monopolies Commission was retitled the Monopolies and Mergers Commission.

Now the Secretary of State could refer specific mergers and monopoly situations or make general references. Similarly, the Director General of Fair Trading could refer monopoly situations.

Since 1980, the Competition Act allowed the Director General to make competition references and the Secretary of State to refer questions relating to public sector bodies.

24. Merger references

All merger offers for quoted companies are subject to the *City Code on*

Take-overs and Mergers and lapse on reference to the Commission. The reference may be made when the merging companies together control at least 25 per cent of the market or where gross assets exceed £30m, and after the OFT has decided that there are sufficient public interest reasons for an in-depth examination by the Commission.

25. The meaning of 'the public interest'
Under the 1973 Act the Commission must take the following into account when considering the public interest:

(a) maintaining and promoting competition in the UK;
(b) the development of new products and the reduction of costs;
(c) the balanced distribution of industry and employment; and
(d) competitive activity by UK companies in overseas markets.

26. Monopoly references
Under the 1973 Act the Director General may refer where a company, or connected companies in the same group, supplies or receives at least 25 per cent of all goods or services of a particular description.

The Commission handles the reference in the same way as a merger reference. Facts are collected and opinions invited. The monopoly situation is analysed and discussed with the monopoly company before the report is published.

The Secretary of State may then make an order to remedy or prevent any adverse effects found to be against the public interest, or require the Director General to negotiate suitable undertakings.

27. Financial Services Act 1986
More recent developments in regulation have been the Financial Services Act and the effects of the Treaty of Rome on UK companies. The Financial Services Act replaced the Prevention of Fraud Act 1958 and deals with acts, practices or courses of conduct likely to defraud or deceive investors. Only authorised investment businesses have a statutory right to advertise or promote the sale or purchase of investments. Supervision is delegated via the Securities and Investment Board, to five self-regulatory organisations run by practioners who specialise in particular aspects of the investment business.

28. The Treaty of Rome
Although none of the legislation is directed towards mergers and acquisitions, it can influence such transactions, e.g. Articles 85 and 86 contain wide anti-trust legislation. The Commission can take action

against any company which already has a dominant position within the EC in any particular section of industry which acquires another company producing similar goods. The objective is to ensure that monopolies and cartels do not hinder the integration of the common market.

29. Regulation of privatised utilities
Watchdogs were established when the public utilities were privatised to ensure that they did not abuse their strong monopoly positions by overcharging their customers. These watchdogs, known as 'Ofgas, Oftel, Ofwat and Offer', regulate the British Gas, British Telecommunications, and the water and electricity companies. But ultimately the utilities are accountable to the Monopoly and Mergers Commission. For example, in 1993 the MMC probed into British Gas's near monopoly position and was asked to adjudicate in the dispute between the company and Ofgas.

There are critics of the current system who argue:

(a) The regulators have too much power and the absence of detailed rules gives them too much discretion.
(b) They do not always give sufficient financial details about the reasons for their decisions.
(c) They are not sufficiently accountable. Ultimately they are answerable to the MMC which would adjudicate but only in cases of dispute.

Conglomerates

30. Definition
A conglomerate is a holding company with a number of interests widely diversified throughout different industries.

31. Doubtful value of lateral integration
The term 'cult of giantism' was coined in 1968 to describe the unprecedented level of takeover and merger activity, which in value terms amounted to £2312m, of which some two-thirds was for concentration and one-third for diversification purposes. While many could appreciate the advantages of large-scale organizations which concentration might bring, the merits of diversification were less apparent. The increasing number of amalgamations of this latter nature, coupled with doubts about their economic value, placed the conglomerate at the centre of a controversy.

The Department of Trade and Industry surveys, on which Table 4F

Table 4F *Analysis of acquisitions and mergers by category of expenditure*

	Expenditure (£m) Total	Cash	Ordinary shares	Fixed interest securities	% of Expenditure Cash	Ordinary shares	Fixed interest securities
1988	22 839	15 993	4 993	1 853	70	22	8
1989	27 250	22 356	3 520	1 347	82	13	5
1990	8 329	6 402	1 533	393	77	18	5
1991	10 434	7 278	3 034	121	70	29	1
1992	5 850	3 679	2 123	47	63	36	1

is based, indicated that between 1988 and 1992 acquisitions were financed more and more by the issue of company securities.

32. Disadvantages of conglomerates

The chief fears and criticisms of conglomerate mergers may be summarized as follows:

(a) These amalgamations were taking place and their economic consequences were unknown. Fears were expressed that:

(*i*) conglomerates possessed potential monopoly powers which might be used to dictate to retailers, consumers and employers;

(*ii*) the increased cost and inflexibility of their administration in the enlarged organization might outweigh other expected economic benefits. Consequently diseconomies might result.

(b) Trade unions were concerned about redundancies resulting from large-scale amalgamations.

(c) Lateral integration hindered rationalization of industries.

(d) Competition was constrained because:

(*i*) risk capital was used to buy established companies and not for investment in innovation or re-equipment in the parent company's business;

(*ii*) subsidiaries had disproportionate economic power when they drew on the group's resources;

(*iii*) the group was less responsive to competition in the various industries; and

(*iv*) the spread of conglomerates weakened the stimulus of competition in the economy.

(e) Diversification by any group of limited resources inhibited its economic growth in any industry compared with large-scale specialization, although some economies in overheads, finance, R & D and marketing were probable.

(f) A group might, however, grow in financial terms when it used its shares which have a high profit–earnings ratio to buy 'victim' companies with lesser profit–earnings ratios. This might lead to a false appreciation of the results of the merger and an over-evaluation of the company's shares which might be used for further acquisitions.

A company growing financially is less stable than one expanding by 'organic' growth.

For example, if the earnings available for ordinary dividend of two companies A and B are equal and each has an earnings per ordinary share of £0.25, and A, the offeror, has a P/E ratio of 30:1 and B, the offeree, a P/E of 15:1, then after a merger financed by an exchange of one of company A's shares for two shares of B, total earnings of the merged company have doubled immediately and earnings per share have risen from £0.25 to £0.30 without any internal growth whatsoever.

(g) The failure of a group precipitated by an excessive debt-capital burden, coupled with a bearish market, could seriously affect investors' confidence and the supply of capital.

(h) Conglomerates gave insufficient information about their different activities. It was therefore difficult for investors to assess the real profitability of the group.

33. Advantages of conglomerates
On the other hand, there are conglomerates whose performance, whether measured in terms of return on capital, of innovation or of market growth, is superior to the performances of many other companies. Any interest by such companies in an industry is certain to ginger up competitors, perhaps forcing them to innovate, streamline their organization and generally improve their efficiency, in order to maintain market shares or to resist acquisition. Furthermore, the emergence of conglomerates is to be expected for the following reasons:

(a) Any aggressive management will seize profit opportunities which are more numerous laterally than horizontally and vertically combined.

(b) The 'conglomerate umbrella' gives small companies access to specialised management skills, personnel and finance, and allows cross-fertilization of ideas.

(c) Companies tend to diversify when they find their original business expanding too slowly.

(d) Developments in management techniques mean that increasingly larger organizations may be controlled.

(e) Integration by means of a holding company is cheaper than by complete integration.

(f) A holding company's structure allows constituent firms a high degree of autonomy which may realize benefits of decentralization.

(g) This suggests that large-scale redundancy is not inevitable.

34. Demergers

In the 1990s a number of large companies whose activities extended across several different businesses decided to demerge. In 1991, Racal sold off its mobile telecommunications business in the form of Vodaphone and in 1992 sold its security business as Chubb Security plc. In 1993 ICI demerged. The reasons for demerging are as follows:

(a) Managers of a separate company can concentrate on its core business and focus on its own particular corporate objectives.

(b) Managers can concentrate on the specific operating, financial and investment policies of the company.

(c) Shareholders of the original company are given shares in the demerged company which are listed on the stock exchange, and which are likely to increase in value.

(d) The threat of a hostile takeover is reduced if the demerger pre-empts others by removing the object of a bid.

Progress test 4

1. How do you think a prolonged Government policy of privatisation would affect a country's concentration level? (1–2)

2. How important do you think the existence of economics of scale are to an industry's concentration ratio? (1–5)

3. What do you think the relationship between the state of the economy and the level of acquisition activity is?

4. What do you understand by the Takeover Panel and Code? (7–8)

5. The City Panel lacks adequate disciplinary powers and should be replaced by the equivalent of a Securities Exchange Commission.' Discuss. (9–11)

6. 'Self regulation doesn't work.' Discuss. (9–11)

7. To what extent do you agree with Puxty's diagram on degrees of regulation? **(11)**

8. Explain the circumstances which brought into being the Monopolies Commission, its purpose and objects in operation. **(12–13)**

9. Explain the term 'monopoly power'. **(13)**

10. A manufacturer could continue with a restrictive agreement after 1956 only if he could prove its worth by passing through the 'gateways and tailpiece'. Explain. **(16–18)**

11. Assess the effectiveness of the Restrictive Practices Act 1956, and its consequences. **(17)**

12. 'The Monopolies and Mergers Act 1965 strengthened Government control over monopolies.' Comment. **(19)**

13. Describe how the Fair Trading Act 1973 provided greater consumer protection. **(23–26)**

14. The Treaty of Rome complements existing UK legislation concerning dominant companies. Discuss. **(28)**

15. 'The watchdogs of privatised utilities should themselves be regulated more tightly.' Discuss. **(29)**

16. **(a)** What is a conglomerate?
(b) Discuss the pros and cons of conglomerate mergers. **(30–33)**

17. 'Mergers were the hallmark of the 80s, demergers will stamp the 90s.' Discuss. **(34)**

Part two
Finance for industry

5
Long-term finance for industry

The capital market

1. The capital market

Generally speaking, saving (making money available, for borrowers) and investment (using money for the purchase of capital goods or equipment) are undertaken by different parties, and some mechanism is needed to co-ordinate these forces of demand and supply. This is done by the capital market through its many different specialist institutions, which act as intermediaries and channel the savings of companies and individuals to borrowers. The main institutions are as follows:

(a) commercial banks;
(b) merchant banks;
(c) discount houses;
(d) insurance companies and pension funds;
(e) investment trusts, etc.;
(f) the Stock Exchange.

2. Categories of capital

In order to examine more closely the main sources of capital, and the roles of the financial institutions, it is convenient to classify these funds under broad headings. They may be grouped according to risk, e.g. low-, medium- and high-risk capital. However, it is more satisfactory to use liquidity as the criterion. In this way, the institutions are members either of the money market or of the capital market. The former provides industry, in the broadest sense, with very short-term loans for the financing of Treasury and commercial bills of exchange. The latter is concerned with longer-term loans but will include some institutions which also operate in the money market, e.g. the commercial banks, whose advances contribute towards industry's working capital. The main categories of capital are as follows:

(a) long-term capital (i.e. 'permanent' share, loan capital);
(b) short- and medium-term capital (i.e. working or circulating capital).

Two other types of highly specialized capital merit special attention. They are:

(c) Export finance.
(d) Specialist finance.

The new-issues market

3. Advantages of private companies

(a) Private companies are likely to be small enough to benefit from the following factors:
  (i) close contact between directors, staff and employees;
  (ii) greater flexibility;
  (iii) the stimulus of members' self-interest.
(b) They possess the following privileges:
  (i) fewer documentary requirements compared with public companies;
  (ii) fewer procedural requirements.
(c) Control is exercised by members who can manage the company in their own interest, uninfluenced by public opinion, i.e. they are not in the public eye.
(d) They are secure from takeover bids.
(e) They can discount current profitability for longer-term development, which would reduce the market valuation of public companies and invite takeover bids.

4. Advantages of public companies

(a) Public companies may invite the general public to subscribe capital and thereby raise more money than by private subscription.
(b) They may secure the advantages of quotation (*see* 5).
(c) Their status lessens the impact of death duties on shareholders who may more readily sell shares to realize funds.

(d) Public subscription may avoid the 'close company' status of the Finance Act 1965, and its special tax provisions.

Generally, these advantages outweigh those for private companies; hence the tendency for conversion at some stage in the development of firms.

5. Reasons for share quotation

Every year several privately owned companies seek admission to the Stock Exchange official list for one or more of the following reasons:

(a) Shareholders of unquoted companies may request a 'flotation' which, while adding nothing to the capital resources of the company, does provide them with cash or marketable shares which may be used for a variety of purposes: the spread of investment risk, consumption, estate duty, etc.

(b) Capital commitments may outstretch net cash flow, in which case the new-issues market may be the suitable source of new permanent capital or long-term loans. In addition, banks, a main source of working capital, may react more sympathetically to requests from quoted companies. On the other hand, companies wishing to reduce their dependence on bank finance, which may be withdrawn in times of severe credit squeeze, may be attracted towards the long-term finance of the new-issues market.

(c) Quotation may lessen the impact and uncertainties of death duties and avoid the problem of valuation of unquoted shares.

(d) Quoted shares are readily marketable and acceptable and may be given as consideration in merger and takeover transactions.

(e) Quotation can avoid the tax disadvantages of 'close' companies.

(f) Quotation seems to invest companies with a superior status. This may be important to customers, who often like to know the trading patterns and financial resources of their suppliers.

(g) The market tends to place a higher valuation on quoted companies than private investors do, and this is naturally to the benefit of shareholders.

6. Disadvantages of quotation

Against the above advantages must be set the following disadvantages.

(a) Quotation may be accomplished at a cost to some shareholders in the form of loss of control in the conduct of the business. However, it is not essential that equity should be made public, and it may be possible to raise capital by an issue of quoted loan-stock instead, so that equity and control is retained.

(b) The exacting Stock Exchange requirements place greater responsibilities on the board of directors. Quotation also demands a fair distribution policy and consistent profits. Failure on the part of directors will damage the company's public standing.

(c) The disclosure of information for shareholders reviewing progress (e.g. growth prospects and circumstances which might materially affect share prices) may be useful to competitors.

(d) Going public is expensive.

(e) The company is vulnerable to takeover bids.

7. Requirements for quotation

Generally speaking, a company seeking Stock Exchange quotation needs to fulfil the following conditions.

(a) It should be of reasonable size. The Stock Exchange will not normally consider any application unless the initial expected value of the company security is £700 000.

Nevertheless, a company in this situation may take the following actions.

(*i*) It may exchange its unquoted shares for the shares of a quoted company by means of a 'reverse takeover', although the Stock Exchange is certain to suspend quotation if the new company is materially different, until the necessary information about the new company is supplied.

(*ii*) It may merge with companies in a similar situation whose group valuation and collective pre-tax profits are sufficient for quotation.

(b) A sufficiently large proportion of shares must be made available to the public to create a market, i.e. at least 25 per cent of an issue of equity securities should be made available to the public.

(c) The company must have a satisfactory trading record for three years and must be financially sound. Ideally it should have a record of profitable trading with adequate levels of fixed and working capital in relation to liabilities.

8. Types of issues

A company may make its securities available to investors by the following means.

(a) An issue by prospectus:

(*i*) a public issue by the company;

(*ii*) an offer for sale; or

(*iii*) an offer for sale by tender.

(b) Placing:

(*i*) a private placing;

(*ii*) a Stock Exchange placing.

(c) An introduction.

(d) A Rights Issue.

(e) A Bonus Issue.

All are methods whereby companies raise new capital (except the introduction and Bonus Issue) and all except the private placings by the issue of quoted securities.

9. An offer for sale

This method either permits a company to raise new capital by means of an issue of shares, or allows existing shareholders to realize their shareholdings in cash. In the former case, the issuing house buys the shares from the company and, in the latter case, from the shareholders. As principal, it offers them for sale to the public either by offering the shares at the purchase price, charging the company a fee for the Stock Exchange quotation and administrative services, or by re-selling them at a higher price, and making a profit on the transaction, or it does both.

10. Preliminary work for an issue

The members of the Issuing Houses Association play an important role in the new-issues market, acting as intermediaries between companies seeking long-term capital and those who are prepared to supply it by investing. Companies desiring quotations seek the sponsorship of a specialist merchant bank whose high standing will inspire the confidence of investors. This is essential for a successful issue. However, before committing its name to the venture, the bank will naturally examine the company very carefully, its memorandum and articles of association, trading record, directors and management, shareholders and true financial position.

If satisfied, the bank then works out a programme dealing with the following points:

(a) Capital reorganization schemes.

(b) The size of the issue.

(c) The timing of the issue.

(d) Classes of securities, their terms and the estimated issue prices.

Once these proposals are agreed, a detailed programme is then planned for the preparation of reports by solicitors, accountants and stock brokers. These are required for the registrar of companies, the Stock Exchange, the prospectus (*see* **11**), publication and advertising.

11. Prospectus
This is the invitation to the public to apply for securities in the company. Prospectuses are probably familiar to most people, since they are widely advertised in the Press. Briefly the details they contain, which must conform to Companies Acts and Stock Exchange regulations, are:

(a) The name of the company, its share capital, names of directors, bankers, solicitors, auditors, brokers and secretary, and the arrangements for application.

(b) The chairman's report, which deals with the following points:
   (*i*) history and business;
   (*ii*) management and staff;
   (*iii*) premises;
   (*iv*) net assets;
   (*v*) working capital;
   (*vi*) profits and dividends;
   (*vii*) prospects.

(c) The accountant's report, which contains the following information:
   (*i*) the company's profits (pre-tax and depreciation) for the previous ten years (five years since 1973);
   (*ii*) the company's assets and liabilities;
   (*iii*) the rates of dividends paid on each class of share for the past five years.

(d) General information, including the following information:
   (*i*) directors' interest;
   (*ii*) whether or not the company is a close company;
   (*iii*) articles of association;
   (*iv*) details of subsidiaries;
   (*v*) details of the contract between the shareholders and the issuing house, and other contracts not in the ordinary course of business;
   (*vi*) details of capital reorganization.

12. Application and allotment
After the application lists are closed, work proceeds on allotment. If the issue is undersubscribed, then all applications can be accepted in

full and the shortfall borne by the underwriters (*see* **13**). In the case of oversubscription, ballots are held or applications scaled down, usually to the advantage of smaller applicants.

Letters of acceptance and allotment are posted so that they are received by the allottees before dealings commence.

13. Underwriting

For a fee, the issuing house underwrites the issue, guaranteeing a full subscription at the agreed terms. Thus the risk to the company, that adverse market conditions might endanger the issue, is removed, since any deficiency in public subscription is made good by the issuing house and its sub-underwriters (other merchant banks, insurance companies, pension funds and other institutional investors) in return for a sub-underwriting commission of about 1¼ per cent on the offer price. Thus, of the £20m Agricultural Mortgage Corporation 9½ per cent debenture stock 1983–6, applications were received for 7 per cent. The remaining 93 per cent were taken up by the underwriters.

In spite of this extreme case, sub-underwriters are apparently in a privileged position. If the issue is fully subscribed, they earn a commission without further obligation on their part, and if not they possess sound quoted securities which are marketable, perhaps eventually at a premium, in addition to their fee.

14. A public issue by the company

Here the company raises capital by offering shares directly to the public. The procedure is much the same as for the offer for sale outlined above. However, in this case the issuing house does not assume the role of principal and is not normally required by the issuing company to deal with advertising, allocation and allotment, although it usually arranges underwriting.

15. Offer for sale by tender

The procedure is similar to that for issuing Government Treasury bills. It has been used by a number of public utilities since 1945 and by other companies throughout the period 1960–93.

The offer for sale quotes a minimum price to guide investors in tendering a price which they judge will secure for them the allotment they want. However, shares are finally allotted at a single 'striking' price, which is the lowest price at which the issue is fully subscribed. Obviously, this is to the advantage of applicants who have quoted excessively high prices.

The extent to which this method has been used has varied according to the issue and the experiences of companies raising capital in this manner. When striking prices are necessarily set below the minimum offer and dealings open at a discount, the attitude of issuing houses and investors to further issues by tender is certain to be influenced. The approval of the Stock Exchange is always required.

16. Advantages of tenders

(a) Tenders may be preferred by issuing houses in unsettled markets or where a company seeking quotation has no counterpart for comparison. By 'charging what the market will bear', they are relieved of the full responsibility for pitching the terms of the issue exactly right and are spared the embarrassment of a large premium should they pitch the offer price too low in an offer for sale.

(b) In a buoyant market an optimistic valuation by the public will mean that vendors may get a better price for their shares. However, they should also consider that they may be driven up to levels which they cannot hold, which could jeopardise future issues.

(c) Tenders reduce stagging activities because the parties who tender and establish the likely striking price are generally the long-term investors.

In view of these changing conditions, tenders seem to come into vogue for short periods.

17. Stags

The difficulty of issuing successfully a large number of shares or loan stock over a short period is reduced by the activities of stags, who acquire shares for resale at a profit when dealings commence. However, they are most active when the risk of losses from unfavourable changes in market conditions is lowest and may be discouraged if the issuing house believes that permanent investors will subscribe sufficient amounts. Investors who must compete for allotment naturally wish them to be discouraged. They may be discouraged in the following ways.

(a) Since stagging is encouraged when part of the issue price is payable on application and the balance by calls, the issuing house can demand payment in full on application.

(b) Evidence of sufficient bank facilities to match total applications may be required. Alternatively all cheques may be 'presented'.

(c) Multiple applications, which increase their chances of reasonable allotments in ballots and drastic scaling-down arrangements, may be banned. Following the privatisation issues of 1987, several stags were fined heavily, and one imprisoned, for false declarations involving multiple applications.

(d) Banks are unlikely to provide facilities for these purposes in times of severe credit squeeze.

18. Private placings
Companies not requiring quotation or only limited amounts of capital may approach issuing houses with a view to private placings. Institutional clients may be more interested in the security of the investment, return and growth, rather than marketability of the securities. Alternatively, companies may place their shares or loan stock direct with interested finance houses.

19. Stock Exchange placings
The Stock Exchange may agree to a placing of securities which are likely to be of limited interest to investors. Small issues of fixed-interest securities which fall into this category are placed with institutional investors, brokers and jobbers on the Stock Exchange, from whom the general public may purchase.

20. Costs of new issues
The expenses of placings are substantially less than those for public issues and offers for sale, for the following reasons.

(a) Printing costs of limited numbers of application forms and prospectuses are lower.

(b) Bank charges for application and allotment are lower.

(c) No underwriting is required.

(d) Advertising charges are minimal.

The Stock Exchange introduction is certain to be the least costly method.

Costs vary not only between the method of issue, but according to the size of the issue. Naturally a large issue will incur higher charges than a smaller one. However, this is a source of real economies of scale, since costs do not increase in proportion to the size of the issue.

21. Stock Exchange introduction
Where a company's shares are held by, say, 100 shareholders, quotation

or 'permission to deal' may be obtained by means of an introduction. This does not raise new capital and so does not require a prospectus, although advertisements similar to those for placings are needed. Information is also required by the Shares and Loans Department of the Stock Exchange, as for a quotation of shares by public issue.

22. Rights issue

When raising new capital, companies very commonly give existing shareholders an opportunity to subscribe for shares at a preferential price in proportion to their existing holdings. For instance, in a 'one for two' issue, a shareholder with 200 shares is entitled to a further 100.

23. Valuation of the rights

Assuming the information contained in **22** and that the market price of the share is currently £1.00 and the rights issue is made at 75p per share, then the value of rights is found by formula:

$$\frac{\text{Market price} - \text{Issue price of new shares}}{\text{No. of shares required for a right to the new share} + 1}$$

$$= \frac{100p - 75p}{2 + 1}$$

$$= \frac{25p}{2 + 1}$$

$$= 8.3p$$

Thus an investor wishing to acquire shares in this company can either buy in the market at £1.00 or buy the rights of 8.3p per existing share and then subscribe at the issuing price of 75p.

24. Advantages to the company

(a) A rights issue is relatively cheap and simple.
(b) It is usually successful.
(c) It provides publicity.
(d) Additional shares may create a more active market.

25. Disadvantages to the company

(a) The company may forego higher premiums obtainable in the open market.

(b) It must increase profits proportionally to maintain the dividend rate and share prices.

(c) Extra supplies may in the short term depress the share price.

(d) A rights issue may raise the problem of fractions.

26. Advantages to shareholders

(a) They buy shares at a preferential price if rights are taken up.

(b) They can sell rights to third parties. Either way no loss is incurred. (Details of current rights offers are published daily in *The Financial Times*.)

(c) They may maintain their relative shareholding and control position.

(d) They can make up their mind whether to sell or accept on the basis of their past experience with the company.

(e) The lower share price may make them more marketable.

27. Disadvantages to shareholders

(a) Those who fail to sell rights or accept will suffer losses from lower share prices. For example:

Already issued:	
100 000 ordinary shares (market value £1)	= £100 000
Rights Issue:	
100 000 ordinary shares issued at 80p	= £80 000
Total capital:	
200 000 ordinary shares	= £180 000
1 ordinary share	$= \dfrac{£180\,000}{£200\,000}$

= 90p per share, compared with the original £1.

Shareholders who accept lose 10p per share on those held but gain 10p on new shares.

(b) They may lack funds.

(c) They face increased risks arising from their increased shareholding. Diversification may be preferable.

(d) They may incur capital gains liability on the sale of rights.

28. Bonus issues

A bonus issue does not raise fresh capital but represents a capitalization of accumulated reserves, which brings nominal capital into line with the value of capital employed.

Example *X Co. balance sheets and bonus issues of shares*

	Before bonus issue £	After bonus issue £
Issued share capital	50 000	200 000
Capital reserves	200 000	50 000
Revenue reserve	25 000	25 000
Shareholders' funds	275 000	275 000
Represented by:		
Assets	275 000	275 000

Thus the bonus issue of 3:1 has not raised any additional funds; it has merely transferred £150 000 from capital reserve into shares. This is clearly seen by examination of the total shareholders' funds figure, which is unchanged at £275 000.

Assuming that the market price was £4.00 prior to issue, then the new price will be as follows:

$$\text{New share price} = \text{Market price} + \frac{\text{Original No. of shares}}{\text{New No. of shares}}$$

$$= 400\text{p} \times \frac{50\ 000}{200\ 000}$$

$$= \underline{\underline{£1.00}}$$

29. Share split
A split or subdivision of shares, like a bonus issue, does not provide the shareholder with any direct monetary advantage, for although he or she holds more shares, the average price falls (the extent depending on market sentiment) and total dividends are unlikely to change since corporate earning power is unchanged. Nevertheless, the smaller valuation tends to make them slightly more attractive to investors and therefore more marketable. Shareholders' relative voting powers are also unchanged.

30. Timing the issue
There is no set of rules for the timing of issues, a process which is so important for success. To companies this means the best possible price for their shares and the lowest fixed-interest charges on long-term loans. They have to rely to a large extent on the judgment of the issuing house which can best interpret market trends. There are a multitude of factors which may influence the climate of the market and the success or otherwise of an issue. An issuing house will consider the following factors, in timing an issue:

(a) the general level of prices of securities;
(b) the general market trends and trade expectations;

(c) political and international crises;
(d) budgets;
(e) taxation changes and company legislation.

Table 5A indicates the relative importance of the various sources of company finance.

Table 5A *Sources of finance for industrial and commercial companies 1988–1992 (£b)*

	1988	1989	1990	1991	1992
Internal funds	39.9	34.6	33.8	32.7	32.2
Bank borrowings	31.5	33.9	19.9	−0.9	−1.9
Loans and mortgages	5.8	9.1	8.0	3.6	2.5
Ordinary shares	4.3	1.9	2.9	9.7	5.1
Debentures and preference shares	6.9	13.9	11.1	11.0	7.9
Capital from overseas	8.0	11.2	11.7	10.3	6.5

Source: Central Statistical Office

Issuing houses

31. Types of issuing house
There are basically three types of issuing house.

(a) *The merchant bank.* Originally specializing in merchanting business, these banks today deal in accepting bills of exchange and advising companies on share issues, e.g. Hill Samuel.
(b) *The finance house.* These houses have taken on issuing-house work in addition to their traditional role of financing companies themselves, e.g. Investors in Industry.
(c) *The clearing banks.* In recent years the large joint-stock banks have entered into the new-issue business.

32. Role of issuing houses
In 9 we saw that the issuing houses act either as principals or as agents to the companies making the issue of securities. This distinction is essentially a legal one and does not affect their role as issuing houses. Their functions are summarized as follows.

(a) They advise companies on the best method of issue, and
(b) what type of security to issue, and
(c) the issue price.
(d) They have a responsibility to the investing public. Consequently

they make detailed investigations not only to meet the demanding legal and accounting requirements, but to guarantee as far as is possible the claims made in the prospectus and credentials, reputation and integrity of all persons concerned with the issue to avoid exploitation of the public. These investigations are carried out thoroughly (for the reputation of the issuing house is also involved) and will involve checks by issuing house staff who visit the company's premises to interview staff, agencies and possibly police enquiries.

(e) They devise the flotation timetable and act as co-ordinators of the many specialists engaged in the programme.

33. Expenses incurred in the flotation

A typical extract from a prospectus to illustrate the various fees and expenses involved in an Offer for Sale is as follows:

'X Merchant Bankers has contracted to purchase 800 000 ordinary shares of 25p each at a price of 124p per share and to offer such shares for sale to the public (Note: at a price of 125p). The company will pay the costs and expenses of and incidental to the increase in and reorganization of the share capital and the application for quotation for and permission to deal in the issued Ordinary Shares, its accountancy and legal expenses, the stamp duty on the increase in the share capital, the cost of printing, advertising and circulating their Offer for Sale, the fees and expenses of the receiving bankers and the Registrars and a fee to X Merchant Bankers. The aggregate costs and expenses payable by the company in respect of the Offer for Sale are estimated to amount to £45 000. X Merchant Bankers will pay their own legal expenses, a fee to the Brokers and an underwriting commission of 1¼ per cent on the offer of each share.'

34. Hypothetical timetable for a flotation of shares

(i.e. original shareholders sell shares to the Issuing House).

Weeks commencing:

Monday 3 June	1.	Directors of company seeking a flotation of shares by Offer for Sale meet with Issuing House to decide on strategy and timing.
Monday 15 July	1.	Solicitors, Brokers, Reporting Accountants appointed and instructed by Issuing House.
	2.	Solicitors begin drafting new Memorandum and Articles of Association to conform to the Stock Exchange Requirements.

Monday 22 July	1.	Meeting with company's joint-stock bank or other organization appointed Receiving Bankers.
	2.	Issuing House receives details of company's directors, management and staff.
	3.	Decision *re* extent of advertising of Prospectus in newspapers.
	4.	Application to Stock Exchange to make Offer for Sale of, say, 20 per cent of share capital.
Monday 29 July	1.	Meeting of Directors, Reporting Accountants, Brokers, Solicitors, Issuing House to discuss the draft of the Accountants' full report.
	2.	Meeting to discuss narrative sections of the Prospectus, i.e. General and Legal sections.
	3.	Draft sent to printers.
Monday 5 August	1.	All parties meet to discuss the first proof of the Prospectus.
	2.	Draft of Accountants' report for inclusion in Offer for Sale discussed.
	3.	Memorandum and Articles of Association proofed and discussed.
	4.	Second proof of Offer for Sale submitted to the Stock Exchange for comment.
Monday 12 August	1.	Application form, letters of Allotment and letters of Acceptance proofed.
	2.	Service agreements between company and executives completed and executed.
	3.	Powers of Attorney obtained from each director authorising signature of issue documents on his behalf.
Monday 19 August	1.	Full meetings to discuss second proof of Prospectus and Stock Exchange comment and Accountants prepare draft of current year's profit forecast and projection for following year.
Monday 2 September	1.	Accountants finalize current and following year's profit projections.
	2.	Full meetings to consider third proof of Prospectus.
Monday 9 September	1.	Book advertising space.
	2.	Draft of Purchase Agreement between the Issuing House and the Shareholders presented.

3. All necessary consents received, i.e. from Stock Exchange, Bank of England *re* exchange control and timing, and Bankers.
4. Certificates of borrowings and facilities supplied by bank.
5. Statement of company's adequacy of working capital and profits prepared by Auditors.
6. Final proofs of all documents circulated to all parties.

Monday 16 September

1. Finalize all documents and fix the offer price of the shares for printing.
2. Agree notes for City Editors for preliminary press release and announcement to employees.
3. Bulk orders to printers.
4. Extraordinary General Meeting of company to increase capital and adopt new Articles of Association.
5. Board meeting to:
   (*a*) Capitalize reserves and allot shares.
   (*b*) Approve Offer for Sale.
6. Purchase Agreement signed.
7. Prospectus filed with Registrar of Companies.
8. Printers commence delivery of documents.
9. Brokers send underwriting letters to sub-underwriters.
10. Press announcement and announcement to employees released.

Monday 23 September

1. Offer for Sale published in newspapers.
2. Submit documents to Quotations Dept. of Stock Exchange to support application for quotation.

Wednesday 25 September

1. Quotation granted by Stock Exchange.

Thursday 26 September

1. Application List opens and closes.
2. Cheques paid in.
3. If over-subscribed Issuing House decides on methods of allotment.
4. If under-subscribed Broker informs underwriters of the shortfall and their commitments.
5 Press announcement giving result of the Offer and basis of allotment.

Friday 4 October	1	The Issuing House posts Letters of Allotment.
Monday 7 October	1.	Dealings commence.
	2.	Receiving bank pays Issuing House the proceeds of the offer.
Monday 14 October		Last day for share splitting.
Wednesday 16 October		Last day for renunciation.
Monday 11 November		Share certificates available.

Responsibility for documents. There may be as many as fifty documents involved in an offer for sale issue. Table 5B summarizes the main documents and letters needed for the typical programme outlined above and indicates the responsibility of the parties engaged in the flotation.

The Unlisted Securities Market

35. Types of Stock Exchange trading
There are three ways in which company securities may be traded on the Stock Exchange.

(a) Through admission to the Stock Exchange official list giving full quotation (*see* **5**).
(b) Through Stock Exchange rule 163(2) which allows dealers to occasionally buy and sell unlisted securities. However, as no formal relationship exists between the Stock Exchange and the unlisted company, the Stock Exchange acted to form a regulated market for the increasing number of company securities traded outside the official list. From 1980 the Stock Exchange would restrict dealings under rule 163(2) to genuinely occasional transactions and formalize the existing unlisted securities market by setting up (**c**).
(c) Through the Unlisted Securities Market (USM). This began in November 1980, providing a regulated market for the securities of smaller companies as an alternative to official listing.

36. Admission requirements
The requirements for admission are less onerous than for official listing.

Table 5B *Who is responsible for flotation documents*

Letter/Document	Company	Solicitors	Issuing House	Accountants	Registrars
			Responsibility		
Bank of England Timing Consent			x		
Surtax clearance				x	
Current year's accounts	x			x	
Service agreements		x			
Notice of EGM		x			
Print of Resolutions		x			
New Memorandum and Articles		x	x		
Powers of Attorney		x			
Copies of contracts listed in Prospectus		x			
Accountants' Report				x	
Accountants' Statement of Adjustments				x	
Accountants' Consent				x	
Bank's letter of consent	x				
Stock Exchange forms			x		
Bank certificates re company borrowings	x			x	
Statement of working capital	x			x	
Profit forecast	x			x	
Shares certificates					x
Share purchase agreement		x	x		
Offer for Sale			x		
Application forms			x		
Letter of Acceptance			x		
Press announcements			x		
Underwriting letters			x		
Statement re working capital for Stock Exchange			x		
Printed copies of Accountants' Report			x		
Authorization of adverts			x		
Order of printing			x		
Distribution list			x		
Letter to Stock Exchange re splitting			x		
Letter of regret			x		

(a) Only 10 per cent of the company's issued capital must be in public hands, compared with 25 per cent on the listed market.

(b) Financial statistics need be provided only for two years or for whatever lesser period the company has been trading, instead of the full accounting report for listed companies.

(c) The company must be registered as a public limited-liability company.

(d) Sponsorship by a broker must normally be supplied by two firms of jobbers prepared to register as dealers in the securities.

37. Method of issuing securities
A company admitted by the Quotations Committee may issue its securities in the following ways.

(a) *Introduction*. This would be the appropriate method where the securities are already fairly widely held as a result of dealings under rule 163(2).

(b) *Placing*. This would be the usual method for a newly admitted company. Securities are sold to clients of brokers, although at least 25 per cent of the issue must be offered to jobbers who may make them available to the general public.

(c) *Offer for sale*. This method would suit the larger, more mature company that is more attractive to the general investors.

(d) *Offer for sale by tender*. This method would suit companies who have no comparable quoted companies. Consequently they issue the shares by tender so 'charging what the market will bear'.

38. USM companies by industrial sector
The USM has attracted a broad cross-section of companies, many in high-technology products and processes, computers and electronics. Table 5C indicates the number by industrial sector and generally how small the companies are.

39. Benefits of the USM
The USM provides many benefits.

(a) Small relatively young companies can raise capital for development.

(b) Company promoters can realize their investments by selling their shares.

(c) Companies can use their marketable securities to finance acquisitions.

Table 5C *USM companies by industrial sector (quoted in* The Financial Times *July 1993)*

	No.	%	Capitalization £m	%	Average Capitalization £m
Brewers, distillers	3	1.3	37.77	0.7	12.6
Building materials	12	5.2	96.44	1.8	8.0
Business services	9	3.9	93.0	1.8	10.3
Chemicals	2	0.9	6.5	0.1	3.3
Conglomerates	1	0.4	2.3	0.0	2.3
Construction	17	7.4	129.4	2.5	7.6
Electronics	32	13.9	1030.1	19.7	32.2
Engineering	6	2.6	30.1	0.6	5.0
Finance, insurance	5	2.2	149.1	2.8	29.8
Food manufacturing	5	2.2	45.3	0.9	9.1
Food retailing	2	0.9	67.7	1.3	33.9
Health, household	13	5.7	1510.2	28.8	116.2
Hotels, leisure	18	7.8	124.7	2.4	6.9
Media	16	7.0	307.7	5.9	19.2
Metals	3	1.3	30.7	0.6	10.2
Miscellaneous	32	13.9	557.0	10.6	17.4
Motors	6	2.6	107.2	2.0	17.9
Oil, gas	12	5.2	169.2	3.2	14.1
Paper, printing	9	3.9	124.8	2.4	13.9
Property	13	5.7	167.5	3.2	12.9
Stores	6	2.6	388.4	7.4	64.7
Textiles	7	3.0	49.0	0.9	7.0
Transport	1	0.4	13.4	0.3	13.4
Total	230	100.0	5237.51	100.0	

40. Disadvantages of the USM
The disadvantages are as follows.

(a) Investors find difficulty in valuing small, young companies operating in new-technology fields.

(b) Prices of securities may be forced up because of the relatively small issues in relation to demand and the prevalence of placing, which means that potential purchasers in an offer for sale must buy in a secondary market.

(c) The investor faces higher risks than on the Stock Exchange.

The Third Market

41. Over-the-counter share market
An unofficial over-the-counter share market has existed in London for several years. The market makers were licensed dealers offering limited protection to the investor against their own failure. Some of the shares in the market were in new companies that did not have the backing of large financial sponsors. Consequently, the risks facing the investor were higher in this market than for the investor in securities adopted by the Stock Exchange.

42. The Third Market
In January 1987 the Third Market was created when the Stock Exchange brought under its aegis the shares in the over-the-counter market. Now the investor is covered by Stock Exchange compensation schemes.

43. The advantages of the third market
The main advantages are:

(a) Only a small advertisement announcing the dealing is required.
(b) There is no minimum size criteria.
(c) There is no requirement for specific percentages of equity to be made available.
(d) The sponsor confirms that the company is suitable to join the market and arranges shares with at least two market makers.
(e) It provides a more liquid market for company shares than other sources of venture capital.
(f) Share prices are quoted in *The Financial Times*.

Progress test 5

1. Compare and contrast the advantages of private and public companies. **(1–4)**

2. For what reasons do companies seek quotation? **(5)**

3. What are the prerequisites for a company seeking a Stock Exchange quotation? **(7)**

4. Describe the steps taken by a company leading up to an offer for sale. **(10–13)**

5. Describe the main features of an offer by tender. **(15–16)**

6. Compare placings and introductions as methods of making company securities available to investors. **(18–21)**

7. What are the pros and cons of a rights issue? **(22–27)**

8. Explain the following terms:
(a) issuing house;
(b) stagging;
(c) underwriting and sub-underwriting;
(d) convertible loan stock;
(e) application and allotment;
(f) bonus issues. **(13–28)**

9. What does Table 5A show you about the role of the banks as a source of company finance?

10. Describe the nature of issuing houses and their role in floating new issues of shares. **(31–32)**

11. Draw up a typical timetable for a flotation of shares and indicate the responsibilities of the various parties concerned. **(34)**

12. Describe the role and development of the USM. **(35–39)**

13. (a) From Table 5B determine which industrial sectors are most reliant on the USM as a source of finance.
(b) Give reasons for your results.

14. Describe the role and development of the Third Market. **(41–43)**

6
Short-term, export and specialized finance for industry

Short-term finance

1. Trade credit
It is an impossible task to measure this value accurately. Nevertheless, the Radcliffe Report in 1959 indicated that the total amount of trade credit outstanding surpassed the total of bank credit. Little is known about its distribution pattern, but it is thought that it is relatively more important to small firms and fast-growing firms. The latter are likely to be net takers, as their need for working capital runs ahead of their resources. Larger firms on the other hand are perhaps able to economize on working capital, holding a smaller proportion to turnover.

2. Forms of trade credit
Credit terms, which vary between businesses, may be arranged as follows.

(a) They may be recommended by the industrial trade association.
(b) They may be a trade custom.
(c) They may be specially arranged by the parties. For example:
  (*i*) customers may advance loans to manufacturers to buy materials;
  (*ii*) customers may supply manufacturers with materials (to guarantee quality), paying for manufacturing costs with an allowance for material wastage (i.e. 'free issue materials');
  (*iii*) customers may advance loans towards the costs of equipment.

3. Cost of trade credit
There are costs to firms giving and taking credit, as follows.

(a) Although invoices are usually submitted 'terms net monthly', it may in practice be six weeks before settlement is made. This costs the creditor more than 1.5 per cent (if annual interest is taken as 8 per cent) in addition to the accounting and collection costs. There is evidence that firms now consider the opportunity cost of this credit, i.e. profitable alternative uses to which this money can be put, as judged from the growth of factoring services.

(b) Customers who take credit and thereby waive cash discounts forgo returns which for large-scale purchases may amount to substantial sums per annum.

For example, a customer who is offered a cash discount of 2.5 per cent if payment is made within seven days, or alternatively full payment at thirty days, is really paying interest of 40.6 per cent for this credit. This cost may be calculated by formula:

$$\text{Cost of credit} = \frac{\text{Percentage discount}}{100 - \text{Percentage discount}}$$
$$\times \frac{365}{\text{Final payment date} - \text{Period of discount}} \times 100$$
$$= \frac{2.5}{97.5} \times \frac{365}{23}$$
$$= 40.6\%$$

Clearly the customer should borrow to take advantage of the cash discount. However, one should remember that the gain to the customer is the loss to the supplier, who is paying dearly to get payments in earlier.

4. Risks
Dependence on trade credit carries the following risks.

(a) Middlemen may find themselves in an impossible dilemma when placed between creditors, who withdraw or grant credit on less liberal terms, and their customers, who may attempt to extend their credit.
(b) As a result, customer goodwill is lost.
(c) Reliance on powerful creditors might result in a loss of independence.

5. Bank credit
Commercial banks prefer not to advance long-term loans which conflict with their basic objectives of security and liquidity of funds. However, although theoretically repayable on demand, overdrafts are generally renewable by negotiation and constitute a flexible and a relatively cheap source of working capital since interest is only payable on money borrowed.

6. Rates of interest
The rates charged to a businessperson will be influenced by the following factors.

(a) The current base rate, to which overdraft and loan rates are linked (Bank Base Rate plus 1.5 to 3 per cent).
(b) The credit-worthiness of the borrower, which will depend on:
  (*i*) the records of profits;
  (*ii*) the relation of assets to liabilities;
  (*iii*) borrowers' integrity and commercial goodwill; and
  (*iv*) the quality of available collateral and securities.

7. Classification of bankers' advances
The importance of bank credit to the various sectors of the British economy is indicated in Table 6A.

8. Bank bill finance
Bank bills of exchange are drawn on acceptance-credit facilities granted by merchant banks to their customers, preferably against short-term self-liquidating transactions, which realise funds to meet the bills at maturity. They are termed 'fine' bills in that their payment is guaranteed and are second only to Treasury bills for the lowest rate of discount when sold by the customer in the discount market. Thus they offer the businessperson a relatively cheap and reliable source of short-term credit.

9. Cost of bank bills
The cost of this credit depends on the following factors.

(a) Current and expected short-term market rates of interest.
(b) The period of credit.

Table 6A *Analysis of bank lending to UK residents 1992*

	Total Advances £m	%
Manufacturing sector	49 126	11
Agriculture, oil, gas, energy, construction	30 389	7
Services sector	128 272	28
Financial sector	107 114	24
Personal sector	135 758	30
Total	450 659	100

Source: Bank of England

(c) The rate of commission charged by acceptance houses, which is determined by:
- (*i*) the credit-worthiness of the borrower; and
- (*ii*) the nature and quality of security.

10. Trade bills

This is a bill of exchange drawn by a trader on another in exchange for goods where the purchaser (acceptor) is granted a period of credit and makes payment on its maturity. However, should the creditor want immediate payment, then he or she discounts the bill. His or her success and the cost (discount) depends on the following factors.

(a) The general financial and commercial standing of both parties to the transaction.

(b) The nature of the transaction. There are no obstacles if the parties customarily finance their business by bills. However, banks may refuse to discount accommodation bills which are issued without valid consideration.

(c) The number of bills already in the discount market and particularly those bearing the acceptor's name. As a result of these factors, the differential on trade bills can be as low as 0.5 per cent and as high as 2 per cent a year.

11. Invoice discounting

Expanding companies often find that rising sales bring increased book debts. However, there are today a number of firms prepared to advance finance to alleviate the problem of insufficient liquidity which hinders further growth, by invoice discounting. Generally an invoice-discounting facility is agreed for sound established traders who 'offer' to sell to the specialist sales debts up to this limit and who guarantee the payment of any debts so bought. If the offer is accepted, then the trader receives a cheque for perhaps 75 per cent of the total amount and accepts a bill of exchange for the same amount as security for his or her guarantee. The trader then acts as the specialist's agent, collecting sales debts in the usual manner to honour the bill. The following advantages are claimed for the trader.

(a) The increased liquidity will mean that the trader can take advantage of cash discounts offered by suppliers which may exceed the overall cost of the facility, which is about 1 per cent per month.

(b) Greater credit terms can be extended to customers.

(c) More working capital is available for peak production periods in seasonal trades.

(d) Improved credit rating through prompter payments.

(e) Since the trader may use the facility at his or her option, it may be a more economical source of finance than fixed-interest loans.

12. Factoring

Factoring, established in Britain in 1959, is similar to invoice discounting in that the specialist advances finance when it buys a trader's book debts, but in addition it may assume responsibility for the sales ledger and the credit risk. Naturally, the cost varies accordingly. The cost of the cash flow may be base rate plus 2 per cent, in addition to the service charge which will vary between 1 and 3 per cent on turnover, depending on:

(a) the size of the company;

(b) the amount of work (i.e. the number of invoices); and

(c) the degree of risk.

13. Advantages of factoring

The main advantages to a firm using the services of a factor may be summarized as follows.

(a) There are clerical and administrative savings, particularly for firms selling repetitively on credit, as follows:

(*i*) In effect the firm has one customer only, the factor. Even if the factor is 'undisclosed' to the firm's customers, it is a simple matter for the firm to endorse cheques and pass them on.

(*ii*) The firm is no longer concerned with bad-debt controls.

(*iii*) There are economies in management and staff salaries, since fewer supervisors and clerical workers are needed. Also there are corresponding savings in recruitment and training.

(b) There are also the following financial benefits.

(*i*) Capital locked up in sundry debtors' balances is available for use within the business, as all sales become in effect cash sales.

(*ii*) With this improved liquidity it can offer improved credit terms to its customers in order to increase orders.

(*iii*) It can take advantage of suppliers' cash discounts and make prompt payments.

(*iv*) This improves its credit rating.

(*v*) The turnover of stocks into cash is speeded up and this allows a larger turnover on the same investment.

(*vi*) Undisclosed factoring does not prejudice customer goodwill.

(*vii*) Since factoring is not borrowing, the company's balance sheet liquidity is not weakened nor its borrowing potential impaired.

These administrative and financial savings may be more than sufficient to cover the cost of the factoring service.

(c) The company is free to concentrate on the main jobs of producing and selling.

14. The economics of factoring
The following example indicates the areas in which a company using factoring services might obtain savings.

Savings:		£
(a) Salaries of staff working on credit control, say		20 000
(b) Discounts taken with funds provided by the factor: 2.5 per cent on say £200 000 of purchases		5 000
(c) Economies through bulk buying, using funds provided by the factor: 10 per cent on say £5 000		500
(d) Discounts no longer allowed to customers as inducement for prompt payments: 2.5 per cent on say £200 000		5 000
	Total	30 500
Less factoring service charge say 1.5 per cent on £600 000 turnover		9 000
	Notional savings	21 500

15. Factoring and invoice discounting compared

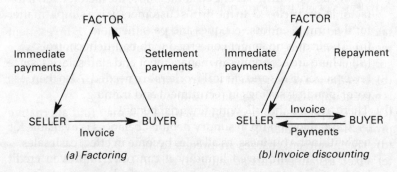

Figure 6.1 *Factoring and invoice discounting compared*

16. Financing of retail sales by HP
Many retailers selling goods on hire purchase or rental basis use the services of the many specialists in this field, so as to maintain the liquidity of working capital. Retailers have a choice of either placing customers with the HP company to draw up the agreements and arrange the payments of instalments direct, or using 'block'

discounting facilities where they sell their HP debts for immediate payments of a high proportion of the value of HP sales. The retailers then collect the instalments in the normal way to repay the finance company.

17. Financing industry by HP
This is an increasingly important source of medium-term finance for the purchase of capital goods, ranging from plant and equipment to commodities and vehicles and their insurance.

18. Types of HP agreement

(a) *Ordinary HP agreement.* The seller invoices the goods to the HP company, which agrees with the customer on a charge to be added to the amount financed. This 'balance of hire' is then repaid in equal instalments by the customer over, say, twenty-four months.

(b) *Machine life finance.* This recent innovation in the UK allows customers to purchase equipment over its anticipated working life. Once this is agreed, periodic payments are calculated by adding to the reducing balance a percentage finance charge which is linked to and slightly above base rate.

19. Advantages of HP agreements
Advocates of HP financing point out the following advantages.

(a) HP encourages firms to take a longer-term view of investment requirements, since they no longer have to buy only when they have sufficient funds for outright purchase.

(b) It is the use of equipment which is important for profits and this is gained on payment of the first instalment.

(c) Since capital is not tied up immediately, it may find alternative profitable employment.

(d) The instalment charges are predetermined.

(e) Fixed instalments are advantageous in inflation.

(f) A variety of flexible HP agreements are available to suit the customer.

(g) If the goods qualify for capital allowances and grants, these benefits are retained by the user.

Legally, finance houses are entitled to repossess goods if the terms of the agreement are broken. Consequently, they are generally reluctant to finance equipment in this way, when it becomes a fixture within a building, or it has restricted marketability, e.g. furnaces (where a secured loan is more suitable). Instead they favour identifiable goods with working lives exceeding the term of the agreement.

20. Leasing
The post-war practice of renting equipment from finance houses is now well established in the UK. It has long been a method of equipping business offices, but latterly, with the development of complex and costly equipment which needs regular servicing, firms have taken advantage of leasing schemes. The parties negotiate a primary lease period of between three and seven years, according to the anticipated working life of the equipment, in which time the capital cost and service charges are recouped. Thereafter, for the indefinite secondary period, the lessee may continue to use the equipment at a nominal rental. In 1971 the annual value of business of members of the equipment leasing association was £130m. By 1992 this total had increased to £8955m.

21. Reasons for the growth in leasing
The main reasons for the growth of leasing are as follows.

(a) Leasing provided a major source of medium-term finance, filling a gap that existed in the 1970s between short-term bank overdrafts and long-term finance from banks, insurance companies and pension funds.

(b) Companies with little scope for traditional borrowing turned to leasing. Moreover the leasing obligations were not always shown on the balance sheet: Court Line, for example, had 'off-the-balance-sheet finance' amounting to £40m for the lease of Tristar aircraft.

(c) The tax advantage. In March 1973 first-year capital allowances were set at 100 per cent for purchasers of plant and equipment, which meant that a company with taxable profits of £200 000 can offset against the profit the purchase price of equipment costing, say, £100 000; consequently, tax amounting to £52 000 is saved and the equipment acquired effectively for £48 000 compared with £100 000 if the company had insufficient profits to claim the full tax relief:

	Equipment not purchased	*Equipment purchased*
Taxable profit	£200 000	£200 000
First-year allowance 100%	—	100 000
Taxable profit	200 000	100 000
Corporation tax at 52%	104 000	52 000
Profit after tax	£96 000	£48 000

Many companies needing new equipment but lacking sufficient profits to claim tax relief turned to leasing from banks which as profitable service companies needed to purchase plant and equipment to reduce their tax liability and were prepared to pass on some of these savings by way of lower rentals.

During the mid 1980s capital allowances were phased out and by 1987 withdrawn completely, so that this tax advantage was lost (except for a relatively small number of companies in qualifying activities and locations). However, many companies with experience of leasing, and perhaps originally attracted by the high capital allowances, continue to lease equipment.

22. The size of the credit business
Today, the total value of credit outstanding on and credit agreements with finance houses, other specialist credit grantors, building societies, retailers and bank credit cards is very high and increasing. This is apparent from Table 6B.

Table 6B *Amount of credit outstanding (£m)*

	1988	1989	1990	1991	1992
From Banks:					
Credit cards	6 711	7 251	9 012	9 786	9 888
Personal loans	27 563	31 917	33 659	33 747	33 178
Other credit grantors	5 891	6 852	7 460	7 569	7 192
Retailers	2 378	2 383	2 447	2 507	2 605
Mortgages	223 736	257 980	294 909	321 544	339 793
Other bank lending	31 436	40 120	44 074	43 181	40 099
Total	297 715	346 503	391 561	418 334	432 755

The figures show the total value of credit outstanding from 1988 to 1992. In the early period they grow strongly but after 1990 the growth falters as the recession deepens and people, fearing unemployment, reduce their financial commitments.

23. Differences between HP and leasing
Lease and HP financing have many advantages in common, although there are the following basic differences:

(a) The whole leasing rental is tax allowable compared to just the interest charge of HP.
(b) Unlike the case with HP financing, it is the finance house which

receives any capital allowance, although it can pass on these benefits to the lessee by way of lower rental charges.

(c) Deposits are not required, which helps cash flow.

(d) Leasing agreements are not borrowings and so do not increase company gearing or limit a company's borrowing powers.

(e) The lessee may use the equipment after the first payment.

(f) Leasing is not subject to government controls of maximum repayment periods and minimum deposits.

The finance of foreign trade

24. Methods of payment in international trade
There are basically five methods of payment in international trade:

(a) Countertrade.

(b) Cash with order.

(c) Open account.

(d) Bills of exchange.

(e) Bankers' documentary credits.

25. Countertrade
There are several variants of countertrade:

(a) *Counter purchase.* In return for receiving a sales order, the exporter must purchase goods as services from the importer's country. The value of the counter purchase normally varies between 10 and 100 per cent of the export order. Payments are made by cash or on credit terms.

(b) *Barter.* This is a direct exchange of goods and involves no cash.

(c) *Buy-back.* Here the exporter might sell capital plant and allow the importers to pay by buying some of the plants' output in the future.

(d) *Offset.* This is becoming increasingly common in international trade in defence equipment. For example, the exporter agrees to incorporate in the final product items of equipment produced in the importing countries.

26. Cash with order
This is not a commonplace method. It might be insisted upon by the seller who is in a strong position.

27. Open account
The exporter treats the importer like any domestic customer, debiting

his or her account for goods dispatched and receiving direct payments at agreed times upon the customer's receipt of the documents of title. This is done by:

(a) telegraphic transfers;
(b) mail transfers from the debtor's bank;
(c) personal cheques where exchange-control regulations permit; or
(d) banker's draft, drawn on the debtor's bank in favour of the creditor's bank or a correspondent bank. This is the simplest and cheapest method of payment.

28. Bills of exchange
A bill of exchange is defined as 'an unconditional order in writing addressed by one person to another, signed by the person giving it, requiring the person to whom it is addressed to pay on demand or at a fixed or determinable future time, a sum certain in money to, or to the order of, a specified person, or the bearer'.

The exporter draws the bill on the importer who accepts its terms by signing it. A bill is to the advantage of both parties (and therefore figures prominently in foreign trade) for the following reasons.

(a) The exporter may realize cash by discounting it prior to maturity.
(b) The importer receives a term of credit. The transaction may be 'self-liquidating', realizing funds to meet the bill's payment.

29. Types of bills
They may be either:

(a) *documentary bills*, i.e. bills of lading indicating title to the goods are attached to the bill of exchange; or
(b) *clean bills*. Here documents are not attached but are sent direct to the purchaser. Naturally clean bills are used only when the purchaser's integrity is unquestioned.

30. Bankers' documentary credits
Here the importer arranges for his or her bank to pay the exporter, in the exporter's country, on presentation of specified documents evidencing shipment of the goods within a given time period.

31. Forms of documentary credits

(a) *A confirmed and irrevocable credit*. This guarantees payment to the exporter, since the terms of payment cannot be altered without the agreement of both parties (it is irrevocable). Furthermore, such a bill will be honoured by the correspondent bank (it is confirmed by the bank).

(b) *An unconfirmed and revocable credit.* This offers the exporter no such guarantee.

(c) *Revolving credits.* Here the importer specifies the maximum amount which may be drawn on his or her bank at any one time or may be drawn in any period by an exporter.

(d) *Transferable credits.* This prior arrangement with the importer allows the exporter to transfer part or all of the benefit of the credit to another party, usually his or her supplier.

32. Nature of risks

There are two types of risk facing exporters, as follows.

(a) *Normal commercial risks*:
   (*i*) physical damage to the goods; or
   (*ii*) default of payment through insolvency of buyer, etc.
(b) *'Political' risks*:
   (*i*) the introduction of exchange control prior to payment;
   (*ii*) import licensing changes; or
   (*iii*) local wars, etc.

33. Insurance cover

The normal commercial risks can be covered by insurance with commercial organizations, and is sufficient for those transactions where the political risks are negligible. However, when full cover is required, it is provided by the Government's Export Credits Guarantee Department (ECGD). The reduction in risk makes firms more export-orientated and able to offer better credit terms. Even so the ECGD does not accept the whole risk but insists that the exporter carries a small share (up to 10 per cent) in order:

(a) to deter overtrading;
(b) to encourage prudence; and
(c) to encourage the exporter to press for payment on default.

34. The Export Credit Guarantee Department (ECGD)

The purpose of the government body, ECGD, is to help exporters of UK goods and services to win business and UK firms to invest overseas by providing guarantees, insurance and reinsurance against loss.

The total business insured is:

1982–83	£19 090m
1990–91	£16 755m
1991–92	£12 186m

The 1991–2 reduction needs an explanation. In this year ECGD sold its short-term business to a private sector credit insurance company (it was privatised) as a result of emerging legal challenges within the EC to the unrestricted operation of state credit insurance in the short-term area. Consequently, its business is now principally medium- and long-term credit guarantee work although it will insure UK exporters by providing short-term export credit when private companies refuse to accept the risk.

Specialized finance

35. The Investors in Industry Group
Investors in Industry (3i) is an independent, private-sector group whose main business is providing long-term and permanent investment capital and advice to companies of all sizes. These facilities are provided through specialist groups with particular skills in different segments of the market, either directly or through 3i's network of 25 regional offices. Between 1983 and 1987 Investors in Industry invested a total of £1587m in 4500 companies.

For smaller companies it provides long-term loans and share capital, and short-term hire-purchase, leasing and guarantees. It also provides business premises through its Properties division. For the larger company its City operation provides equity and loan capital up to about £50m, or more through syndication with other investors.

For high growth companies, particularly those in high technology areas, the Ventures team provides capital and advice. The advisory services of the group are carried out by the following subsidiaries:

(a) 3i Portfolio Management Ltd. Provides investment management services and also manages the group's listed investments.
(b) 3i Corporate Finance Ltd. Provides advice and specialist services with mergers, acquisitions and new issues.
(c) 3i Consultants Ltd. Provides a management consultancy in all industrial and commercial sectors.

36. The Agricultural Mortgage Corporation Ltd (AMC)
This was established in 1928 with the Bank of England and other banks as its shareholders. Its objectives were:

(a) to make loans on first mortgage of agricultural, forestry and farming estates.

(b) to make loans in accordance with the Improvement of Land Acts 1864 and 1899 for effecting and paying for improvements for agricultural purposes.

37. British Technology Group (BTG)

The group's primary function is to promote the development of technology from universities, polytechnics, Research Councils and government research bodies. It also takes responsibility for licensing and protecting inventions, providing funds for developing the inventions and their subsequent industrial applications and negotiating license agreements with industry.

Venture capital

38. The sources of capital for small businesses

The sources of capital for business start-ups and business development are as follows:

(a) Business Expansion Scheme.
(b) Loan Guarantee Scheme.
(c) Banks.
(d) Unlisted Securities Market.

39. The Business Expansion Scheme (BES)

The BES was introduced in 1983 as the successor to the Business Start-up Scheme. It quickly became an established part of the venture capital market, raising a record £148m from investors in 1987. The features of the scheme are as follows:

(a) the investor can offset against one's top rate of income tax, investments of between £500 and £40 000 per year in the shares of certain companies. Moreover, if the investor holds onto the shares for five years there is no tax on the profit from their sale;

(b) the investee company must not be quoted on the Stock Exchange or Unlisted Securities Market; and

(c) it must be in a qualifying business. The excluded sectors are financial services, e.g. commodities and share trading, leasing, banking, businesses doing more than half their trade overseas, and property companies.

40. The Loan Guarantee Scheme

This scheme was introduced in 1981 to provide capital for companies unable to meet the banks' normal criteria for lending. The main features are as follows:

(a) Loans of up to £100 000 are available from participating financial institutions (English, Scottish and Irish commercial banks, etc.) guaranteed by the Government.

(b) The guarantee was originally 80 per cent, since reduced to 70 per cent. It is 85 per cent in the government's Inner City Task Force Areas. These areas are those regarded as the most deprived parts of the inner city within Urban Programme Areas. They are not mandatory or permanent (by 1990, 20 had been started and four had already closed).

(c) The interest rate includes a premium of 2.5 per cent and 2 per cent when inner city.

(d) Borrowers do not have to pledge their personal assets.

41. Banks

There are hundreds of sources of capital available in the form of loans or equity capital for companies that may not qualify for the BES or Loan Guarantee Scheme.

(a) All merchant banks have funds available for loans.

(b) Equity finance is available from merchant banks, pension funds and insurance companies. The British Venture Capital Association provides a list of members.

However, these investors prefer to make large scale investments in developing companies with a proven track record and a high probability of well above average returns.

Progress test 6

1. Indicate the various sources of working capital available to a quoted company engaged in manufacturing activities. **(1–18)**

2. Compare and contrast Trade and Bank Credit as sources of working capital. **(1–6)**

3. Explain the terms 'invoice discounting' and 'factoring' and the advantages of these services to the businessman seeking funds. **(11–15)**

4. Compare and contrast hire purchase and leasing as methods of financing industry. **(16–22)**

5. What is meant by trading an open account? **(27)**

6. Outline the methods by which an exporter may be paid. **(24–31)**

7. Describe the main risks facing exporters and how these risks can be avoided. **(32–34)**

8. (a) Describe the work of the ECGD. **(33–34)**
   (b) Account for the reduction in ECGD insurance in the 1990s. **(33–34)**

9. Discuss the activities of the Investors in Industry Group. **(35)**

10. Write notes on the following:
   (a) British Technology Group. **(37)**
   (b) The Agricultural Mortgage Corporation. **(36)**

11. What do you understand by the term 'Venture capital'? **(38–41)**

Part three
The search for profitability

7
Objectives of the business firm

Profit maximization

1. Profit maximization: the traditional objective

Alfred Marshall's *Principles of Economics*, 1890, a statement of contemporary economic theory, contained a convincing and impeccably argued theory of the firm that explained the behaviour of firms operating in the highly competitive markets of the late 1800s. Furthermore, Marshall and contemporaries established plausible theories showing how monopolists behave; and subsequently to fill in the middle ground between these two extremes and thereby mirror the actual market situation the neo-classical economists (notably Robinson and Chamberlin) turned their attention to 'imperfect competition' and 'monopolistic competition'. Throughout this extended development of micro-economic theory, one fundamental assumption subsisted, i.e. that firms endeavour to maximize profits.

2. Perfect competition

In view of the prevalence of this profit-maximizing goal in modern micro-economic theory, an objective which many writers on economics and corporate behaviour take for granted, it is surely relevant in an examination of firms' objectives to analyse the basis of this goal, its strengths and weaknesses and appropriateness to the modern business organization as a prime motivating force. For this reason, let us first examine the classical theory of the firm in a competitive situation.

The theory of the firm in a perfectly competitive market predicts how a firm behaves and reacts to changes in market forces. This may be summarized by the following analysis and by reference to the supporting Figs. 7.1 and 7.2.

At the outset, the assumptions that are usually made for perfect competition must be stated. They are:

(a) the firm's objective is profit maximization;
(b) firms are free to enter the industry;
(c) all goods are homogeneous (i.e. no trade marks or branded goods);
(d) there is perfect knowledge regarding production methods;
(e) consumers are rational and wish to maximize satisfaction;
(f) there are very many suppliers and buyers.

3. Determination of the market price
The very many buyers behave collectively in a manner characterised by the demand curve DD in Fig. 7.1. This means that they conform to the Law of Downward-Sloping Demand, preferring to buy smaller quantities of the product if the price is high and larger amounts if the price is low. Sellers' attitude towards price is summarized by the supply curve SS in Fig. 7.1. The Law of Upward-Sloping Supply states that they are prepared to supply larger amounts for higher prices.

Consequently, buyers and sellers interact in the market place to establish an equilibrium price (OP) where the quantity offered for sale exactly equals the amount buyers are prepared to purchase (OQ).

4. The firm – a price-taker
A careful examination of the assumptions in 2 reveals that the market price OP is the ruling selling price for the typical competitive firm (Fig. 7.2). Clearly, any attempt to sell above OP means it will fail to meet its fundamental objective of maximum profits because of assumptions **(c)** and **(e)** above. Moreover, any attempt to sell below OP is out of the question because it can sell its entire output at the ruling (higher) market price. Thus the firm has no choice regarding price: it must accept the ruling market price.

5. The optimum output
However, the profit-maximizing firm can exercise choice in its output policy if not in its selling price. Furthermore, if it is to secure its goal it must first clearly understand its cost/production relationship and, secondly, achieve a unique balance between its level and cost of

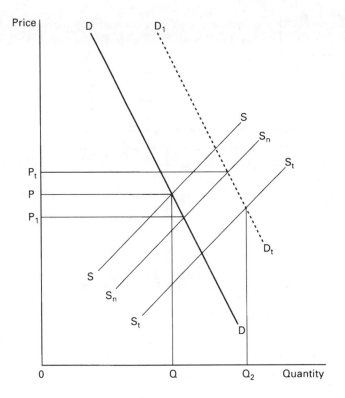

Figure 7.1 *Perfect competition – the market*

production and its selling price. The first step in this process requires an appreciation of the relationship between average and marginal costs. The second step is to select the exact level of output/sales that maximizes profits, given the selling price.

6. Average and marginal costs

The economist who is interested in the relationship between costs and output over the whole production range conventionally graphs U-shaped average and marginal cost curves to illustrate the influence of increasing and decreasing returns to a fixed factor of production. In other words, if extra variable factors, e.g. workers, are employed, with a fixed factor, e.g. a factory, then variable costs rise less steeply than output because of the operation of the law of increasing returns; and eventually at high levels of operations the law of diminishing returns (*see* Fig. 7.3) causes variable costs to rise faster than output. Table 7A

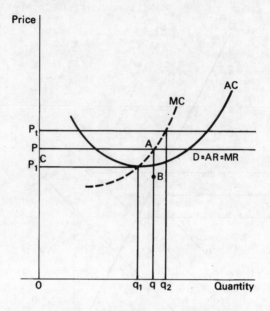

Figure 7.2 *The firm in perfect competition*

Table 7A *Cost/output relationships*

Workers	Total output	Variable costs	Marginal costs	Average costs
		£	£	£
1	10	15		1.50
			1.00	
2	25	30		1.20
			0.75	
3	45	45		1.00
			0.60	
4	70	60		0.85
			0.75	
5	90	75		0.83
			1.00	
6	105	90		0.85
			1.50	
7	115	105		0.91

illustrates typical cost/output relationships based on hypothetical productivity figures over a company's range of output (*see* Fig. 7.4).

Note: Variable costs consists of wages of £15 per worker. Marginal cost is the additional cost of one unit, e.g. the second worker adds 15 units to total output at an extra cost of £15. Therefore MC = £1 and since it is an 'average', value corresponds to the 17.5 unit which is the midpoint between the 10 units produced by the first worker and the 25 units subsequently produced when the second is employed.

Output/Sales	MC	MR	Loss – or Gain +
22	8.0p	10p	2.0p +
23	8.5p	10p	1.5p +
24	9.0p	10p	1.0p +
25	10.0p	10p	–
26	11.0p	10p	1.0p –

By increasing output-sales, the *additional* profit is less and less, and total profits are maximized at 25 units; at 26 units the cost of the extra unit is 11p and therefore a loss of 1.0p is incurred. Consequently, profits are not maximized at output/sales below or in excess of MC = MR levels.

7. Output that maximizes profits

The concept of marginal analysis provides the answer: profits are maximized at that level of output/sales where the marginal cost (i.e. the incremental cost of producing/selling one extra unit) is equal to the marginal revenue (i.e. the incremental revenue of selling one extra unit) (*see* Fig. 7.3). Thus, in the examples shown on pp. 95 and 96, the firm produces and sells Oq at a price of OP to realise the largest possible profit (CPAB in Fig. 7.2).

Total revenue = Average revenue × output
                = OP   × Oq
                = OPAq

Total cost   = Average cost   × output
                = OC   × Oq
                = OCBq

Profit   = Total revenue – total cost
                = OPAq   – OCBq
                = CPAB

8. The equilibrium state

However, newcomers are attracted by these excessive profits being earned by the industry (termed super-normal profits because they are the surplus above the minimum reward necessary to keep the

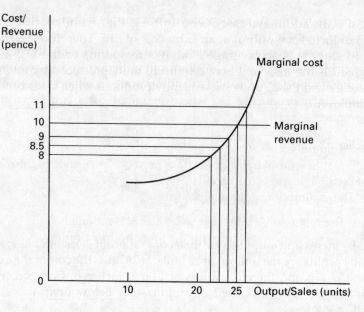

Figure 7.3 *Maximum profits where MC = MR*

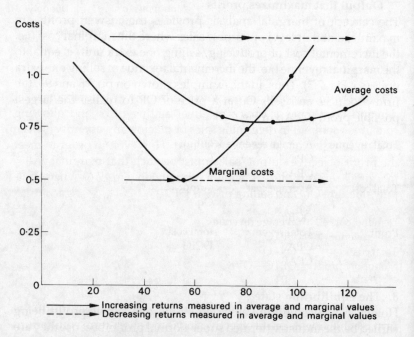

Figure 7.4 *Average and marginal costs*

resources in their present employment). Supply increased to Sn—Sn and price falls to Op_1.

Here total revenue just matches total costs (including the normal profit). Consequently, the surplus profits are competed away, supply and market price are stabilised and firms are in a short-run equilibrium, each producing Oq where marginal costs equal marginal revenue.

9. Monopoly

Monopoly is the extreme opposite of perfect competition in the range of possible market structures (*see* Fig. 7.5).

The assumptions for monopoly are:

(a) The monopolist is the sole seller and acts rationally.
(b) There are no substitutes for the monopolist's product.
(c) The monopolist's objective is profit maximization.

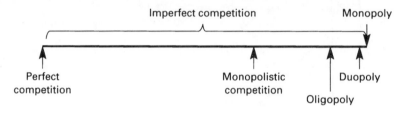

Figure 7.5 *Degrees of competition*

Here the monopolist, faced with the downward-sloping market demand curve, has a choice of either setting price and allowing consumer demand to determine sales or placing any quantity on sale and charging what the market will bear. However, in order to meet the profit objective output/sales must be such that marginal cost = marginal revenue and is shown visually in Fig. 7.6, where output/sales are OQ and selling price is OP.

Demand curve	= average revenue
Sales revenue	= OPTQ
Total costs	= OVLQ
Monopoly profit	= OPTQ – OVLQ
	= VPTL

No other price-output combination can secure a larger profit: the firm is achieving its profit objective and is in a short-term equilibrium situation.

10. Demise of profit-maximization assumption

The foregoing analysis of the theory of the firm in perfect competition and monopoly has been included to give the reader an insight into the nature of neo-classical micro-economic theory and to demonstrate its dependence on the profit-maximization objective. Many people still unquestioningly regard this profit objective as the entrepreneur's motivating force; its proponents find it intellectually appealing and of practical value in that marginal analysis, in contrast to behavioural motivation theories, can be relied on to provide solutions in every situation; its logic is faultless, its underlying assumption of rational behaviour suggests that firms should act as hypothesised in the theory. Indeed the amount of profit made by businesses, the conventional acid-test of their managerial ability and performance, reinforces this view that firms should in practice try to maximize profits.

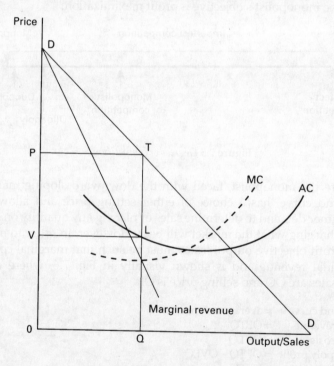

Figure 7.6 *Equilibrium situation in monopoly*

Nevertheless, this most powerful hypothesis of business motivation is severely criticized.

(a) It does not deal effectively with the *dynamic situation* for it is essentially a statement of general short-term equilibrium situations describing the *status quo* at one point in time. For instance, if as in Fig. 7.1, demand increases to $D_t - D_t$ the temporary equilibrium is upset by a price rise of $P - P_t$. New firms are attracted into the industry ($S_t - S_t$) by the super-normal profits made by firms selling a quantity Oq_2 at a price of OP_t (Figs. 7.1 and 7.2) and the *status quo* is re-established where the industry and firm are in equilibrium once more at outputs of OQ_2 and Oq_1 respectively. However, the theory is incapable of predicting the longer-term equilibrium situation where the *status quo* is fundamentally upset, where, for instance, a firm or group of firms are prepared to discount short-term profits for stability of trade in order to guarantee maximum longer-term profits.

(b) There is no place in the theory for the *decision-maker*. However, firms are made up of individuals who may have personal business objectives and whose behaviour on occasion is certain to be different and perhaps incompatible with that predetermined by the theory of the firm.

Other objectives of the business firm

11. Objectives of technocrats

J. K. Galbraith in *The New Industrial State* hypothesised on the motivation of business behaviour by examination of the technostructure of the modern corporations which consisted of individuals who identified their own personal and pecuniary success with that of the corporation, i.e. 'corporation men' who possessed powers of decision-making because of their specialized technical knowledge and skills necessary for the success of the corporation (*see* Chapter 4).

(a) Their first objective was to preserve the technostructure for self-interest by securing a minimum level of earnings for the corporation. Failure to do so would mean:

(*i*) The company going to the capital market for additional funds where lenders might impose limitations on managerial freedom.

(*ii*) Loss of office and power through shareholders' actions or takeovers.

(b) The next objective was corporate growth (with sufficient earnings to guarantee growth in rates of dividend for the shareholders and to finance investment projects) since this would increase the power and size of the technostructure.

(c) Technical innovation was pursued as a means to secure (b) and in its own right because it further increased the prospects of the technical managers.

(d) They strove to build up a sound corporate image.

Moreover, the justification for and power of the technostructure was further enhanced if their personal objectives of higher output and sales, innovation and corporate growth coincided with the goals of society.

12. Organizational objectives

Cyert and March in *A Behavioural Theory of the Firm* argued that corporations *per se* did not have objectives. Instead, business organizations are made up of persons with individual goals, viz. managers, staff, shareholders, creditors, suppliers, customers etc. who by means of bargaining, established compromise objectives for a coalition of individual interests.

13. Formation of coalition objectives

Cyert and March hypothesised also that coalition goals were fixed by the following processes.

(a) Individuals made *demands on the organization* either in the form of monetary or policy commitments. For instance:

(*i*) shareholders demanded monetary payments which if realized meant that they might adopt a passive role in further coalition bargaining;

(*ii*) managers demanded and strove to secure monetary payments, plus authority and policy commitments;

(*iii*) workers' goals were basically monetary.

Consequently, there was a trade-off between conflicting demands with the result that joint preference or compromise objectives emerged. Shareholders whose demands, expressed in dividend income or capital growth, were satisfied would leave management to pursue policy-making that achieved among other things managers' monetary and non-monetary aspirations. Workers would accept the organizational objectives but only for a price that satisfied their monetary demands.

(b) *Mutual control systems*. Coalition members needed a system to enforce the organizational objectives. Examples cited were:

(*i*) *The budget system* that controlled coalition members within the agreed plan.

(*ii*) *Allocation of functions*. Areas of responsibility and discretion of coalition members, if clearly defined, constrained members from pursuing their own self-interest.

(c) *Objective change through experience.* Coalition members would shift their attention to new or modified goals in the light of experience. Certainly the achievement of the individual and of others within that person's reference group caused a modification of current aspirations quantitatively and qualitatively, e.g. higher incomes or more stable dividend payments.

14. Economic goals

The size, composition and bargaining power of individuals within the coalition group resulted in economic objectives with the following areas:

(a) *Production.* Here the objective would be expressed in terms of:

   (i) Stability of output.

   (ii) Level of output.

The interpretation and relative emphasis placed on each depended on the demands and aspirations of the coalition members concerned with output.

(b) *Stocks.* Individuals concerned with stocks, e.g. stock controllers, accountants, sales personnel and customers would pressurize for individual goals which through negotiations were reduced to compromise goals for:

   (i) Level of stocks.

   (ii) Range of stocks.

(c) *Sales.* The sales goal in unit or monetary terms summarized the objectives of individuals who were concerned with stability of production, earnings and employment and survival.

(d) *Market share.* Individuals interested in comparative performance or growth would demand market-share goals.

(e) *Profit goals* were expressed in absolute terms or in relation to capital employed. A variety of individuals were interested in the former; shareholders demanded that they be sufficient to pay satisfactory dividends and that ploughed-back profits covered internal investment opportunities for future capital growth, and managers demanded that retained profits were adequate to finance the capital investment needed for corporate growth. Top managers might set profitability objectives to see how efficiently they had used shareholders' and total resources at their disposal in comparison with managers in other organizations.

15. Nature of shareholders' demands

The profit objective referred to above was the outcome of the various motives and the relative bargaining strengths of shareholders' groups. Possible motives were as follows:

(a) *Maximum current dividends*. Certain shareholders wished to maximize dividend payments, e.g. persons living on investment income and company controllers who as 'dividend strippers' exploited their position for maximum short-term gain.

(b) *Maximization of share values*. There was a difference of opinion as to whether share prices were an increasing function of retained earnings or of dividends. M. J. Gordon stated that higher dividends improved share values on the grounds that capital gains were less certain and more risky than immediate dividend expectations. Therefore, a company pursuing a policy of earning retention commanded a lower P/E ratio than one that maximized dividends. Friend and Puckett, on the other hand, argued that the value of ploughed-back profit was more significant. The controversy continues. However, there is one situation when earnings retentions contribute to capital gains.

The newly-established company at the innovative and subsequent growth stage of the life cycle of the firm is likely to be permanently short of funds. Shareholders in this situation are usually prepared to discount present income and reinvest earnings for the substantial gains that are anticipated in the subsequent maturity stage of the firm's life cycle. Thus, at this point in time, the prerequisite for success is additional funds which may be raised either externally or internally: however, additional funds raised outside will dilute the equity so that shareholders must share the anticipated gains, hence their preference for self-financing.

16. Objectives a management tool

In the preceding sections, we examined briefly various theories that have attempted to explain the principal goals of business firms and how they are selected. But whatever the selection process and choice of goal, objectives once decided on provide a valuable management tool.

(a) The goal provides management with a purpose and direction and pace of operations.

(b) Management can appraise their performance by comparison of actual performance with the standard.

17. Desirable characteristics of objectives

Objectives possessing the following characteristics provide a most valuable management tool.

(a) They must be quantified and measurable, e.g. to increase Return on Capital Employed (ROCE) from 10 per cent to 20 per cent.

(b) They must be qualified by a time-scale, e.g. to increase ROCE from 10 per cent to 20 per cent by 31 December.

(c) They must be ends in themselves and not means, e.g. to secure good labour relations could be considered as a prerequisite for profits.

(d) They should be realistic and attainable, yet stretch management.

(e) They should be capable of revision.

(f) They should be communicable and communicated to all staff on whose shoulders implementation rests.

(g) They should be limited in number and reflect the compromise between coalition members' conflicting interests.

Visual representation of economic objectives

18. Objectives and break-even analysis

A logical progression in an examination of company objectives is to consider the impact of selected goals on the company's operational policy. Consequently, we shall select four of the most frequently-quoted goals and show diagrammatically by means of break-even analysis how the chosen goal influences corporate sales, costs and output. The objectives chosen for this purpose are as follows:

(a) maximization of profits;

(b) maximization of sales volume;

(c) maximization of sales revenue;

(d) maximization of sales volume or revenue subject to a profit constraint.

19. Total costs: the economist's viewpoint

The first step in this exercise is the construction of a break-even model to illustrate the typical behaviour of sales revenue and costs over the company's entire range of activity. Let us start with costs. Total costs are the sum of all costs incurred in an operation. Therefore, if we classify costs under the heading of fixed costs and variable costs, then we have the familiar equation

$$\text{Fixed cost} + \text{Variable cost} = \text{Total costs.}$$

Now of course we must quantify these costs and for this purpose let us imagine that a company supplies the hypothetical cost/revenue data contained in Table 7B. From it, we may graph the continuous total cost of production to see how costs behave over the range of operations from zero units to 115k units.

Table 7B *Total cost of production*

(i) Output k	(ii) Fixed cost k	(iii) Variable cost k	(iv) Total cost k	(v) Selling price	(vi) Total revenue k	(vii) Profit k
0	£100	£—	100		—	(£100)
10	£100	15	115	4.50	£45	(70)
25	£100	30	130	4.00	100	(30)
40	£100	45	145	3.75	150	5
70	£100	60	160	3.00	210	50
90	£100	75	175	2.40	216	41
105	£100	90	190	2.00	210	20
115	£100	105	205	1.64	189	(16)

Column (*ii*) states the value of fixed costs: the first element in the cost equation. Thus we see that fixed costs are constant at £100k and represent rent and rates, interest on loans, management salaries and other costs that do not vary with output.

In contrast, variable costs (column (*iii*)) by definition change with the level of activity, e.g. wages of direct labour, materials and power, etc. However, they may not vary directly. In fact, at low levels of activity, variable costs probably rise less steeply than output as additional workers are taken on, because of the operation of the law of increasing returns and eventually at high levels of operations beyond optimum worker–capital combination the law of diminishing returns will cause variable costs to rise faster than output. The summation of these two costs (column (*iv*)) is the basis for the continuous non-linear total cost curve, *see* Fig. 7.7.

20. Total revenue: the economist's viewpoint
Economic theory, supported by empirical studies, states that most firms are subject to the law of downward-sloping demand. This means that they are incapable of supplying an infinite quantity of any good at a fixed price. Inevitably there comes a point where, at high sales-volume, suppliers wishing to further extend sales encounter consumer resistance and/or reaction by competitors which forces

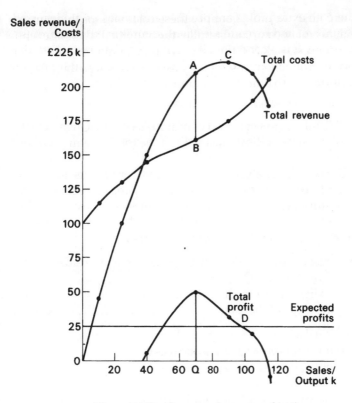

Figure 7.7 *Break-even and company objectives*

them to reduce price. Naturally, this has an immediate and direct effect on sales revenue: it declines relative to sales volume when price cuts are made and falls absolutely if demand for the product is inelastic. The sales data in Table 7B is based on this assumption and is expressed as the non-linear sales revenue line graphed in Fig. 7.7.

21. Maximization of profits goal
A basic tenet of economic theory is that profit maximization **(7)** is achieved at a level of activity where marginal cost and marginal revenue are equal. This means in general terms that if at a certain level of activity the extra sales proceeds from the sale of an additional unit exceed the extra cost of producing and selling it, then total profits can be improved by producing and selling this marginal unit. If, however, the extra cost exceeds the extra revenue of an incremental unit of output, less total profit is made. The intermediate level of output and

sales where no extra profits are possible and no losses are incurred, i.e. marginal cost and revenue are equal, secures maximum profits.

Furthermore, it is a condition, if profits are to be maximized, that total sales revenue must exceed total costs by the greatest possible amount since:

Profit = Total sales revenue – Total costs.

In Fig. 7.7, this occurs at a level of output/sales of OQ where AB is the longest possible vertical line between the total revenue and total cost curves.

Thus break-even analysis, based on the continuous total sales revenue and cost lines that reflect the economist's view of cost/revenue/output behaviour, indicates that profits are realized when sales/output is in the range of activity 37k–114k units and that the profit maximizer's goal is realized at 70k units where:

(a) The vertical distance between these curves is maximized (£50); and
(b) where marginal cost must equal marginal revenue; and
(c) where the slope of the total revenue curve equals the slope of the total cost curve.

The profit maximizer's selling price will be

$$OA \div OQ,$$

i.e.

$$£210k \div 70k = £3.00,$$

which is confirmed by examining the appropriate selling price for 70k units.

22. Maximization of sales volume goal

This assumed objective is only realized when sales/output are at the highest level possible, and in this example is achieved at 112 units where the company breaks even. Its selling price will be

$$£198k \div 112 = £1.77.$$

Sales/output activity beyond this level, although desirable, is unrealistic because losses are incurred because total costs exceed revenues. Nevertheless, although the higher break-even level of operations satisfies the assumed goal, it is doubtful whether it is any more than a very short-run equilibrium, for although no losses are incurred, neither are any profits made. It is obviously an unhealthy situation for survival but may be qualified at a later stage in this analysis to represent a realistic and variable long-term objective by building in a profit constraint, on the grounds that many companies do actually pursue the highest possible sales figures as long as they are making satisfactory profits.

23. Maximization of sales revenue goal
The assumed goal is achieved at 90 units where the total revenue curve is at its highest point C (in the economist's terminology, where marginal revenue is zero). Here the selling price is

£216k ÷ 90k = £2.40 per unit.

24. Maximization of sales with a profit constraint
We assumed in **18 (b)** and **(c)** that the sole objective was maximization of sales in unit and revenue terms. However, more realistic goals (which are intuitively satisfying and supported by several studies) are likely to include a prescribed level of profit which checks the firm's ability to pursue sales *ad infinitum*. For example, management may require a £25k profit in order to satisfy the demand of shareholders and to provide internal funds for new investment. In this case:

(a) The sales-volume-maximizing firm will produce and sell less than before, i.e. 102k units. (Point D on the graph.)
(b) The sales-revenue-maximizing firm will wish to produce and sell 90k units. In fact, the inclusion of a profit constraint of £25k is quite compatible with revenue maximization and will not affect the sales-revenue maximizer's policy, since 90k units already realize profits of £31k.

In this example, the sales-volume maximizer who is subject to this profit constraint is forced to cut back sales from 112k to 102k units and raise prices from £1.77 to £2.08. Furthermore, this illustrates a typical compromise demanded by a coalition of members representing the sales and profit interests referred to by Cyert and March (*see* **12**). Thus shareholders are presumably satisfied with the profit of £25k, leaving managers to sell as much as they can to maximize their satisfactions.

Progress test 7

1. Compare and contrast the theory of perfect competition and the theory of monopoly. **(1–9)**

2. Critically analyse the 'profit-maximization' objective. **(10)**

3. 'Organizations *per sę* do not have objectives.' Discuss. **(11–12)**

4. Describe the process whereby coalition objectives are formed. **(13–15)**

5. Explain the principal goals of business firms and how they are selected. **(1–16)**

6. 'Objectives to be useful must be qualified and quantified.' Discuss. **(17)**

7. Explain by means of break-even graphs how the selection of objectives affects company operations. **(18–24)**

8

The choice of finance for companies

Types of capital

1. Classification of company capital
The capital of a joint-stock company can be summarized as follows:

(a) *Share capital*. This consists of variants of preference shares and ordinary shares.
(b) *Loan capital*. This consists of loans, debentures and mortgages.

2. Ordinary shares
These equities issued to individuals subscribing towards a company's share capital confer on shareholders a residual claim to dividends and repayment of capital in the event of liquidation after all prior charges have been met. Normally they carry voting rights by way of compensation.

Since the demise of the owner-manager (who traditionally performed the entrepreneurial functions of risk-bearing, decision-making and co-ordinating factors of production) and the development of large-scale industry, it has become more difficult to identify the entrepreneur. One may regard the ordinary shareholders of joint-stock companies (the typical business unit) as the entrepreneurs of the twentieth century, since they perform the main entrepreneurial functions of risk-bearing for profit. Despite apathy on their part, which has led in some cases to a divorce between ownership and control, in theory they exercise control by voting on boards and delegating authority to managers who perform the other entrepreneurial functions of decision-making and factor-coordination.

3. Risk and control
The 'golden rule of capitalism' (i.e. 'where the risk lies, there the control lies also') described a situation where, as in sole proprietorship, the risk-taker and business controller were one. However, today this rule needs to be modified in view of the divorce between ownership

and control which has occurred with the development of the joint-stock company.

4. Causes of this divorce
The factors responsible for this situation, where the board of directors in effect controls business affairs, are as follows:

(a) the usual provision in articles of association making directors fully responsible for management;
(b) the unwillingness of shareholders to dismiss the board in order to overrule decisions;
(c) diversity of shareholdings, which hinders unanimity in policy and action;
(d) the apathy of shareholders while dividends are maintained;
(e) the reluctance of institutional shareholders to 'act as a public watchdog' and to set an example by intervening and criticizing boards when necessary;
(f) the difficulties involved in attending shareholders' meetings;
(g) the clash of interests between controllers and shareholders.

5. The interests of shareholders
The following conditions serve the interests of shareholders.

(a) Their company earns for them at least long-term normal profits appropriate to the degree of risk in that trade.
(b) Dividends are maximized to give shareholders the choice of reinvesting most profitably. Undistributed profits are regarded by some as a source of cheap funds for management. On the other hand sufficient profits should be retained to secure long-run growth objectives.
(c) Shares are freely marketable so that investments may be realised.

6. Interests of controllers
The following conditions serve the interests of controllers.

(a) The 'corporation people' identify themselves with the company and may plough back a high proportion of their earnings for capitalization since corporate success brings personal success by way of increased authority, status, prestige and remuneration.
(b) They have a duty to shareholders and pursue policies which serve their interests. However, they may be tempted through self-interest to:

    (*i*) favour other companies in which they have financial interests with advantageous contracts;

(*ii*) use inside information (e.g. for profitable transactions in the company's shares, directly or indirectly);
(*iii*) selfishly advise shareholders on a certain course of action in a takeover situation.

It must be emphasized that these are temptations only. It would be wrong to conclude that directors generally abandon the interests of shareholders by benefiting personally from the opportunities which their privileged position affords.

7. Deferred shares
Deferred ordinary shares rank after ordinary shares in profit-sharing and are sometimes issued to companies' promoters and underwriters with various voting rights.

8. Preference shares
These shares carry the prior right to a fixed dividend (a fixed percentage of the nominal value) from profits and to preferential payments before ordinary shareholders in the event of winding-up (if the articles allow). They may be:

(a) *cumulative* (i.e. shareholders receive full payment of dividends in arrears before any other shareholders are paid);
(b) *non-cumulative* (i.e. shareholders receive a yearly dividend when sufficient profits are available);
(c) *participating* (i.e. shareholders receive a fixed dividend and participate in surplus profits with ordinary shareholders);
(d) *redeemable* (i.e. shareholders may redeem their shares for cash at or before a date specified at the time of issue).

9. Debentures
A debenture security is a written acknowledgement of a debt incurred by a joint-stock company. It provides for repayment of the debt with a fixed interest, usually twice yearly. A debenture may be one of the following kinds.

(a) A simple 'unsecured' or 'naked' debenture, so called because the holder has no lien or pledge on any assets of the company and ranks after secured creditors for payment in the event of winding up.
(b) A debenture having a 'fixed' charge on specified assets, e.g. property. Stockholders are entitled to interest and repayment of the loan out of the sale of these assets should it be necessary.
(c) A debenture having a 'floating' or general charge on the company's unpledged assets.

10. Convertible debentures and loan stock

Such issues may be made when a company needs to raise capital when rates of interest are high. Investors are induced to subscribe for these securities (which carry a lower coupon and are generally unsecured) by the option which allows them to convert their stock on predetermined dates and terms into the company's ordinary shares. Success is assured if the investors feel that corporate success and inflation are certain to lift the price of the share above the conversion price. On the other hand they offer some security by way of fixed interest even if things go ill with the company. Reactions of shareholders will be favourable for the following reasons:

(a) prior charges on earnings are less than for normal debentures;
(b) equity holders enjoy the benefits of high gearing when earnings are large in relation to these fixed-interest charges;
(c) equity is not immediately diluted;
(d) assets are not generally pledged, so that borrowing powers are unrestricted.

11. Mortgages

A mortgage is similar to a debenture in that it is a loan secured by assets of the borrower, but it differs in that it is a debt to a single lender, the mortgagee. The provision of mortgages is especially well known in the private sector, but it is also a valuable source of long-term capital for commercial undertakings. Insurance companies, pension funds and finance companies are the main mortgagees, although limited funds are available from solicitors and building societies. Organizations like the Ship Mortgage Finance Company and the Agricultural Mortgage Corporation make special-purpose loans.

Gearing

12. Capital gearing

The gearing ratio or coefficient indicates the relative proportions of the types of capital employed in a company. The gearing ratio can be measured by the ratio,

$$\frac{\textit{Borrowed funds, i.e. interest–bearing loans}}{\textit{Ordinary shareholders' funds, i.e. equity}}$$

13. Determinants of the gearing ratio

The ratio varies between firms and industries and is influenced by the following factors.

(a) The borrowing powers in a company's articles of association.
(b) The existence of charges on the company's assets.
(c) The attitude of shareholders towards control. They may resist attempts to diffuse their equity holding and prefer 'debt' capital as a source of new finance.
(d) The relative costs of raising debt and share capital.
(e) The level of anticipated profits in relation to the fixed interest charges on debt capital.

14. Effect of gearing on profits

A simple example (overleaf) illustrates the effect of different gearing ratios on company dividends. Let us assume there are two equally capitalized companies but with different capital structures: A is low-geared and B is high-geared. Profits in each case for years 1, 2 and 3 are £9000, £7000 and £4000 respectively. Company A has a share capital of 20 000 at £1, preference at 5 per cent, 80 000 ordinary at £1. Company B has a share capital of 70 000 at £1, preference at 5 per cent, 30 000 ordinary at £1.

Thus if one ignores taxation and profit retention one sees that the high gearing in company B produces higher dividends at higher profits and lower dividends at lower profit-levels, in contrast to company A. This has important implications for companies and shareholders.

15. Advantages of gearing

(a) When profits are high in relation to total fixed-interest charges, the ordinary shareholders in a highly geared company benefit immediately

	Years					
	1		2		3	
Company	A	B	A	B	A	B
Total profits for distribution	£9000		£7000		£4000	
Total dividends for 5 per cent preference shares	1000	3500	1000	3500	1000	3500
Dividends for ordinary shares	8000	5500	6000	3500	3000	500
Dividend percentage	10	18.3	7.5	11.6	3.7	1.6

from additional dividends, or in the future from the earnings generated by the retained profits.

(b) It enables a company to increase its capital without dilution of equity and shareholders' control.

(c) The interest is tax-deductible.

16. Disadvantages of gearing

(a) High gearing is disadvantageous to equity holders when profits are falling since they receive disproportionately less by way of dividends.

(b) The company is committed to fixed-interest payments which could cause cash flow problems.

(c) Charges may be placed on company assets.

(d) Once assets are pledged, further gearing may be accomplished only by offering higher yields to lenders to compensate for the lack of security.

(e) Gearing demands that management produce sufficient profits to pay interests and dividends and meanwhile establish a sinking fund for the redemption of debentures.

(f) Companies whose incomes fluctuate (perhaps their products are elastic in demand) will find it difficult to maintain satisfactory dividend rates and share prices.

(g) Investors will be reluctant to subscribe new capital.

17. The choice of finance

A company in need of additional finance has a wide choice, its final option being influenced by the following considerations.

(a) The *relative cost* of borrowing by different methods.

(*i*) The 'cost of capital' is the interest which has to be offered on debentures, the dividends on preference shares and yields on ordinary shares to attract investors' capital.

Obviously the opportunity cost of capital is relevant, but in addition it is influenced by the investors' attitudes towards risk, reward and control offered by various securities. For instance, lenders will demand higher rewards on ordinary shares and unsecured loan stock than on preference shares or secured debentures, to compensate for the higher risks. But they will demand less if they confer control with its attendant advantages.

(*ii*) The administrative costs involved in raising the capital.

(b) The *term of the finance*. Projects which mean that expenditure will not be recouped in the short-term suggest long-term finance, which is generally more expensive. However, in times of high interest rates, a company should consider financing a long-term project by redeemable securities and by short-term borrowing when there is a good chance that it can be re-financed later when rates are lower.

(c) The *effects of taxation*, e.g. loan interest is allowable against profits (unlike dividends) in the assessment of corporation tax.

(d) The *value and nature of corporate assets* available as security.

(e) The nature of *conditions imposed by lenders* on a company's freedom of action, e.g. restrictions on future borrowing ability if assets are pledged.

(f) The company's *ability to earn a sufficient cash flow* to pay fixed charges and repay loans, e.g. redeemable debentures.

(g) The company's *existing capital structure* and the effect of new borrowing on capital and vote-gearing.

(h) *Market conditions*, e.g. a severe 'credit squeeze' may make it difficult to obtain short-term bank finance, or the capital market may already be 'saturated' with new issues.

18. Recent trends in capital gearing

There are benefits in borrowing capital when, for example, you can borrow at 10 per cent and use the money to earn 11 per cent. You have made a profit of 1 per cent using another's money.

In the boom of the late 1980s, companies increased their levels of borrowing. A survey of leading plcs shows their average gearing levels to be:

1988	1989	1990	1991
19.6%	21.9%	26.2%	23.6%

Without doubt they were encouraged by the widespread availability of credit, but found themselves in financial trouble with the onset of the recession. Their earnings fell and interest rates rose so that they were unable to service the interest charges. Many companies as a result collapsed or were saved through the intervention of others, and this experience was not confined to the UK. Examples of companies with these high gearing levels are: Bond Corporation of Australia, Olympia and York of Canada, and in the UK, Brent Walker, Heron, Coloroll, Maxwell, Allied Carpets.

Table 8A *Debt structure of industrial and commercial companies*

	1989 (£m)	%	1990 (£m)	%	1991 (£m)	%	1992 (£m)	%
Bank borrowing	33 950	48	19 911	37	−878	−3	− 1 881	−9
Other loans	9 120	13	8 045	15	3 585	11	2 519	13
Ord. shares	1 880	3	2 851	5	9 746	29	5 117	25
Debentures	6 367	9	3 645	7	5 466	16	1 641	8
Miscellaneous	18 718	27	19 213	36	15 822	47	12 726	63
Total	70 035	100	53 665	100	33 741	100	20 122	100

Source: Central Statistical Office

Debt and equity finance

19. Effect of corporation tax
This tax, introduced in 1965, replaced the system of income and profits tax on company profits, and has changed industry's method of raising new capital in the following ways.

(a) Equity, traditionally employed, was replaced by loan capital.
(b) Issues of preference shares virtually disappeared.

The impact of this tax was severe. Preference and ordinary capital as a percentage of total new issues fell from 2.6 and 40.8 in 1964, to 0.6 and 9.0 respectively in 1965. Loan capital rose sharply from 56.5 to 90.3.

20. Effect of corporation tax on company financing
The method of corporation tax assessment makes it cheaper for a company to service loan capital than to pay dividends on equal amounts of equity.

(a) Corporation tax is assessed on profits after interest charges, but not ordinary and preference dividends, have been deducted.
(b) Ordinary and preference dividends, which were charged net of tax to the company, are now charged gross.

If corporation tax is assumed to be 50 per cent, it costs a company just as much to pay a 5 per cent dividend as it does to pay interest on a 10 per cent debenture. For example see the table below.

Thus to retain the same profits, Company B can afford to pay total dividends of £5000, equivalent to 5 per cent against 10 per cent for debentures by Company A.

Another example illustrates the effect that gearing has on earnings

Company A: 100 000 £1 debentures at 10 per cent		Company B: 100 000 £1 ordinary and preference shares	
Company profits	£50 000	Company profits	£50 000
Debenture interest	£10 000	Corporation tax	£25 000
	£40 000		£25 000
Corporation tax 50%	£20 000	Dividend	£5 000
Profits retained	£20 000	Profits retained	£20 000

per share (EPS). Here the comparison is between a wholly equity-financed company and one which has a gearing ratio of 1:1. Profits of £50 000 are assumed and corporation tax and debenture interest are taken to be 50 and 10 per cent respectively.

	Company A	*Company B*
Ordinary shares £1.00	£100 000	£50 000
Debentures at 10%	–	£50 000
Capital employed	£100 000	£100 000
Profits	£50 000	£50 000
Less Debenture interest	–	£5 000
Profits before tax	£50 000	£45 000
Less Corporation tax 50%	£25 000	£22 500
Profits available for shareholders	£25 000	£22 500
Earnings per share	25p	45p

Clearly both companies are equally efficient in terms of profitability; both realized a return on capital employed (ROCE) of 50 per cent. However, Company B having earned a 50 per cent return on its borrowed funds which cost only 10 per cent to service, retains the surplus earnings for the benefit of the shareholders so that £22 500, although a smaller absolute profit than A's, is spread among only half the number of ordinary shares. Consequently earnings per share amount to 45p compared with 25p for Company A.

21. Effect of gearing on profitability
The above advantages of gearing on the ordinary shareholders' earnings per share may also be expressed in a slightly different way in terms of return on investment. For instance, the 50 per cent ROCE for Company B in the previous example lifts the return on investment (ROI) to 45 per cent because it is trading on the equity (i.e. £22 500 ÷ £50 000 share capital × 100). In fact, at the profit level of £50 000 shareholders

receive the substantial benefit of an extra 20 per cent return over the shareholders in Company A whose ROI figure is 25 per cent. This information is plotted in Fig. 8.1 (points a and b). A third plotting is O where for a ROCE of zero the wholly equity-financed company's ROI would also be nought: the fourth point is C that shows that a ROCE of 5 per cent must be earned by the geared company B to cover its interest charge of £5000, thus leaving the ordinary shareholder with a zero ROI. Then by joining these points we establish two lines that indicate the relationship between ROCE and ROI for the two companies with their very different capital structures.

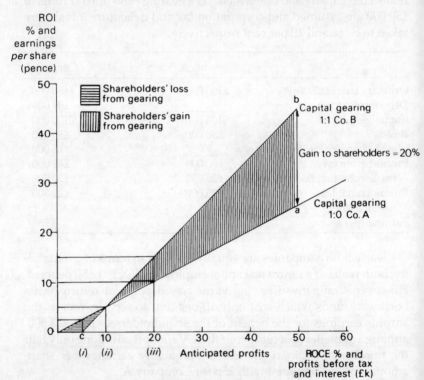

Figure 8.1 *Relationship between ROCE and ROI, profits before tax and earnings per share for given capital-gearing structures*

This visual representation of gearing confirms the conclusions drawn in (14) that gearing operates against shareholders' interests when profits are very low but is beneficial when profits are high. In fact, when the ROCE is less than 10 per cent gearing actually reduces the

ROI return; consequently whole-equity financing is preferable. However, when the ROCE exceeds 10 per cent a degree of gearing is desirable.

These important principles of financial management may be summarized as follows.

(a) An equity-financed capital structure is recommended if the anticipated ROCE is inadequate to service the cost of borrowing.
(b) A degree of capital gearing is recommended when the ROCE exceeds the cost of borrowing.
(c) When the ROCE exceeds this break-even point, then the higher the gearing the higher the return to the shareholders.

22. Forecasting earnings per share

The principle underlying Fig. 8.1 may be usefully extended into the areas of financial forecasting. For example, it provides the financial accountant with a simple method (once he has drawn in the company's appropriate gearing line) of translating targeted or anticipated earnings figures for the company into the appropriate EPS values. Furthermore, by considering only the numerators of the percentages on the two axes, i.e. profits before tax and interest on the horizontal axis and profits available to the ordinary shareholders expressed as earnings per share on the vertical axis, we can forecast the earnings per share for any given level of profits. Thus if profits so defined are (*a*) £5k for both companies, A's shareholders earn 2.5p per share, B's earn zero pence per share; with profits of (*b*) £10k, A and B's shareholders earn 5p per share; and with profits of (*c*) £20k, A's shareholders earn 10p and B's earn 15p per share. This analysis shows clearly that if anticipated profits are greater than £10k (the real cost of servicing the debt since the company must earn £10k before tax to leave £5k after deduction of 50 per cent corporation tax) then a geared capital structure is in the interest of shareholders in that earnings per share are improved.

23. The best measure of performance – ROI or EPS?

Although EPS is widely used as the measure of financial performance (it must be disclosed in published accounts) it can be criticized on the grounds that it does not take into account the total investments of the shareholders that generate the profits. In the previous examples EPS and ROI were the same because revenue reserves were ignored but in reality they do form a substantial part of total shareholders' funds and must be included if the measure of profitability is to be meaningful. For example, if Company A's ordinary-share capital consisted of

$$100\,000 \text{ ordinary shares of } £1 = £100\,000$$

plus Reserves	100 000
Total shareholders' funds	200 000

then the EPS would still be 25p, i.e.

$$\frac{\text{Earnings after tax}}{\text{No. of ordinary shares}} = \frac{£25\,000}{100\,000},$$

but the ROI is lower at 12.5%, i.e.

$$\frac{\text{Earnings after tax}}{\text{Total shareholders' funds}} = \frac{£25\,000}{£200\,000}\%.$$

24. Comparisons between EPS and ROI
Generally, EPS is higher than ROI and will rise over time because:

(a) companies tend to retain some profits so that the denominator in the ROI calculation increases;
(b) earnings increase during times of inflation, but the number of shares may not change;
(c) the EPS method of company assessment is a short-term assessment concentrating on the profit-and-loss account while ROI is a long-term measure concentrating on total shareholders' funds in the company to date.

25. Advantages of issuing loan capital

(a) The effect of corporation tax makes it cheaper for a company to service its debts than to make dividends on equal amounts of equity.
(b) It encourages higher gearing, which is to the advantage of equity holders, while long-term corporate earnings exceed debt interest.
(c) Long-term capital may be raised without dilution of ordinary shareholders' holdings and control.

26. Limitations to debt financing

(a) Every company has a maximum equity to debt capital ratio. Beyond this point:
  (*i*) the burden of debt interest and perhaps sinking fund provisions becomes unacceptable;
  (*ii*) the risk of default increases; and
  (*iii*) future borrowing is restricted.
(b) Companies' articles of association limit their borrowing capacities.
(c) Companies have to offer higher coupons in order to attract investment funds if the supply of debt securities in the market is increasing. This reduces the cost advantage of debt over equity capital.

(d) Rising share-prices reduce yields and thereby the cost of making rights issues *vis-à-vis* loan stock.

(e) Potential lenders are disinclined to advance funds when they feel that their money is at risk. Therefore companies with above-industry-average debt ratios and times-interest-earned ratios may be unable to attract additional debt capital.

(f) Investors may find debt securities unacceptable in continuing inflation. However, companies may overcome this reluctance by offering convertible loan stock.

27. Demise of preference shares

Today, preference shares actually form only a negligible part of new capital issues. Indeed they have not been generally popular, since in their usual form they are unsecured, possess no voting rights to influence company policy and, unlike ordinary shares, do not partake in the success of the company. They are less attractive, too, from the viewpoint of companies, since their dividends are not allowable for corporation tax and are therefore costly.

Convertible debt *v.* other debt issues

28. Significance of convertible debt

New convertible debt and loan stock securities (*see* **10**) ranged between 5 and 20 per cent of total issues in the London capital market over the period 1973–6.

29. Why issue convertibles?

Company financial managers may decide to issue convertibles in preference to straight debentures or loan stock, for the following reasons.

(a) Lenders of funds may require the added inducement of *potential capital gains* over and above the guaranteed interest payment to persuade them to advance funds. In effect, the lender receives a minimum-risk security that offers a hedge against inflation and deflation, i.e. capital gains and a minimum floor value determined by the coupon.

(b) The company can normally offer convertibles at *lower coupons* than straight debt securities. Consequently, the company can minimize the burden of interest charges until the conversion date, which may be set at the outset to coincide with the anticipated fall in market interest rates. Alternatively, they may provide cheap short-term finance, say, during the development and growth stage of the product life-cycle when the company is generally short of funds.

(c) The company may use convertibles as a *delaying tactic for issuing new shares*. For instance, if the current market share-price is depressed but expected to improve, then the company may issue convertibles with the option to convert later into equities. Consequently, the company may gain a premium by floating shares at the higher price.

(d) The low risk associated with convertible investment means that the company can demand a redemption premium payment. Consequently, the conversion price is increased and since fewer shares are issued at conversion equity is less diluted compared with a straight equity issue.

30. The price of convertibles

The determination of the price of convertibles is complicated by their hybrid nature, i.e. their ordinary shares and fixed-interest security characteristics. For example, a company may decide when market interest rates are 12 per cent to issue convertibles for £1.00 each earning 10 per cent p.a. convertible at four years into three ordinary shares. Consequently, the conversion price is:

(*i*) *Situation 1*. If the share price is 33p prior to conversion then the convertible's price will also be 33p per share, the value at which it is freely converted.

(*ii*) *Situation 2*. If the share price declines to, say, 11p then ordinary shareholders will have incurred a capital loss of 66 per cent. By contrast, convertible bond holders will have lost only 17 per cent because of the straight debt value of 27.5p, i.e.

$$\text{Bond price} = \frac{\text{Bond interest rate}}{\text{Market interest rate}} \times \text{Bond issue price}$$
$$= \frac{10}{12} \times 33\text{p}$$
$$= 27.5\text{p}$$

In fact the price is likely to be higher than 27.5p because of the lower risks of holding convertibles in comparison with equities and straight debt securities.

(*iii*) *Situation 3*. If the share price is expected to increase over the four years by 5 per cent per annum from an original value of 33p, then the conversion value can be forecast as follows:

Value at end of
Year 1 = Initial conversion price × (1 + Share growth rate)

$$= 33p \times (1.05)$$
$$= 34.6p;$$
$$2 = 33p \times (1.05)^2$$
$$= 36.4p;$$
$$3 = 33p \times (1.05)^3$$
$$= 38.2p;$$
$$4 = 33p \times (1.05)^4$$
$$= 40.1p.$$

31. Convertibles and earnings per share

In (14) we considered the effect of capital gearing expressed as the ratio of preference share capital to equity capital and concluded that at a high level of net profits a higher ratio benefited ordinary shareholders in terms of higher earnings per share and thereby dividends available for the equity. The result would be similar if instead we had substituted debenture or loan stock and in fact more beneficial to the equity than preference capital because of the further advantages of tax shielding illustrated in (21). Let us now summarise this analysis by comparing the relative advantages of equity and debt financing in the forms of debentures and convertibles using as a criterion maximization of earnings per share.

Imagine that a company requires additional capital of £1m which may be raised by issuing 1 000 000 ordinary shares at 100p, bringing total issued shares to 3 000 000. Alternatively, it may issue £1m worth of debentures at 12 per cent p.a. or convertibles to the same value paying 10 per cent p.a. convertible into 600k ordinary shares. If corporation tax is taken to be 50 per cent and anticipated profits £800k the effect on EPS is as follows:

	(i)	(ii)	(iii)	(iv)
			Convertibles	Convertibles
	Equity	*Debentures*	*(undiluted)*	*(diluted)*
Net profit before interest	800 000	800 000	800 000	800 000
less interest	—	120 000	100 000	—
Net profit after interest	800 000	680 000	700 000	800 000
less tax at 50%	400 000	340 000	350 000	400 000
Earnings available for equity	400 000	340 000	350 000	400 000
No. of shares	3 000 000	2 000 000	2 000 000	2 600 000
EPS	13.3p	17p	17.5p	15.4p

Conclusions:

(*i*) Conversion price = $\dfrac{\text{Issue value of convertible}}{\text{No. of shares receivable}}$

$= \dfrac{100}{0.6}$

$= 166p$

(*ii*) Since the conversion price is significantly above the proposed equity issue price, there must be some doubt whether the company can raise the market price by the required amount before the option date, particularly if it is close at hand. Perhaps the equity issues market is depressed at this point in time and hence the interest in convertibles, which delays the issuing of new shares until perhaps a bullish market exists. Alternatively, if the market capitalises this company's earnings at 12–13 times then the company can afford to convert on the basis of its diluted EPS of 15.4p.

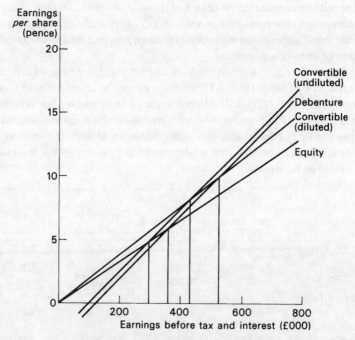

Figure 8.2 *Comparative sources of finance and EPS*

(*iii*) As one would expect with this very-high-profit situation, debt financing scores heavily over equity financing and confirms our earlier conclusions about the benefit of trading on the equity.

Moreover, convertibles undiluted perform more satisfactorily than straight debentures than if fully diluted (i.e. after conversion since the anticipated profits are now shared among 2 600 000 shares).

(*iv*) Convertibles are preferential to ordinary share finance while profits available for equity remain above £100k (or £300k before tax and interest); below this level of profits, the interest charge of £100k works against the interest of shareholders.

32. Convertibles *v*. straight debt

The above example shows that if the company objective is to maximise EPS then convertibles may score over straight debt while earnings are undiluted because of the lower coupon.

Furthermore, it provides the company with greater flexibility over straight debt issues, allowing them either to postpone equity issues or to redeem the debt for cash or to convert into equity or possibly to raise additional straight debt either in the interim, since the bondholders are subordinated creditors, or upon redemption if bondholders are unwilling to take up their option and require cash redemption.

33. Choice of finance and EPS

The level of anticipated profits will naturally influence the choice of finance. The reason, of course, is gearing, which is explained in principle in **14** but for a wider comparison of financing possibilities we must consider Fig. 8.2. It is based on the data contained in **31**, and by assuming different profit levels (before tax and interest) examines the effect of the choice of finance on EPS values.

(a) If anticipated profits are £200k then the methods of financing ranked in order of preference that maximize EPS are:

(*i*) Convertible (fully diluted)	: EPS	3.8p
(*ii*) Equity	:	3.3p
(*iii*) Convertible (undiluted)	:	2.5p
(*iv*) Debenture	:	2.0p

(b) If anticipated profits are £300k:

(*i*) Convertible (fully diluted)		:	5.7p
(*ii*) Convertible (undiluted)	} break-		
(*iii*) Equity	even	:	5.0p
(*iv*) Debenture		:	4.5p

(c) If anticipated profits are £365k:

(*i*) Convertible (fully diluted)	:	7.0p
(*ii*) Convertible (undiluted)	:	6.6p

(iii) Equity ⎫ break-even : 6.1p
(iv) Debenture ⎭

(d) If anticipated profits are £430k:
(i) Convertible (undiluted) ⎫ break- : 8.2p
(ii) Convertible (diluted) ⎭ even
(iii) Debenture : 7.7p
(iv) Equity : 7.2p

(e) If anticipated profits are £520k:
(i) Convertible (undiluted) : 10.5p
(ii) Debenture ⎫ break- : 10.0p
(iii) Convertible (diluted) ⎭ even
(iv) Equity : 8.6p

(f) If anticipated profits are £800k:
(i) Convertible (undiluted) : 17.5p
(ii) Debenture : 17.0p
(iii) Convertible (diluted) : 15.4p
(iv) Equity : 3.3p

34. Choice of finance and capital requirements

Different conclusions as to the optimum financing method, however, are drawn if the objective is to maximize capital receipts. In this case, the key determining factor is the present and anticipated market value of the ordinary shares.

(a) If the current market value is low, then the order of preference is:

(i) *Straight debt*, e.g. debentures. This could be redeemed and replaced by equity when the share price has recovered, subject of course to the company's attitude to risk and its borrowing capacity.
(ii) *Convertibles*. Presumably a high interest rate would have to be offered because of the small capital gains anticipated by investors.
(iii) *Ordinary shares*. An equity issue would raise only limited amounts for this company's shares in the depressed market.

(b) If the current market value is high, then the order of preference is:

(i) Ordinary shares
(ii) Convertibles
(iii) Straight debt

Determining the level of gearing

35. General determinants of the gearing ratio

In **13** we noted the main determinants of a company's gearing ratio, i.e. its borrowing ability, the level of anticipated profits in relation to the interest charges on debt capital, the relative costs of raising debt and equity funds and shareholders' attitude towards control. These general influences now serve as a basis for a more comprehensive examination of a company's capital structure and its gearing factor.

36. Borrowing capacity

The first two factors mentioned above are closely related. The first, borrowing ability, is subject to a constraint contained in the company's articles of association and by the attitudes of company officials and shareholders towards borrowing. In other words, the company promoters who originally framed the articles and defined the limits and the managers who determine and implement the financial policy must assess the risks inherent in borrowing:

(a) loans have to be repaid;
(b) loans have to be serviced.

Thus, a decision to borrow, places on managers an obligation to generate sufficient earnings to service and redeem the debt. However, success cannot be guaranteed: management is faced with the ever-present possibility that cash holdings may be insufficient to meet these continuing commitments and repayment of the capital. In this event, default on interest payments has serious repercussions for managers and shareholders in that creditors can legally take control and petition for the winding-up of the company for repayment of their debt: the former lose the benefits that control affords, the latter may lose part or all of their investment.

What then determines a company's borrowing policy? It is suggested that a decision to borrow and the degree of borrowing is a compromise decided by the size and composition of the coalition members within the company who, as individuals, possess different attitudes to risk, ranging from the optimistic risk-takers to the pessimistic risk-averters.

The second factor influencing the company's borrowing capacity is management's view of the level of anticipated profits in relation to the interest charges on the debt capital. Clearly, risk of default on debt servicing, with its attendant detriment to coalition members' interests, is minimized where earnings are expected to remain stable and well above the fixed-interest payments. Thus the company's past record of earnings and the anticipated earnings cover on a proposed loan, i.e. the expected margin of safety, may cause coalition members to qualify their attitudes towards the risk inherent in a borrowing decision.

37. The lender's attitude

So far, we have not mentioned the attitude of the other party in the transaction, i.e. the lender of the finance. The lender too is concerned with minimizing risk, and tends to:

(a) *Diversify lending* so that not all of the eggs are in one basket.
(b) *Advance money at a price*. This means that:
(*i*) A price or rate of interest will be stipulated by the lender that is a satisfactory trade-off between the anticipated return on his or her investment with the company's quantity and quality of expected future earnings;
(*ii*) The lender will set a price that is a trade-off between the return on the investment and the probability that the capital will be repaid.

38. Quantifying the lender's expectations

Let us imagine that X Ltd approaches Advance Ltd with a view to obtaining two loans, i.e. £100 000 secured and £100 000 unsecured. X Ltd provides the following data:

Balance sheet of X Ltd	£k		*Break-up value of assets*	
Fixed assets				
Land and buildings	450		500	
Plant and machinery	200		100	
Total		650		600
Current assets				
Raw materials	25		25	
WIP	75		25	
Stocks of finished goods	100		33	
Debtors	150		135	
Cash	50		50	
Total	400		268	
Less Current liabilities				
(unsecured creditors)	100	300	100	168
		950		768
Net assets				
Financed by:				
Equity	550			
Debenture 8% (secured				
on land and buildings)	400	950		

Advance Ltd will consider the following:

(a) *Earnings cover*. If X Ltd has a good record of stable profits and forecasts annual earnings before tax and interest of £80k for the duration of the loans then Advance Ltd can determine with the help of the balance-sheet information the terms of the loans.

(*i*) Loans ranked in order of repayment on winding up	(*ii*) Annual cost of servicing loans	(*iii*) Available earnings before tax and interest	(*iv*) Earnings cover (*iii*) ÷ (*ii*)
10% Debenture £400k	£40k	£80k(–£40k)	2.0
12% Secured loan £100k	£12k	£40k(–£12k)	3.3
15% Unsecured loan £100k	£15k	£28k	1.8

Advance Ltd should start by applying the opportunity cost rates, i.e. 12 per cent and 15 per cent for secured and unsecured loans respectively, which means a satisfactory margin of safety for the secured loan (earnings cover 3.3 times). However, the 1.8 times earning cover for the unsecured loan is rather low, as is the 2.0 times cover for the debenture, and Advance should decide whether their loans become callable if earnings cover falls to a predetermined level.

The next step is to trade-off between the interest rates and the risk of default, i.e. to raise the rate to compensate for the slim margin of safety (although this will necessarily reduce the earnings cover further). Thus if 0.5 per cent is added to each loan we have:

(*i*)	(*ii*)	(*iii*)	(*iv*)
10% Debenture £400k	£40k	£80k	2.0
12.5% Secured loan £100k	£12.5k	£40k	3.2
15.5% Unsecured loan £100k	£15.5k	£27.5k	1.7

Advance Ltd should next consider the security of the investment, i.e. asset cover.

(b) *Asset cover.* Advance Ltd should next compare X Ltd's assets valued on a going-concern basis with realistic market values on the break-up value (*see* balance sheet for X Ltd *above*).

Land and buildings valued at £450k in the balance sheet provide the security for the debenture holder. However, its market value may be currently £500k, in which case there is a surplus of assets of £100k available for other creditors. The asset cover for the debenture holder is:

$$\frac{\text{Value of secured asset at break-up value}}{\text{Amount of the loan}} = \frac{£500\text{k}}{£400\text{k}}$$

$$= 1.25 \text{ times.}$$

The asset cover for the secured loan of £100k on a break-up valuation is the total of fixed and current assets less the prior claim of the debenture, i.e.

$$£600\text{k} + £268\text{k} - £400\text{k} = £468 \div £100\text{k} = 4.68 \text{ times}$$

(assuming that there are no preferential creditors, e.g. tax, wages and salaries owing).

The asset cover for the unsecured loan is

$$£368\text{k} \div £100\text{k} = 3.68 \text{ times.}$$

Advance Ltd might consider the asset cover to be satisfactory and confirm the interest rates of 12.5 per cent and 15.5 per cent, with the proviso that the loans become callable if earnings cover falls below a minimum level, on the grounds that the low overall-earnings cover, i.e. only 1.17 times (i.e. £80k ÷ £68k total annual interest charge) puts the interest at risk.

39. Shareholders' attitudes to control

Another factor influencing a company's gearing ratio is the attitude of shareholders towards control. If they are unwilling to dilute the equity and thereby weaken their control, they will borrow additional funds when required and pay the higher interest premiums demanded by lenders as compensation for the inevitable deterioration in earnings or asset cover.

40. Relative costs of raising finance

This is another consideration influencing capital gearing which has been discussed earlier. In summary, the financial planner will compare:

(a) The net proceeds of equity/debt issues in relation to capital requirements.

(b) The tax treatment of dividends and interest payments to establish the true cost of shares and debt capital financing.

(c) The coupon rate that the company must offer, which depends on:

  (*i*) the company's potential earning capacity;
  (*ii*) the opportunity cost of capital at the time of issue;
  (*iii*) the asset cover.

41. Summary
Financial planners attempting to fashion a satisfactory capital structure should proceed in the following manner.

(a) The determination of the economic objectives of the coalition, e.g. maximization of EPS either for dividends or retention, dilution or extension of control by shareholders. Naturally, these objectives will be tempered by attitudes to risk.

(b) The determination of the broad long-term financial policy to secure these objectives and in particular the selection of a target gearing ratio which the company could reasonably support, bearing in mind the anticipated earnings.

(c) A consideration of the alternative methods of debt financing available to the company.

(d) Selection of the financing method that minimizes the cost of capital.

42. Gearing levels and the cost of capital
Let us consider the alternative courses of action available to the financial planners mentioned above whose objective is to minimize the company's cost of capital. The required level of gearing to achieve minimum cost of capital is explained by two different theories of company capital structure:

(a) the traditional theory of capital structure and

(b) the Modigliani and Miller theory.

43. The traditional theory
At low levels of gearing, as the proportion of debt to total capital increases, the average cost of capital falls because the cost of debt is lower than the cost of equity. This is because equity investors will require a higher yield on their investments than suppliers of debt capital to compensate for the higher risks associated with post-interest earnings. They will not, however, demand higher returns in proportion to increasing gearing while the absolute level of gearing is low to moderate because, although the risk is rising, it is still relatively small. However, when gearing levels become excessive the average cost of capital increases because the company must then offer shareholders higher yields to compensate for the higher risks of low post-interest profits.

Similarly, suppliers of loan capital must be offered higher yields because their interest may not be guaranteed at very high levels of gearing. Therefore there must be a level of gearing between these two extremes where the unit cost of capital is minimized. This level is OA in Fig. 8.3.

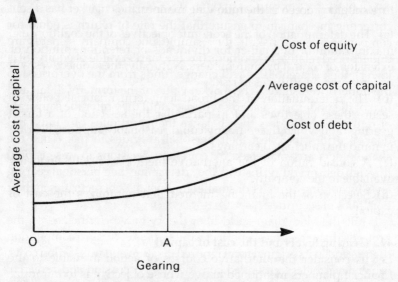

Figure 8.3 *Gearing levels and the cost of capital*

44. The Modigliani and Miller theory

Developed in a series of articles dating from 1958, it is at variance with the traditional theory. It argues that the cost of capital is independent of the capital structure.

The theory holds that for all companies of comparable risk, the rate of return on total capital (R) is constant and related to the companies' earnings before interest (E), the value of their shares (S) and the value of their fixed interest bonds (i.e. total debt securities) (B), as follows:

$$\frac{E}{S + B} = R$$

For example, consider two companies with equal risks, A and B.

		A £	B £
Expected earnings before interest	(E)	1 000	1 000
Value of total shares	(S)	50	40
Value of total debt securities	(B)	50	60

Both companies have the same expected earnings but Company B is more highly geared. Applying the formula $E \div (S + B)$ to both, we have identical values of R.

Modigliani and Miller argue that the securities market has a self-correcting mechanism to ensure that the rate of return is equal for companies of equal risk. If, for example, one company's shares are underpriced relative to another's (i.e. the market value of equity (S) is lower), then shareholders will change funds from the overpriced to the underpriced shares. The market value of the former will fall and that of the underpriced shares will rise, until they offer the same rate of return. Shareholders then balance their portfolios of equity and debt securities to reflect their personal attitudes to risk. Thus the shareholders are unaffected by company decisions to raise capital through debt or equity. Instead, they determine their personal gearing level by holding a greater or smaller number of debt securities in their portfolios of securities.

While the Modigliani and Miller theory may be criticized on the grounds that it assumes a perfect capital market of pure competition theory, and in its original form ignored taxation and transaction costs, it has nevertheless provoked considerable discussion and research, and a better understanding of the attitudes of investors to rates of returns and the effects of gearing on those returns.

Progress test 8

1. Compare the main features of ordinary shares, preference shares and debentures. **(1–2, 7–9)**

2. What do you understand by 'the divorce between ownership and control in modern joint-stock companies'? What are the causes of this divorce? **(3–6)**

3. Compare and contrast the interests of shareholders and company controllers. **(5–6)**

4. Compare debentures, convertible loan stock and mortgages as sources of long-term capital for industry. **(9–11)**

5. What do you understand by 'capital gearing'? Outline the pros and cons of a high gearing ratio. **(12–18)**

6. (a) Indicate the main considerations which affect a company's choice of capital to finance a long-term project. **(17)**

(b) What effect do high interest rates have on companies with high gearing? **(18)**

7. What has been the effect of corporation tax on the choice of company finance? **(19–20)**

8. Consider the pros and cons of loan capital as a means of long-term company finance. **(20–26)**

9. Compare and contrast ROI and EPS as measures of company performance. **(23–24)**

10. Compare the effects on earnings per share if finance is raised by ordinary shares, debentures and convertibles. **(28–34)**

11. Explain how the gearing level is determined with specific reference to the company's borrowing policy and the attitude of lenders. **(35–44)**

12. Explain Modigliani and Miller's theory. **(44)**

13. 'Borrowing is crucial to a firm's survival.' Discuss. **(1–44)**

9
Principles of investment

The choice of investment

1. Investment objectives

In theory, the ideal investment is one which offers perfect security, maximum income and perfect liquidity. In practice there is no such ideal investment, for these objectives are basically contradictory: liquidity and income, and income and security generally vary inversely. Investors are forced therefore to compromise and choose investments with the specific features which best suit their circumstances.

Age, anticipated future earned and unearned incomes, attitude towards risk, liquidity preference and tax liability are important considerations influencing the individual's investment choice. For example, a person who does not pay standard-rate income tax would lose by investing in building societies, since no tax refund is possible. The investor's attitudes towards future interest rates and economic conditions are relevant, too, to the investment decision. Generally the following rules hold.

(a) Liquid securities are preferred if high interest-rates are anticipated.

(b) Illiquid securities are preferred if low interest-rates are anticipated.

(c) Equities are preferable if economic expansion is anticipated.

(d) Fixed-interest securities are preferable if depression is anticipated.

(e) Equities, particularly foreign securities, are preferable if devaluation is threatened.

(f) Equities are preferable in moderate inflation.

(g) A balance between cash, equities and bonds is advisable if no change is expected in interest rates and economic conditions.

(h) Cash is preferable in times of economic and financial uncertainty.

2. Types of investment

The investor may choose between the following three broad categories of investments.

(a) fixed-capital investments, which guarantee security and high liquidity, although this must be sacrificed for high returns (*see* **3**);

(b) fixed-income investments, which guarantee a certain annual income but less security of capital (*see* **4**);

(c) investments which guarantee neither capital nor income but which may produce above-average returns (*see* **9**).

3. Fixed-capital investments

There are several types of competitive deposits which afford the investor security of capital (albeit in money terms in inflation) with a high degree of liquidity. They are:

(a) commercial bank 'time' deposits;

(b) building society deposits;

(c) finance company deposits;

(d) British Government Savings Bonds;

(e) National Savings Certificates;

(f) Post Office and Trustee Savings Banks;

(g) local authority loans.

4. Fixed-income investments

There are many fixed-income securities available to the investor. They are:

(a) British Government stocks (gilt-edged);

(b) British corporation and county stocks;

(c) public board stocks;

(d) Commonwealth Government stocks;

(e) Commonwealth municipal stocks;

(f) Foreign Government stocks;

(g) industrial loan stocks;

(h) preference shares.

5. Categories of fixed-income stocks

Fixed-income stocks fall into two groups.

(a) Irredeemable or undated securities, issued in the form of industrial loan stock, certain preference shares and gilt-edged stock on the understanding that the capital will not be repaid.

(b) Redeemable or dated securities which will be repaid on predetermined dates and terms. They fall into the following three categories:

(*i*) short-term, with lives up to five years;

(*ii*) medium-term, with lives over five and under fifteen years;

(*iii*) long-term, with lives over fifteen years.

6. Fluctuations in capital values

Changes in interest rates are certain to affect the capital value of fixed-interest stocks. For example, the Government (in the Dalton 'cheap money era') offered Consols at 2.5 per cent, guaranteeing an annual interest of £2.50 on £100 investment. When, however, investors attempt to realize this investment later when market rates are, say, 5 per cent, they find that prospective purchasers will not pay £100 but only £50, which at 2.5 per cent (on £100 nominal value) yields the market rate of return of 5 per cent. The price of 2.5 per cent Treasury stock (£15.5 at Aug. 1974) indicates the size of possible capital losses under inflation for this type of investment.

7. The yields of stocks

The prospective purchaser of gilt-edged stocks will compare the return, or 'yield', of the investment with its opportunity cost, i.e. what it could earn elsewhere at current interest-rates. Two yields may be calculated, as follows.

(**a**) *Flat yield.* This is the annual return on the investment. It is appropriate for irredeemable stocks. Suppose 2.5 per cent undated Consols are quoted at £30. Then:

$$\text{Flat yield} = \frac{\text{Coupon rate}}{\text{Market price}} \times 100$$

$$= \frac{2.5}{£30} \times £100$$

$$= 8.33\%.$$

(**b**) *Redemption yield.* The true return on dated stocks must include the rate of interest and any capital gain which results from differences between their cost and redemption price. Suppose 5.25 per cent Conversion Bonds redeemable at par in 1998 were quoted at £84 in 1992. Then:

$$\text{Flat yield} = \frac{5.25}{£84} \times 100$$

$$= 6.25\%.$$

In addition, the investor will make a capital gain of £16 over six years since the bond was redeemable for £100 in 1998. Capital gain may be expressed as an annual yield for the period. In practice this is found in actuarial tables, which allow for compounding, but it may be estimated as follows:

$$\frac{\text{Capital gain}}{\text{Years to redemption}} = \frac{£16}{6} \times 100$$

$$= 2.66\%.$$

Redemption yield   = flat yield 6.25% + 2.66%

$$= 8.91\%.$$

8. Factors determining yields
The general level of yields on stocks is determined by a complex of factors:

(a) *The bank rate and the corresponding level of interest rates.* A change in interest rates will affect security prices and yields as follows:
    (*i*) a fall in interest rates brings about a rise in the price of fixed-interest securities and a fall in yields;
    (*ii*) a rise in interest rates has the opposite effect.

(b) *The borrower's financial standing.* The Government offers absolute security for its debts so that yields on gilt-edged are the finest in the market and establish a standard for other yields. Since the standing of other borrowers is lower, investors expect higher yields. This difference is known as the 'yield differential' or 'yield gap'.

(c) *Duration of the loan.* The element of risk increases with the duration of the loan so that, *ceteris paribus*, investors expect higher yields on long-term bonds than for short, by way of compensation. However, in reality other things are not equal, for there are other considerations which affect the outcome, not least the investors' expectations about the direction of future interest rates. Ideally one should buy long when rates are highest and short when they are lowest. However, in practice expectations regarding these trends will differ between individuals. Their decisions to switch between securities will cause distortions in the general pattern of yields between short-, medium- and long-term stocks, with short-term rates even exceeding long-term rates if lower interest-rates are expected.

(d) *The general economic outlook.* A bullish outlook for industry or the prospect of inflation and high rates of interest will cause investors to switch to equities to depress the prices of gilts and to raise their yields.

(e) *Political events.* Prices and yields are also influenced by political events, e.g. changes of government, industrial unrest, publication of trade figures, international crises or any events likely to affect business confidence, e.g. confusion surrounding Britain's stance on the Maastricht Treaty.

9. Variable income and capital investments

Ordinary shares are known as risk capital because neither income nor capital is guaranteed. Companies pay shareholders an income or dividend, expressed as a percentage of its ordinary shares' nominal value, the size of which depends finally on its trading profits. These may, of course, vary considerably and in bad years shareholders may receive nothing. The price of shares tends to fluctuate as well, according to the forces of supply and demand, so that investors are liable to capital gains or losses.

10. Methods of investment

Investors wishing to take up equities may do so in the following ways.

(a) *Direct investment.* They may take up shares in a company or from issuing houses when new issues are available, or they may buy existing shares through a stockbroker.

(b) *Investment intermediaries.* Instead they may rely on the expertise of professional managers of investment or unit trusts to select a portfolio of shares which are expected to produce above-average returns.

Investment intermediaries

11. Investment trust

An investment trust is a limited company which uses the capital subscribed by its shareholders to build up a portfolio of securities for income and long-term capital growth. Despite its name, which dates from last century, it is not a trust in the legal sense: its directors are not trustees, nor are its shareholders beneficiaries, and the normal director–shareholder relationship exists.

12. Organisation

Since the ordinary share capital of these companies is fixed at any time and increases are made by rights issues to existing shareholders, their shares are normally available on the Stock Exchange at prices reflecting supply and demand and not necessarily the current market value of their securities in their portfolios. However, this share capital represents only one source of funds available for investment. There is also borrowed money, undistributed profits, investment income and any capital gains on the sale of shares in their portfolios.

13. Advantages of investment trust

Generally speaking, the investment trust offers investors several advantages, as follows.

(a) Diversification of investment. An investment trust can minimise the risk of unstable income and capital associated with equity investments by building up a portfolio spread between companies, industries and countries. Thus it may average its yields in a way which is beyond the resources of individual investors.

(b) Professional management. If investment is regarded as a science rather than an art, then professional management, using investment analysis to make efficient security and portfolio selections, may be expected to predict returns and risks more accurately than non-specialists.

(c) An investment trust can select investments which have different dividend dates to produce a steady flow of income for distribution or reinvestment.

(d) An investment trust can realize economies in brokerage and administration charges through bulk buying and the selling of shares.

(e) Shareholders may benefit from an investment trust's high gearing factor. Long-term finance, raised through issues of preference shares and debentures at keen rates of fixed interest, because of the trust's high-class security, forms a good proportion of total capital. This may be used to buy securities earning a higher rate of return. This net income is available either for distribution or reinvestment. However, this satisfactory situation exists only while average returns exceed the fixed-interest charges. If returns are insufficient, then dividends can fall considerably, although trusts have built up large reserves to ensure stability of dividends. The discount on highly-geared investment trusts' ordinary share prices (i.e. the difference between market price and the higher break-up value), which is general except for those with particularly impressive dividend records or under bullish market conditions when premiums may be established, reflects the doubts of investors that gearing may act against them.

(f) The financial strength of an investment trust with unified management secures privileged market dealing and an influence over companies in which the trust has shares which outmatches individual or unorganized shareholders.

(g) An investment trust secures the privileges which membership of merchant banks' sub-underwriters and placing lists afford.

14. Unit trust
A unit trust is an association of investors, established by a trust deed approved by the Department of Trade and Industry, which employs professional management to build up a portfolio of securities for income and capital appreciation.

15. Organization
Most trusts have a banker or insurance company as trustee, to register and hold investments and see that the terms of the trust are observed, and a professional management company for the selection of securities and overall investment policy.

Unit trusts were first introduced into the UK from the United States in the 1930s as 'fixed' trusts, which meant that investments were limited to a definite selection of securities listed in the trust deeds. Later 'flexible' trusts were adopted, allowing managers to switch to securities showing greater promise of income and capital growth.

Blocks of shares bought by the managers are sold to the public in the form of sub-units at a price based on the current asset value per unit, plus expenses covering stamp duty, brokers' commission and an initial service charge. Units are re-purchased by the managers at the current asset value per unit less expenses, should the investor wish to sell. Since new block issues of units are available from time to time, unit trusts are said to be 'open-ended' (no fixed capital) in comparison with the 'close-ended' investment trusts.

16. Portfolios
Although a small number of trusts cater for certain types of investors (e.g. pensions funds, family trusts, and 'offshore' funds for the investor interested in $ securities), the majority are designed to attract the savings of the small investor, although there is a noticeable trend towards the trust aimed at the relatively rich. Some specialize in certain types of investments (e.g. insurance companies, banks, investment trusts and North American securities), but most have portfolios containing a spread of equities in industrial, commercial and financial fields. In addition trusts offer the investor a choice of units, providing for the following factors:

(a) high income yield;
(b) capital growth;
(c) a combination of **(a)** and **(b)**.

17. Development of unit trusts

The last decade has witnessed an impressive increase in the number and type of trusts and also in their financial growth (*see* Table 9A). The reasons for this are as follows:

(a) successful advertising of block issues in national media, backed up by comprehensive marketing facilities, e.g. 'over the counter' sales and sales by instalment credit;
(b) continuing inflation since the war and the outstanding success of certain trusts has focused attention on equity investment as a means of combating it. Unit trusts have benefited from this 'cult of equity';
(c) the introduction of trusts which cater for all types of investors;
(d) the introduction of schemes which link regular purchases of units with life insurance to secure for investors tax relief on the whole of the savings;

Table 9A *Total assets of investment trusts and unit trust companies*

Year ending	Unit Trusts (£m) Home	Overseas	Total	Investment Trusts (£m) Home	Overseas	Total
1984	8 843	5 164	14 007	7 127	8 124	15 251
1989	32 549	23 234	55 783	12 413	10 838	23 251
1990	27 293	14 325	41 618	11 205	7 903	19 108
1991	31 559	18 971	50 530	12 263	10 234	22 497

(e) the willingness of trusts to sell units in small amounts to attract small savers;
(f) the ease with which units can be bought and sold;
(g) investors benefit from lower initial and annual charges for larger-scale transactions, e.g. £1000 plus;
(h) the ability to expand supply to match demand for the units. 'Open-end' trusts merely have to add to their holdings of securities and issue more unit certificates.

18. Insurance companies

The business of insurance companies is the underwriting of risk.

(a) general business (including fire, motor, accident and marine);
(b) life assurance (a very important source of savings).

19. Liabilities and choice of investment

Insurance companies' liabilities from these two types of business are quite different. General business constitutes short-term liabilities by way of claims during the life of the policy, which is generally one year. Life-assurance liabilities, on the other hand, are considerably longer term, perhaps forty to fifty years. One may expect insurance companies, therefore, to distribute their assets in a way which matches their liabilities, in order:

(a) to keep those funds providing general business cover in secure short-term liquid assets; or

(b) to invest life assurance premiums in less liquid securities, which may be expected to achieve income and capital appreciation in the long run.

Table 9B *Assets of insurance companies (£m)*

| | Long-term insurance funds | | | | General insurance funds | | | |
| | Assets | | Net acquisitions | | Assets | | Net acquisitions | |
	1990	1991	1990	1991	1990	1991	1990	1991
British Government securities	31 137	36 585	2 976	9 866	5 464	6 359	531	1 029
Local Government securities	820	577	30	5	22	33	50	16
UK company securities[1]	114 482	145 590	11 563	5 789	10 065	9 877	−940	−531
Overseas company securities	20 067	28 120	4 272	−371	3 233	3 776	−32	−37
Overseas Government securities	4 935	5 996	790	1 276	2 712	3 534	130	487
Loans/mortgages	6 883	7 925	146	79	1 854	983	114	116
Property	34 828	32 185	1 493	663	3 288	3 034	−10	−68
Agents and others	6 997	7 313	715	472	14 704	17 831	1 956	369
Cash	12 165	11 938	−227	3 415	2 874	2 454	−420	644
Total	232 314	276 229	21 758	21 194	44 216	47 881	1 379	2 025

Source: CSO Financial Statistics
Note: ([1]) Includes Unit Trust units

Examination of Table 9B confirms that a larger proportion of assets of general insurance funds are held in liquid forms compared with long-term insurance funds' investments which are more concentrated in equities and property.

20. Role of insurance companies in the capital market

The relative importance of insurance companies as large-scale investors in the capital market and as a medium for marshalling the resources of small savers, is indicated by the magnitude of their total assets spread between different classes of securities and the volume of new premiums channelled into the market each year. This need to find suitable outlets for these funds has caused them to enter the new-issues market as underwriters and as members of issuing houses' placing lists.

21. Pension funds: definition

Pension or superannuation funds are trusts set up to provide employees of private industry and local and central government with pensions on retirement. Pensions are taken out of contributions paid in by employers and employees throughout their working lives. These contributions are invested by the funds' trustees, who have wide powers of action to select securities which will secure incomes for pensioners.

22. Pension funds' investment objectives

Actuaries calculate the size of contributions needed to provide a scale of pensions which is acceptable at the expected level of prices on the basis that invested funds earn a compounded interest of, say, 10 per cent. However, the trustees' investment policy is to exceed this minimum return, for the contributions and calculated rate of appreciation may eventually prove insufficient to provide acceptable pensions in times of inflation.

23. Pension funds as investors

Pension funds, like insurance companies, need to match their investments with their liabilities, which are in the main long-term. Consequently they look to high-yielding but safe long-term investments. A large proportion of their assets are held in the form of government stocks and amounts of property and equities, which can best realize capital appreciation. Only a very small proportion need to be kept in liquid form, since short-term liabilities of current pensions and repayments to employees leaving the pension scheme are more than covered by current contributions. Thus pension funds may be described as permanent net investors. They provide, indirectly through insurance companies (which administer many private schemes) and directly in the case of self-administered funds, a reliable and expanding source of long-term finance for the capital market. While only part of this is used as venture capital, purchase of existing securities releases funds which may take up new issues.

Table 9C shows the growth in market values of the pension funds' assets held in public, private and local authority schemes.

Table 9C *Assets of pension funds (£m)*

	Assets	Net investments
1979	40 825	5 673
1985	156 395	9 107
1990	302 714	N/A
1991	343 667	8 704

Source: CSO financial statistics

24. Institutional investors

The financial institutions play a vital role in the capital market, bringing the savings of individuals to companies. They do this both directly, in their capacity as underwriters and mortgagees, etc., and indirectly when they purchase existing securities and thereby release funds for reinvestment in risk ventures. An examination of their balance sheets reveals an impressive financial involvement.

From this, another advantage follows. Financial institutions tend to exert a stabilising influence on the market, for they are unlikely to engage in short-term switching of investments, although they influence it by their disposition of investment incomes.

25. Disadvantages of institutional investment

(a) Some observers view with alarm the increasing participation of institutional investment in British industry, on the grounds that security of investors' capital, their principal concern, conflicts with risk-taking. Their considerable corporate holdings are sufficient perhaps to moderate management's dynamic policies.

(b) Institutions once taken to task for failing to use their influence to prod companies on efficiency or challenge weak or ineffective management, today play a more positive role, e.g. in July 1993 they forced board changes in Owners Abroad and Spring Ram.

Measuring the performance of investments

26. The imputation tax system

It is advisable to explain the tax system, which changed with effect from 6 April 1973, before examining the fundamentals of investment.

(a) Before 1965, company profits paid *income tax and profits tax*. The balance was paid as dividends on which income tax had already been paid.

(b) After 1965, company profits paid *corporation tax*. The balance was paid as dividends after deducting income tax for the Revenue from the gross dividend. Thus, the cost to a company paying a dividend was the gross instead of the net amount.

(c) Since 1973, we have had the *imputation system*, whereby companies no longer account to the Revenue for the income tax on dividends paid to shareholders. They pay advance corporation tax (ACT) at the basic rate of income tax on dividends but can offset this against the mainstream of corporation tax in the accounting period in which the dividends were paid.

From an individual shareholder's point of view any dividend received is really a 'net' dividend. The basic rate of income tax, say, 25 per cent of the 'grossed up' dividend, is assumed to be already paid, providing him with a tax credit which he could reclaim if his overall income was so low that it did not give rise to a tax liability. Thus an individual's tax represents $25/75$ and the gross dividend $100/75$ of the dividend received: these fractions may be used to calculate the grossed-up dividends and tax credits for any value of dividend (say 14 pence).

Example
_____

Grossed-up dividend	100%	18.7p ($100/75 \times$ 14p)
Income tax	25%	4.7p ($25/75 \times$ 14p)
Net dividend	75%	14p
_____

(d) *Calculation of ACT.* The calculations below show the ACT payable by a company assuming different dividend payments:

	(i)	(ii)
Net profit before tax	£100 000	£100 000
Corporation tax (35%)	35 000	35 000
Net profit after tax	65 000	65 000
Dividend (i) 25% (ii) 50%	16 250	32 500
ACT ($25/75$ of dividend)	5 417	10 833
Mainstream corporation tax	29 583	24 167
Total tax	35 000	35 000

Examination of the figures shows that the corporation tax totals £35 000 in both cases despite the higher dividend payment in situation **(ii)**. In the latter case a larger advance payment of tax is made upon payment of dividend and both ACT payments are offset (relieved) against the mainstream corporation tax payable at a later date.

27. Selection of investments

A useful criterion by which investors may measure the performance of the equities they select is the additional return they realize in the long term over that which could be earned on fixed-interest stocks. This profit they regard as their reward for risk. Naturally, it cannot be assured at the outset, but there are a number of indicators which would-be investors may use in investment decision-making.

The criteria for judging shares are summarized as follows.

(a) Quality of earnings, meaning the amount and reliability of profits. Basically, three standards are employed to measure quality of earnings and how the market judges the company's performance in this respect, dividend yield, dividend cover and price/earnings ratio.
(b) Asset backing of the shares, indicating the value of assets that are attributable to shareholders.
(c) Cash flow, and
(d) Liquidity ratios which indicate the ability of the company to survive when trade is bad.
(e) Institutional backing, on the grounds that the institutions in the forms of pension funds, banks, etc. are unlikely to embarrass the company by short-term switching of shares, but will take a longer-term view of investment.

28. Measuring investment performance

(a) *Dividend yield.* This refers to the current year's dividend and, if used as a measure of future yield, assumes that rates of dividend remain unchanged. Its usefulness, therefore, is limited, although it does give the investor a standard for comparisons between similar investments:

Company X has issued 3 000 000 shares at 33.3p	=	£1 000 000
Post-tax profit	=	500 000
Dividend paid	=	420 000
Dividend per share	=	14.0p

Thus the shareholder who has bought shares for, say, 110p receives a dividend of 14p per share with a tax credit of 4.7p (i.e. $^{25}/_{75} \times 14p$) which he can offset against his tax liability. If he has no tax liability, it is refunded. Thus in effect his 'gross' dividend is 18.7p.

$$\text{Gross dividend yield} = \frac{\text{Gross dividend per share}}{\text{Market price}} \times 100$$

$$= \frac{18.7}{110\text{p}} \times 100$$

$$= 17\%.$$

(b) *Cover for income.* This indicates the number of times dividends are covered by earnings. Naturally, a higher cover is preferred. Similarly, higher dividends and therefore higher dividend yields are preferred, but naturally not at the expense of cover.

$$\text{Cover for income} = \frac{\text{Post-tax profits available for distribution}}{\text{Dividend}}$$

$$= \frac{£500\ 000}{£420\ 000}$$

$$= 1.2.$$

(c) *Earnings per share.* Earnings per share can be calculated on either the 'net' or 'nil' distribution basis. In both cases the starting-point is the published profit figure after tax which is then adjusted to remove exceptional or non-recurring items.

(*i*) Nil distribution basis. The nil basis, as implied, assumes no distributions of profit are made. The resultant earnings figure is divided by the number of issued shares.

(*ii*) Net distribution basis. Here the earnings figure is based on the post-tax profits adjusted for any unrelieved ACT.

Example _____

	Nil distribution	*Net distribution*
Number of shares issued	1 000	1 000
Net profit for year	£100	£100
Less Tax (say 35%)	£35	£35
Net profit after tax	£65	£65
Less unrelieved ACT[1]		£5
		£60
EPS	£65/1 000 = 6.5p	£60/1 000 = 6.0p

Note: ([1]) Generally, ACT can be offset against mainstream UK corporation tax, but not against overseas tax, so that where insufficient UK tax liabilities occur ACT cannot be offset, i.e. it is unrelieved.

The Financial Times uses the 'net' earnings as the basis for price/

earnings ratios since it is closest to the actual results and so enables a realistic comparison to be made between different companies whether or not engaged in UK or international trade.

(d) *Price/earnings ratio.* This is a commonly used indicator of a share's performance.

$$P/E = \frac{\text{Market price of the share}}{\text{Earnings per share}}$$

If a company's share price is £1.00 and net or nil earnings are 10p per share then the P/E ratio is 10:1 or 10. Thus the share price of £1.00 represents ten times the last annual earnings, or, put another way, the investor will recoup capital outlay in ten years if earnings are unchanged. Expressed in yet a different way, the investor must pay £10 to buy company post-tax profits of £1. Generally, a company with a lower P/E ratio than others in the same market sector would be a better buy for an investor; the investment could be recouped faster.

It is quite possible for P/E and dividend yield to move in opposite directions, where, for instance, a company making less earnings in fact raised its dividend payments. Consequently, the dividend yield would rise but investors would probably mark down price on the grounds of the lower dividend-cover.

(e) *Earnings yield.* This is the reciprocal of the P/E ratio and represents the rate at which the market capitalizes the value of a company's current earnings ('net' or 'nil' distribution basis).

Thus if the P/E ratio is 10 and the share price is valued at £2.00 then the

$$\text{Earnings yield} = \frac{1}{10} \times £2.00$$

$$= 20\%.$$

29. Comparison of yields

Having examined the meaning and basis of calculation of yields for fixed-income securities and equities, we are now in a position to compare these relative returns and explain the significance of movements in the yield differential.

At the outset, one should remember that the yield attributed to a security represents the state of mind of investors towards the immediate and anticipated rewards in relation to the inherent risk. Furthermore, this investment opinion, while cognisant of the underlying facts, is susceptible to shifts in investment fashion and is exaggerated by feelings of optimism and pessimism: indeed the opinion may be so extreme as to be irrational, so that yields become excessively high or low in relation to the real underlying situation.

Nevertheless, one important principle of investment is that investors generally expect a higher yield to compensate for higher risk.

Another principle is that opinion takes account of current and anticipated rates of inflation and interest rates. Thus before 1959, when inflation and rates of interest were contained at moderate levels, investors required a 2 per cent premium for holding ordinary shares over gilts in order to compensate for the extra risk (i.e. the yield gap). However, with higher interest rates and inflation, investors saw the capital values of these gilts and their real income whittled away: in contrast, dividends on equities showed greater promise so that the situation was reversed, with investors demanding higher returns for gilts than for equities, i.e. a reverse yield gap existed. In 1993 the reverse yield amounted to 3% when the yields on government stocks and equities were 7% and 4% respectively.

30. Factors determining the P/E ratio

If P/E comparisons are to be meaningful indicators of the relative values of company shares, then earnings must always be measured on a consistent basis. Therefore non-recurring items which affect company profits (e.g. revenue from the sale of a fixed asset or the writing-off of a capital loss) must be discounted.

The factors that determine a company's P/E ratio are as follows.

(a) The value of earnings attributable to each share. The company's dividend policy is also relevant since many investors still cling to dividend yield when valuing shares.

(b) The P/E ratio of similar companies which are in direct competition for the funds of the investor.

(c) The prospects of the company.

(d) The prospects of the industry in which the company lies.

(e) The size of the company:

    (*i*) small companies have good growth records,

    (*ii*) large companies have stable dividend policies.

(f) The net asset value per share.

(g) The prospects of a takeover bid for the company.

31. Capital gains

Investors correctly consider this appreciation as their reward for risk-bearing, part of which may be regarded as an aggregation of deferred income, especially if past dividends have failed at least to maintain the returns of alternative safer investments. Looked at in this way, the imposition of a capital gains tax seems equitable so long as capital losses may be offset against gains. However, the introduction of capital gains taxation raised the problem of determining the correct rate. Since tax liability arises only when investments are realized, the effect of too high a rate is to make capital less mobile in its search for profitable investment, to the disadvantage of industry and the national interest.

32. Factors affecting share prices

The more extreme fluctuations of share prices cannot be explained solely in terms of economic realities. They are more likely to be caused by the following factors.

(a) Investors' response to developments which may affect the fortunes of particular companies, e.g. merger proposals.

(b) Investors' response to 'bullish' and 'bearish' markets:

(*i*) fears or hopes of budgetary measures;

(*ii*) easy or tight monetary measures;

(*iii*) publication of balance of payments figures, e.g. *The Financial Times* Index has fallen considerably on occasions through nervous selling as a result of the publication of poor trade figures and fears of stringent economic measures;

(*iv*) political and economic conditions abroad.

(c) Speculation, which tends to aggravate share movements, e.g. in 1969 Poseidon shares rocketed from 37p each to £120 in a matter of a few months.

(d) Levels of interest rates and yield differentials between stocks and shares.

33. Performance of equities

The Financial Times Industrial Ordinary Share Index, *The Financial Times* Actuaries Share Index and the Moodies Index are the most commonly quoted share indices which indicate to the investor the movements of share prices on the Stock Exchange. Generally, they show a clear upward trend of share prices over the last fourteen years (see Figure 9.1), increasing from 500 in 1979 to over 3000 in 1993.

34. 'Beating the index'

If a share 'beats the index' it means that its market price has risen more than the average for a group of similar shares or that its price has fallen less. Thus it suggests a better than average performance. *The Financial Times*, in association with the Institute of Actuaries in London and the Faculty of Actuaries in Edinburgh, publishes a comprehensive set of daily share-price indices with other information useful for investment analysis, e.g. P/E ratio, earnings and dividend yields for the following industries:

(a) Capital goods industries and for each of the ten sub-sections, e.g. motors, building materials, etc. (a total of 213 stocks).
(b) Consumer industries and for each of the nine sub-sections, e.g. breweries, food manufacturing, etc. (a total of 236 stocks).
(c) Other groups, e.g. chemicals, business services and miscellaneous (a total of 141 stocks).
(d) Oils (a total of 18 stocks).

From these the '500' share index is compiled (actually a total of 608 shares). *The Financial Times* also publishes a financial group share price index with indices for each of the eight sub-sections, which range from banks to property (a total of 93 stocks).

The '500' share index and the financial group combine to form the FT-A all- share index (809 stocks).

Thus the performance of any retailing company's shares may be compared directly with *The Financial Times* Actuaries Stores Share Index. If it is superior the share is said to have 'beaten the index'.

In addition, other indices are given for fixed-interest securities: one covering the market for British Government Stocks and others covering respectively industrial debentures, loans and industrial preference shares.

35. 'The crash of 1987'

The bull market of 1987 (see Fig. 9.1) came to an abrupt end on 'Black Monday', 19 October 1987. The immediate events leading up to the collapse were as follows:

14 October US trade deficit figure of $15.7b was 1.2b worse than anticipated. Immediately, the dollar and the Dow Jones index fell heavily.
15 October US banks increased their interest rates; the Dow Jones and bond rates fell further.

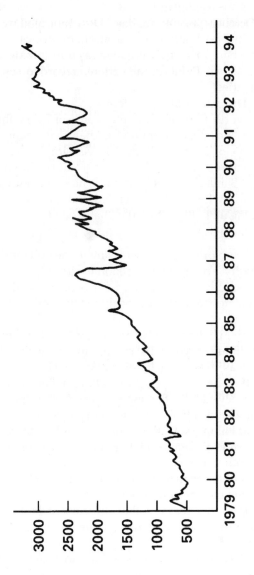

Figure 9.1 *FTSE–100 Share Index*

16 October   Dow Jones was down a record amount on a record level of sales in any one day. The London market was closed because of hurricane damage in Southern England.

19 October   'Black Monday'. Dow Jones fell by 20 per cent and the London Financial Times index by a record 11 per cent. Hong Kong, Singapore, Amsterdam, Brussels and Frankfurt all suffered record losses.

36. The causes of the collapse

It is worth remembering the words of J K Galbraith about the 1929 crash. 'No one, wise or unwise, knew or now knows when depressions are due or overdue. Rather, it was simply that a roaring boom was in progress in the stock market and, like all booms, it had to end.' Similarly, in 1987 there was no single cause of the collapse or one moment when the boom ended. But there were a number of factors leading up to Black Monday that eroded investors' confidence. These were:

(a) Share prices were increasing in the bull market due to increasing liquidity arising from economic growth and declining oil prices. Consequently, people had more disposable income to invest. Speculators and institutional money managers drove the market up further.

(b) The US had a trade and budget deficit. This meant that the US was living beyond its means and financing the trade deficit by overseas borrowing. Foreign governments stopped lending to the US but then had to support the falling dollar under the Louvre Accord (currency stabilisation agreement). This support amounted to a staggering $90b in 1987 which foreign governments raised in their domestic capital markets; the result was higher interest rates. The US then followed suit, but the higher interest rates triggered speculation of an impending US recession.

(c) People began to think in terms of a world recession should the US begin to cut back on imports.

(d) Investors realized that the current high share prices were no longer realistic or maintainable in the increasingly pessimistic market.

(e) Once investors started selling to realize their profits, the fall in share prices was accelerated by computer trading systems which allowed computers to give automatically-triggered sell orders.

Progress test 9

1. 'The investor chooses investments with specific or compromising features which best suit his or her circumstances.' Discuss. **(1)**

2. What are the main features of 'fixed-capital investments'? Give five examples. **(3)**

3. What are the main features of 'fixed-income investments'? Give five examples. **(4–5)**

4. Give an example to show how one can calculate:
(a) the flat yield of an investment;
(b) the redemption yield of an investment. **(7)**

5. Explain the various factors which determine the yield on investments. **(8)**

6. What are the main features of 'variable income and capital investments' ?**(9)**

7. Describe the organization of investment trusts and their advantages as an investment medium for the investor. **(11–13)**

8. Define a unit trust and describe the advantages and disadvantages as an investment medium for the small investor. **(14–17)**

9. Outline the main assets of insurance companies, their distribution and the reasons for such a distribution. **(18–20)**

10. Describe a pension fund, its objectives and the success of such funds as investment media. **(21–23)**

11. 'Many observers view with alarm the increasing participation of institutional investors in the economy'. Discuss. **(24–25)**

12. Explain the following terms:
(a) Dividend yield.
(b) Cover.
(c) Earnings yield.
(d) P/E ratio. **(26–30)**
(e) ACT.

13. Outline the factors which affect share prices. **(32)**

14. How may the investor assess the performance of his equities? **(32)**

15. What do you understand by 'beating the index'? **(34)**

16. Describe the events leading up to Black Monday in October 1987. **(35)**

10
Measuring company performance

Interpretation of company annual reports

1. Meaning of 'Company Annual Reports'

Company Annual Reports refer to the company's Trading and Profit and Loss Account and the Balance Sheet (*see* Fig. 10.1). The former provides an historical assessment of the company's trading position, i.e. a 'true and fair view' of the profit or loss for the financial year; the latter gives a 'true and fair view' of the company's financial position at the time of the statement.

These qualities (true and fair) demanded of financial statements by the Companies Acts are unfortunately undefined, but are interpreted to mean that the auditor applies generally accepted accounting principles and judgment so that the statements reflect 'reality and objectivity'. In other words, there is a duty on the part of the accountant preparing these accounts to interpret all company transactions as objectively as possible, conforming to the generally accepted accounting standards and applying any special accountancy conventions customarily used in that industry or trade. On the other hand, 'reality' calls for the reporting of transactions that are genuinely different or unusual.

Details set out in these reports laid before the company in annual general meeting and thereafter possibly published in the financial press and lodged in Companies House are carefully analysed by interested parties for a variety of reasons.

2. Persons interested in company annual reports

(a) *Management.* Managers naturally wish to compare their performance over the past year with selected market and profitability objectives and with the performance of competitors. Possibly management has set corporate objectives in terms of market share, growth in sales value or units and/or a return on investment, and although there are several sources of information that identify the company's comparative performance in these areas, annual company reports provide a reliable and inexpensive method. Hence senior managers and accountants await the publication of rival companies' annual reports with keen interest.

(b) *Ordinary shareholders.*

(*i*) Short-term income maximizers look for distribution of earnings, i.e. the amount of dividend declared.

(*ii*) Those who take a longer-term view are more interested in profit retention for future growth in earnings and capital appreciation.

(*iii*) Prospective shareholders examine the company's profitability, earning potential and risk *vis-à-vis* alternative investments.

(c) *Preference shareholders.* These look for stable profits at a level that provides adequate dividend cover.

(d) *Debenture holders.* These, as individuals, banks or finance companies, keep a close watch on the level of current and future earnings, dividend payments, company borrowing and the underlying valuation of assets that cover their debt.

(e) *Creditors and bankers.* They ascertain the value of prior charges on company property, since they rely on sufficiency of available assets to provide security for their claims.

(f) *Offerors or asset-strippers.* These are interested in the company's earning potential or the possibility of acquiring assets at a discount, i.e. buying the shares at below their real value.

(g) *Financial analysts, investment advisers and speculators* on the stock exchange. They compare the balance-sheet valuation of the company's shares with the stock exchange valuation and the yield in relation to opportunity cost (i.e. the yield in comparison with the yield of alternative investments).

(h) *Trade Unions.* Unions compare the trends of directors' and shareholders' earnings with union members' wages.

3. Criteria for examination

In summary, these observers are motivated to analyse the published accounts on one or more of the following grounds:

(a) profitability;
(b) activity;
(c) solvency/liquidity;
(d) gearing and capital structure;
(e) ownership and control.

4. Sources of information

The balance sheet with notes to the balance sheet, and the profit and loss account, are the main sources of information because companies are under a statutory duty to publish annually, and include details specified in the Companies Acts, e.g. sales revenue, profit, the company's valuation of its investments, value of fixed and current assets, depreciation provided, authorized and issued share capital, payments to directors, the total of long-term loans made to the company and the interest payable, etc.

Additional information that enables observers to assess company performance in terms of the above criteria is found in the following:

(a) *The Directors' Report.* This is attached to the balance sheet and contains details of the principal activities and any significant changes that have taken place and the dividend the directors are recommending, with a report on the company's state of affairs for the benefit of the shareholders. Naturally, trade secrets or details that could be damaging are not reported. Furthermore, it must contain, *inter alia*:

(*i*)   details of new share and loan capital issues;

(*ii*)   group turnover and profits before tax;

(*iii*)   names of directors;

(*iv*)   the number of shares or debentures of the group owned by each director;

(*v*)   the number of employees and their aggregate annual remuneration.

(b) *The Register of Charges.* This register is kept at the company's registered office and contains details of all charges on the company's property. It is freely available for inspection by shareholders and creditors and to others for a modest fee.

(c) *The Register of Shareholders' Interests.* This records the names and addresses of shareholders of the company and their number of shares. In addition it contains an index of the names of shareholders who have an interest in 5 per cent or more of the shares of any class of capital which carry voting rights. The register is freely available for inspection and in conjunction with the Register of Directors' Interests provides a clue to the true owners of the company.

(d) *Memorandum and Articles of Association.* The former states the constitution of the company and defines its powers and objects, while the latter contains the rules on how company affairs are to be conducted, the rights of members and the duties and powers of directors.

Criteria for examination of company accounts: profitability

5. Introduction

In this section, we consider the five selected criteria for examination of company accounts listed in (3), namely profitability, activity, solvency/liquidity, gearing and capital structure, and finally ownership and control in relation to the sources of information outlined in (4). The whole relationship can be visualized in the matrix found in Table 10A.

Figure 10.1, the balance sheet and summarized profit and loss account of the Auto Co. Ltd, is used to illustrate how company accounts may be interpreted using our selected criteria.

6. Gross and Net Profit

In order to assess the performance of the Auto Co. Ltd in terms of profitability we note from the matrix in Table 10A that the first source of information on this subject is the trading and profit and loss account. This account indicates the 19–4 gross profit and net profit post-tax figures to be £45 000 and £16 000 respectively. However, these figures mean little by themselves; if we compare them with the respective figures for the previous year (£40 000 and £14 000) they become more meaningful. In fact we see that in the year to 31 March 19–4 Auto Co. has been more profitable than in the preceding year. However, this may be due to one of several reasons unconnected with the efficiency of the company. For example, general inflation and sales of old stocks made from low-cost materials may be the reason. In order to assess and interpret company performance more accurately, and on a comparable basis, we rely on a ratio, expressing one figure in terms of another. The matrix indicates the main ones we will use.

(a) *Change in revenue reserve.* The balance sheet shows that the company has retained an additional £4000 after payment of dividends.
(b) *The dividend.* The balance sheet note states that the directors propose a dividend of 11 per cent or 11p per share. By itself, this figure is not very meaningful; an investor receiving the 11p share will calculate its yield or return in relation to the investment and compare this with alternative investments.

If the average yield for this industry is 7 per cent, then present and prospective investors will naturally become disenchanted with the current dividend policy of Auto Co. Ltd, and in consequence the share price of £2.00 will be marked down.

To say that a company makes a profit of, say, £16 000 in 19–4 does not really tell us very much about the performance of the company. It may employ £100 000 capital or £1 000 000 capital to generate this profit. Therefore to assess performance in terms of profitability, we must relate profits to capital employed.

Assume that the current share price is £2.00; then

$$\text{Dividend yield} = \frac{\text{Dividend paid}}{\text{Share price}} \times 100$$

$$= \frac{11p}{200p} \times 100$$

$$= 5.5\% \text{ (or 7.8\% with imputed tax credit added)}.$$

7. Return on capital employed (ROCE)

$$\text{ROCE} = \frac{\text{Net profit before tax and interest}}{\text{Gross capital employed (total assets)}} \times 100.$$

The profit and loss account for the year ended 31 March 19–4 shows the pre-tax figure to be £32 000. However, this is after charging interest on the debenture and so £1000 must be added back, making the numerator in the above fraction £33 000. The reasons for using the profit figure before tax and interest on long-term borrowings are as follows.

(a) Company tax liability varies according to Finance Act requirements. Unfortunately, Finance Acts are beyond the control of managers, and consequently it is useful to use the profit figure that does reflect the internal operating performance of management, i.e. pre-tax profit. Nevertheless, there is a case for taking the post-tax figure, on the grounds that tax minimization is a responsibility of management (who therefore should employ tax specialists to avoid taxation): it is the post-tax profit figure that reflects their performance in this area.

(b) Interest is added back to the profit figure because we want to measure the total return (i.e. profit plus interest payments) resulting from the employment of the total sources of finance whether it be share or loan capital. Clearly interest payments are part of the return on borrowed funds.

If we apply the above formula, then

$$\text{ROCE} = \frac{£33\,000}{£193\,000} \times 100$$

i.e. current + fixed assets

$$= 17.1\%.$$

Table 10A *Selected criteria for examination of company accounts*

Source of information	Profits/profitability	Activity
Register of Charges		
Register of Shareholders' Interests		
Memorandum and Articles of Association		
Trading and Profit and Loss Account	1. Gross profit	1. Sales revenue
	2. Net profit after tax	
Balance Sheet and Notes	1. Change in Revenue Reserve and	1. Movements in assets
	2. Interim and final dividends declared	
Ratio Analysis (Selected)	1. ROCE = $\dfrac{\text{NP before tax and interest}}{\text{Total assets}}\%$	1. $\dfrac{\text{Sales}}{\text{Stocks}}$
	2. $\dfrac{\text{Trading profit}}{\text{Net capital employed}}\%$	2. $\dfrac{\text{Sales}}{\text{Debtors}}$
	3. ROI = $\dfrac{\text{Net profit after tax}}{\text{Equity}}\%$	3. $\dfrac{\text{Sales}}{\text{Current assets}}$
	4. Margins on Sales $\text{Gross} = \dfrac{\text{Gross profit}}{\text{Sales}}\%$	4. $\dfrac{\text{Sales}}{\text{Fixed assets}}$
	$\text{Net} = \dfrac{\text{Net profit}}{\text{Sales}}\%$	5. $\dfrac{\text{Sales}}{\text{Total assets}}$
		6. $\dfrac{\text{Sales}}{\text{Total employees}}$

Solvency/liquidity	Gearing and capital structure	Ownership and control
		1. % of company asset charged and nature of charges
		1. Shareholders with 5% or more of class of voting share capital
1. Value not charged		
1. Company borrowing powers	1. Debentures and preference shares and redemption dates	1. Voting right of classes of capital
1. Capital uncalled	1. Equity capital	1. Authorised and issued share capital and classes of share capital
2. Value of net assets (especially property)	2. Preference and 'loan' capital and annual charges	
3. Estimate of contingent liabilities		
1. Current ratio = $\dfrac{\text{Current assets}}{\text{Current liabilities}}$	1. Times interest earned = $\dfrac{\text{Profit before tax and interest}}{\text{Interest charges}}$	1. Vote-gearing = $\dfrac{\text{Total capital}}{\text{Total voting capital}}$
2. Quick ratio = $\dfrac{\text{Liquid assets}}{\text{Current liabilities}}$	2. $\dfrac{\text{Equity}}{\text{Fixed assets}}$	
3. $\dfrac{\text{Liquid assets + o.d. facility}}{\text{Current liabilities}}$	3. Gearing factor = $\dfrac{\text{Total borrowings}}{\text{Equity}}$	
4. Average collection period = $\dfrac{\text{Debtors}}{\text{Average daily sales}}$		
5. Average payment period = $\dfrac{\text{Creditors}}{\text{Average daily purchases}}$		

The Auto Co. Ltd
Balance Sheet as at 31 March 19–4

	19–3		19–4	
Fixed Assets				
Land and Buildings	£60 000		£60 000	
Plant and Machinery	25 000		20 000	
TOTAL FIXED ASSETS		£85 000		£80 000
Current Assets	40 000		46 000	
Trade debtors	52 000		65 000	
Bank and cash balances	5 000		2 000	
TOTAL CURRENT ASSETS		£97 000		£113 000
Less current liabilities				
Trade creditors	£27 000		£29 000	
Taxation including Corporation tax payable 1st Jan next year	8 000		10 000	
Dividend payable	10 000		11 000	
Bank overdraft	2 000		3 000	
TOTAL CURRENT LIABILITIES		£47 000		£53 000
NET CURRENT ASSETS		£50 000		£60 000
TOTAL NET ASSETS		135 000		140 000
Issued Capital				
100 000 £1 ordinary shares		£100 000		£100 000
10 000 £1 preference shares at 10%		10 000		10 000
Reserves		14 000		18 000
AUTO SHAREHOLDERS INTEREST		£124 000		£128 000
Loan capital 9% Debentures		10 000		10 000
Deferred taxation		1 000		2 000
		£135 000		£140 000

Signed . . . . Directors

. . . .

Notes:

Contingent liability. The contractors who built the plant have brought an action against The Auto Co. Ltd which together with a claim by the Architects could involve liability amounting to £250 000.

The directors recommend a dividend to the ordinary shareholders of 11%.

Preference dividend amounted to £1 000.

(a) Balance sheet as at 31 March 19–4

Figure 10.1 *Published accounts: The Auto Co. Ltd*

Profit and Loss Account for 52 weeks ended 31 March 19–4

		19–3		19–4
Company Sales		£230 000		£245 000
Gross Profit		40 000		45 000
Net profit before tax		28 000		32 000
Is arrived at after charging[1]				
Depreciation	£5 000		£5 000	
Directors' remuneration	2 000		2 000	
Auditors' remuneration	1 000		1 000	
Interest on loans	1 000		1 000	
Less taxation:				
Corporation Tax		£14 000		£16 000
Net Profit after tax		14 000		16 000
Preference dividend 10%		1 000		1 000
Net Profit attributable to				
ordinary shares		13 000		15 000
ordinary dividends		1 000		11 000
Undistributed profit for the				
period		£3 000		£4 000
Earnings per ordinary share				
before tax		27p		31p
Earnings per ordinary share				
after tax		13p		15p

(b) Profit and Loss Account

Note: [1]This is not a complete list of charges but rather items that must be published by law.

Figure 10.1 *Published accounts: The Auto Co. Ltd (cont'd)*

The percentage for the previous year is 15.9, showing a significant improvement in management's performance in its use of total assets. Alternatively ROCE is measured by the fractions:

$$\frac{\text{Net profit before tax and interest }^1}{\text{Net capital employed (net assets)}^2} \text{ or}$$

$$\frac{\text{Net profit before tax and interest}}{\text{Average net assets or average total assets}^3}.$$

Notes:
([1])*Net profit before tax and interest.* The pre-taxation trading profit should be established from the profit and loss account and adjusted as follows: **(a)** Investment income and subsidiary company dividends should be excluded. **(b)** Capital gains or losses, e.g. on the sale of an asset, should be excluded. **(c)** Notional depreciation on revalued assets should be charged against profits.
([2])*Net capital employed (net assets).* Net assets (total assets less current liabilities) should be ascertained from the latest balance sheet and adjusted as follows: **(a)** Asset values may be based on current replacement-cost values. **(b)** Intangible items, e.g. goodwill, should be excluded. **(c)** Fictitious assets, e.g. preliminary expenses, should be excluded.

(d) Trade investments, and (e) investments in subsidiaries should be excluded if the object is to measure the parent company's real trading profitability.

([3])*Average net assets or average total assets.* The average amount of capital used to generate profits before tax and interest of £33 000 is the mid-year value. Expressed in net asset terms this was £135 000 at the beginning of the year plus half the increase in net assets that existed at the end of the year (£2500), i.e. £137 500.

Only the denominator is different, and includes only the longer-term funds employed in the business, consisting of shareholders' funds and borrowed funds. Thus short-term liabilities such as creditors are excluded, since they are used for short periods only before they are paid and replaced by different funds. However, a business that effectively uses short-term funds such as trade creditors and bank overdrafts as long-term sources could regard these funds as semi-permanent and include them in the denominator when calculating ROCE.

Thus the ROCE percentages measured in this way for 19–3 and 19–4 are 21.5 and 23.5 respectively and compare very favourably with the average figures for industrial and commercial companies published by the Department of Trade and Industry (*see* Table 10B).

8. Return on investment (ROI)

This measures the return on the proprietors' investment in the company, being their total share capital plus the reserve that they indirectly own. Naturally they are interested in the profits available for distribution, i.e. the post-tax profit figure.

$$ROI = \frac{\text{Profits after tax}}{\text{Total share capital plus reserves}} \times 100.$$

In this case, the post-tax profit figure accruing to the shareholders in 19–4 is £16 000, i.e.

$$= \frac{£16\ 000}{£128\ 000} \times 100$$

$$= 12.5\%: \text{again an improvement over the preceding year's figure of } 11.2\%.$$

It is possible to develop the concept of ROI further, and to calculate the return on the investment contributed by each class of proprietor.

(a) Return on proprietors' equity investment.

$$= \frac{\text{Net profit accruing to ordinary shareholders}}{\text{Ordinary share capital + reserves}}$$

$$= 19\text{--}4 \frac{£16\ 000 - £1000}{£118\ 000} \text{ preference dividend}$$

$$= 12.7\%.$$

Table 10B *Profitability trends for industrial and commercial companies*
(*Profits divided by capital employed*) *per cent*[1]

1968	9.7	1976	5.9	1985	10.6
1969	9.7	1977	8.1	1986	9.7
1970	8.9	1978	8.4	1987	11.5
1971	9.1	1979	8.1	1988	9.5
1972	9.3	1980	7.4	1989	9.3
1973	8.8	1981	7.3	1990	8.0
1974	6.3	1982	8.1	1991	7.1
1975	5.6	1983	9.2	1992	6.8
		1984	10.2		

Note:([1]) Adjusted for inflation

(b) Return on proprietors' preference investment.

$$= \frac{\text{Net profit accruing to the preference shareholders}}{\text{Preference share capital}}$$

$$= 19\text{--}4 \frac{£1000}{£10\,000}$$

$$= 10\%.$$

In this case, the return on preference capital is that stipulated in the terms under which these shares are used. However, their ROI could be less than 10 per cent if net profits are inadequate to cover their dividend. Alternatively it could be greater than 10 per cent if the shares are participating preference, which entitles them to their fixed dividend plus an extra dividend out of remaining profits when the ordinary shareholders are paid.

9. Margins on sales
These measure the mark-up on cost of sales and therefore the degree of protection to profits arising from inflationary trends in costs. The first ratio – Gross profits to Sales – measures the efficiency of management in converting materials into sales.

$$\frac{\text{Gross profit}}{\text{Sales}} \times 100$$

$$= 19\text{--}4 \frac{£45\,000}{£245\,000} \times 100$$

$$= 18.4\%: 19\text{--}3 = 17.4\%.$$

Naturally the highest possible profit mark-up is preferred, but the limiting factor will always be customers' reactions and competitors' marketing policies if sales prices are raised in an attempt to increase the margin.

The second margin relates Net profit to Sales, i.e. it is the income remaining after charging all indirect expenses and is an excellent indication of the efficiency of management in controlling such costs.

$$= \frac{\text{Net profit}}{\text{Sales}} \times 100$$

$$= 19\text{-}4 \ \frac{\pounds 32\,000}{\pounds 245\,000}$$

$$= 13.1\%: 19\text{-}3 = 12.1\%.$$

Activity

10. Activity
Company accounts contain information that indicates the activity level, or, more specifically, how effectively the company uses its resources.

11. Sale revenue
The figure found in the trading and profit and loss account indicates how successful the company has been in generating income. In isolation it is of limited value, although the trend in sales revenue can be established when comparisons are made with previous years' figures.

12. Movements in assets
Changes in the value of assets should be inspected and any significant movements in items noted and the cause discovered. For example, stocks may have risen disproportionately to other assets, with the result that too much working capital is tied up. However, caution is needed, for on the other hand the company could have adopted different distribution arrangements, e.g. direct selling, which requires higher stock levels because the company is itself performing the wholesale function; or it could be in the process of building up stocks of a new product or model in anticipation of its launch. Similarly, the cause of higher debtor figures should be investigated and credit control tightened, if the cause is non-payment by debtors, rather than a deliberate policy of credit extension by the organization.

13. Turnover of capital employed

The activity ratios (*see* matrix in Table 10A) are the best measures to show how effective the organization has been in using the resources under its control. They relate the various asset items to the sales revenue figure, measuring the appropriate asset turnover, i.e. how many times an asset item has been turned over to generate the sales revenue figure. Naturally, the higher the turnover the greater the efficiency in using these scarce resources.

14. Stock turnover

This is calculated as follows:

$$\text{Stock turnover} = \frac{\text{Sales revenue}}{\text{Stocks}}$$

and in the case of the Auto Co. Ltd is:

$$= \frac{£245\,000}{£46\,000}$$

$$= 5.3 \text{ for } 19\text{--}4 \text{ and } 5.7 \text{ for } 19\text{--}3.$$

The lower turnover figure reveals that the company was less successful in 19–4 in utilizing its stocks. Expressed in a slightly different way, this means that 18.8p worth of stock was needed to generate £1 worth of sales (i.e. £46 000 ÷ £245 000) and only 17.4p in 19–3.

There are two points worth mentioning. First, there is a case for averaging the stock figure for use as the denominator (i.e. opening stocks + closing stocks ÷ 2) because stocks are measured at one point in time whereas the sales revenue accrues over the financial period. Seasonality of sales or an expanding or contracting sales trend add weight for the use of adjusted stock figures. Secondly, 'cost of sales' figures could be employed as numerator, which would then make sales directly comparable with stock values which are measured at cost. This overcomes a possible objection of comparing stocks valued at cost with sales revenue, which may produce unreliable or misleading results if the percentage mark-up is changed.

Thus, in this example, the stock turnover (i.e. how quickly stocks are converted into sales) can be calculated as follows:

$$\text{Stock turnover} = \frac{\text{Cost of sales}}{\text{Average stock of goods held}}$$

$$= \frac{£200\,000}{(£40\,000 + £46\,000) \div 2}$$

$$= 4.6 \text{ times in the year.}$$

Naturally a high turnover figure means that there is less risk to the company if there is a fall in the market price of the goods.

15. Debtors' turnover
This measures the number of times that debtors' balances are turned over to secure the sales revenue.

Debtors' turnover

$$= \frac{\text{Sales revenue}}{\text{Debtors}}$$

$$= 19\text{–}4 \ \frac{£245\ 000}{£65\ 000} = 3.8, \quad 19\text{–}3 \ \frac{£230\ 000}{£52\ 000} = 4.4.$$

However, a convenient method of measuring the effectiveness of debtors' control is to calculate the time it takes on average for debtors to pay for their purchases, which can then be compared with the period of credit allowed to debtors. Thus sales revenue is divided by the number of calendar days in the year and this sales per day figure in turn divided into the debtors' total.

Sales per day

$$= 19\text{–}4 \ \frac{£245\ 000}{365} = £671, \quad 19\text{–}3 \ \frac{£230\ 000}{365} = £630.$$

Average collection period.

$$= \frac{\text{Debtors}}{\text{Sales per day}}$$

$$= 19\text{–}4 \ \frac{£65\ 000}{£671} = 97\ \text{days}, \quad 19\text{–}3 \ \frac{£52\ 000}{£630} = 83\ \text{days}.$$

These calculations reveal that the debtor position has deteriorated since 19–3. Debtors are receiving an additional sales value of £671 every day but are paying more slowly than the previous year, i.e. it takes on average 97 days to collect the cash compared with 83 days in 19–3.

16. Current-asset turnover
This ratio of sales revenue to total current assets measures how effective management is in controlling the more liquid assets.

Current-asset turnover

$$\frac{\text{Sales revenue}}{\text{Current assets}}$$

$$= 19\text{–}4 \ \frac{£245\ 000}{£113\ 000} = 2.2, \quad 19\text{–}3 \ \frac{230\ 000}{£97\ 000} = 2.4.$$

17. Fixed-asset turnover

Fixed assets are basically long-term investments authorized in the past. Consequently, the room for manoeuvre in controlling fixed assets at any point in time is severely restricted by their very nature. Suffice it to say that the fixed-asset turnover ratio, while measuring the company's efficiency in the use of long-term capital resources, tells us more about the efficiency of the capital-investment decisions that authorized such expenditure. Thus the fixed-asset activity ratio measures the turnover of all capital assets including land, building, plant and machinery, furniture and fittings, motor vehicles, etc., although for a detailed analysis the turnover of each category of fixed asset could be calculated.

Fixed-asset turnover
$$= \frac{\text{Sales revenue}}{\text{Fixed assets}}$$

$$= 19\text{-}4 \ \frac{£245\,000}{£80\,000} = 3.1, \quad 19\text{-}3 \ \frac{£230\,000}{£85\,000} = 2.7.$$

18. Total-asset turnover

This measures the efficiency of utilizing all capital employed within the organization, and is calculated as follows:

Total-asset turnover
$$= \frac{\text{Sales revenue}}{\text{Total assets}}$$

$$= 19\text{-}4 \ \frac{£245\,000}{£193\,000} = 1.27, \quad 19\text{-}3 \ \frac{£230\,000}{£182\,000} = 1.26.$$

These activity ratios reveal that 19–4 was a slight improvement on 19–3, and that the company had generated a larger volume of sales revenue from its total investment of assets.

Solvency

19. Solvency

Solvency means the ability of the company to pay its debts.

Assuming that the assets of Auto Co. Ltd. shown in Fig. 10.1 are realistically valued, then the company is clearly solvent, i.e. if all assets are sold then the proceeds are more than sufficient to meet the claims of the debenture holders and creditors.

Liquidity is a closely related concept that measures the ability of the company to find cash to meet maturing obligations. Nevertheless, it is quite possible for a company to fail if it cannot raise sufficient cash funds to meet immediate debts, even though it is solvent in that total assets (when realized) match total debts.

20. Value of assets not charged

Land has long been regarded as suitable collateral for borrowing, since it tends to appreciate and thereby offers the creditor a high degree of safety. Therefore a comparison between a company's fixed assets, particularly land and the Register of Charges, will reveal what assets are free of liens or charges of creditors and available if required as collateral for further borrowing.

21. The company's borrowing powers

These powers and borrowing limits are set out in the Memorandum and Articles of Association.

(a) Company borrowing ability is further restricted by the terms of the debenture deed. In order to protect debenture holders, the borrowing limits are often set very low in terms of today's rate of inflation, which may lead to conflict between the interests of the debenture trustees, who desire adequate security of the debt, and the company, which desires additional liquidity. Alternatively, debenture holders may be induced to waive borrowing restrictions in return for above-average returns.

Moreover, debenture deeds frequently impose further restrictions, e.g. preventing scrip issues and substitution of securities which can conflict with management's financial strategy.

(b) Preference shareholders may have the right to block increases in borrowing powers. Here, the solution may be to buy out these shares, as when George Sandeman, the port, sherry and brandy company, offered to buy out its 426 016 3.5 per cent preference shares in July 1974.

(c) Debenture trustees will look critically at dividend cover and could argue that a distribution out of reserve jeopardizes their security.

22. The authorized capital

In the case of Auto Co. Ltd the authorized share capital is, say, 150 000 £1 shares, of which 100 000 have been issued. This means that the company could issue a further 50 000 shares should it require additional capital.

23. Value of net current assets

The net current assets figure is the difference between total current assets and total current liabilities. Thus the figures for 19–4 and 19–3 in our example are £60 000 (£113 000 – £53 000) and £50 000 (£97 000 – £47 000) respectively. This shows the margin of safety between the company's assets and those debts coming up for repayment and is one of the most important measures of solvency and the ability of the company to continue trading.

24. Estimates of contingent liabilities

This liability becomes payable upon the happening of an event, e.g. a court decision goes against the company, at which time liquid funds must be found to settle the liability. An example is found in the balance sheet of Auto Co. Ltd.

25. Current ratio

The current ratio is the conventional measure that shows whether a company can meet its short-term liabilities out of the assets that are realized into cash within the same time-scale.

Current ratio

$$= \frac{\text{Current assets}}{\text{Current liabilities}}$$

$$= 19\text{–}4 \ \frac{£113\ 000}{£53\ 000} = 2.13, \ 19\text{–}3 \ \frac{£97\ 000}{£47\ 000} = 2.06.$$

These ratios show that the Auto Co. Ltd. had a higher margin of safety in 19–4 to deal with any fluctuations that might occur in cash flow.

The informed manager who fears that sales turnover is increasing too quickly in relation to working capital, i.e. overtrading could be occurring, can confirm this by calculating the current ratio and the ratio of creditors to debtors. If the latter figure is increasing while the former is falling, then there is indication of overtrading, the shortage of cash forcing the organization to finance trade through credit and loans. The consequences are serious, and could, if credit became tight, affect the security of the shareholders' investment, employees' wages, and creditors' debts and therefore demand immediate investigation to identify the cause and remedial measures.

26. Quick ratio or 'Acid Test'

This ratio of liquidity is similar to the current ratio except that stocks, the least liquid of current assets, are eliminated from the numerator.

Thus the quick ratio tests the ability of the company to pay off its immediate debts out of its most liquid assets. It is more useful than the current ratio for general comparisons between companies since it ignores stocks which in practice may be valued by a variety of methods.

Quick ratio

$$= \frac{\text{Current assets—Stocks}}{\text{Current liabilities}}$$

$$= 19\text{–}4 \; \frac{£67\,000}{£53\,000} = 1.26, \; 19\text{–}3 \; \frac{£57\,000}{£47\,000} = 1.21.$$

27. Average collection period
This has already been calculated as 97 days in 19–4 compared with 83 days in 19–3. Obviously these figures should be compared with the terms of sales and a policy of tight credit control implemented if the average collection period is significantly longer than the credit terms.

Gearing and capital structure

28. Gearing and capital structure
Creditors and shareholders have a conflict of interest, and consequently have different views on the ideal capital structure. Creditors firstly require some degree of security and prefer that shareholders have a substantial stake in the company's total capital. Shareholders on the other hand may prefer to control the company through a small share-capital and raise additional capital by means of non-voting debenture and loan capital to take advantage of capital gearing. This means that if the company can earn 18 per cent on capital when interest rates are 10 per cent, it pays the shareholders to finance additional capital through loans and to retain '8 per cent profit' for themselves.

29. Redemption dates
If a company has already issued fixed-interest or dividend securities then it obviously has less room for manoeuvre than one that has relied exclusively on ordinary share capital. However, if these securities have been issued with a fairly wide time span, then the company may redeem and replace with lower interest rates when market rates are lower. Information regarding these redemption dates and classes of

share and loan capital is found in the Memorandum, Articles and balance sheet.

30. Interest cover

This shows the extent to which earnings can fall and still cover fixed-interest charges. Naturally a high margin of safety is preferred. A low interest-cover figure could be serious because a bad trading period resulting in non-payment of interest could result in the creditors petitioning for winding-up and the repayment of their debts.

$$\text{Interest cover} = \frac{\text{Profit before tax and interest}}{\text{Interest charge}}$$

$$= 19\text{--}4 \, \frac{£33\,000}{£1000} = 33, \quad 19\text{--}3 \, \frac{£29\,000}{£1000} = 29.$$

Thus interest payments are well covered in both years.

31. Net worth: Fixed assets

Shareholders should have a substantial contribution of the total capital employed. It is considered desirable for them to contribute funds that finance all fixed assets and a proportion of current assets.

$$\frac{\text{Equity}}{\text{Fixed assets}} = 19\text{--}4 \, \frac{£128\,000}{£80\,000} = 1.60, \quad 19\text{--}3 \, \frac{£124\,000}{£85\,000} = 1.45.$$

Thus shareholders have contributed the whole of fixed assets and part of current assets.

32. Gearing factor

This factor measures the relative proportion of the type of capital employed in a company.

$$\text{Gearing factor} = \frac{\text{Total borrowings}}{\text{Equity}}$$

$$= 19\text{--}4 \, \frac{£23\,000}{118\,000} = 0.19 : 1, \quad 19\text{--}3 = 0.19 : 1.$$

Thus in both years preference shareholders and debenture holders and overdraft have contributed a small proportion of funds in comparison with ordinary shareholders.

Chapter 8 provides a detailed analysis of gearing, and in particular shows how borrowed funds may be employed for the benefit of ordinary shareholders. However, there is a limit to which a company is able or is prepared to use gearing to boost returns for the equity:

(a) Risk may be the deciding factor, especially when company profits are volatile. Shareholders may feel that the risk of bankruptcy which might result from a default on debt interest payment becomes unacceptable at higher levels of gearing.

(b) Creditors may be reluctant to advance additional funds on the grounds that they and not the shareholders are bearing the risk. Clearly lenders of funds will compare the company's gearing ratio with the average for industry generally, and ideally with the ratio for that particular trade, to establish whether it is over-borrowing.

Ownership and control

33. Ownership
The final criterion for examining and interpreting company accounts is ownership.

34. Secured creditors
If the proportion of secured assets is small in relation to total assets, then ownership is unaffected. However, as the proportion increases the company's freedom of action is reduced so that secured creditors may in effect become controllers.

35. Shareholders' interests
The Register of Shareholders' Interests records those shareholders holding 5 per cent or more of share capital. A significant holding of a class of share-capital possessing voting rights gives the shareholder a degree of influence and perhaps control in company affairs. Examination of the voting rights of the classes of share capital can be revealing, e.g. preference shares may have no voting rights except when dividends are in arrears.

36. Vote gearing

(a) For example, the vote-gearing of Auto Co. Ltd, with issued capital of 100 000 £1 ordinary shares (with full voting rights) and 10 000 £1 preference shares, plus 10 000 £1 debentures (without voting rights) is:

$$\frac{\text{Total capital}}{\text{Total voting capital}} = \frac{\pounds 100\ 000 + 10\ 000 + 10\ 000}{\pounds 100\ 000} = 1.2.$$

Here, ordinary shareholders control capital 1.2 times their own nominal capital.

(b) However, vote-gearing of ordinary shareholders is tempered if similar voting rights are given to the preference shareholders:

$$\frac{£100\ 000 + 10\ 000 + 10\ 000}{£100\ 000 + 10\ 000} = 1.09.$$

Use of ratios

37. Value of ratios
We have already established that absolute figures can be misleading when assessing company performance; ratios, however, enable us to summarize and clarify information and throw up interrelationships. Five general rules apply in the use of ratios:

(a) Compilation should be speedy.
(b) Compilation is costly and only those ratios of direct application should be compiled. However, as staff become conversant with their construction and application, ratio analysis may be developed further.
(c) Ratios should be presented in the most appropriate manner for the organization.
(d) Ratios do not give financial control, but pinpoint areas for investigation.
(e) Ratios should not be used in isolation, e.g. if sales increase by 6 per cent per year and profits by 3 per cent, this apparently satisfactory situation is proved otherwise if it is achieved by the injection of a larger amount of capital. Therefore, ratios become more meaningful when compared with others. Comparison may be made within the organization, and is described as 'trend analysis', or with other firms in the industry or industry generally. This latter form of comparison is termed 'comparative analysis'.

Throughout this chapter, we have concentrated on trend analysis to assess the performance of Auto Co. Ltd, i.e. direct comparisons between 19–4 and 19–3 to establish whether the Auto Co. Ltd's performance is improving or deteriorating. The remainder of the chapter will deal with comparative analysis.

38. Comparative analysis
There are a number of sources of ratio statistics available to companies. Trade associations and the Centre for Inter-Firm Comparisons among others supply subscribers with detailed ratios indicating the

range of performance of constituent firms, often with a comment on the subscribers' strengths and weaknesses. Statistics within the following areas are of considerable value for companies wishing to compare their performance with other companies.

(a) Return on assets.

(b) Profit on sales.

(c) Sales to capital employed on operating assets, showing how much capital is 'tied up' to achieve these sales.

(d) Stocks and sales. This shows how many weeks of stocks are carried to maintain current sales. Naturally the length of the manufacturing cycle and material supply delivery situation are considerations in setting stock levels, but as a general rule industry will aim to have approximately two months' stocks.

(e) Debtors to sales. The average length of time for customers to pay invoices is six weeks. If this figure is exceeded, then it represents tied-up funds that cannot be used unless invoice discounting facilities are used.

(f) Current assets to current liabilities. The generally accepted rule of thumb ratio is 2:1. However, this should be interpreted with caution, since much depends on the characteristics of the industry, e.g. the service industry's ratio will be less than that for the manufacturing industry because it operates with relatively smaller values of current assets, i.e. fewer stocks.

(g) Quick assets to current liabilities. The Acid Test's generally accepted norm is in the region of 1:1 or 0.8:1.

(h) Advertising costs to sales.

(i) Production costs to sales. If this increases then the profit margin must deteriorate, and the cause should be investigated.

(j) Administration costs to sales.

(k) Distribution costs to sales.

39. Use of investment ratios
In the post-war period, a number of investment ratios have been used as the yardsticks of investment performance.

(a) Dividend and earning yields in the 1950s.

(b) Price/earnings ratio after the introduction of corporation tax in 1965. This means that if a company's share price is £1.00 and post-corporation tax earnings are £0.10, per share, then the P/E ratio is 10:1 or 10. Thus the share price £1.00 represents ten times the last annual earnings or, put another way, the investor will recoup his capital investment in ten years, if earnings are unchanged.

Companies with good prospects of high future earnings command a higher P/E and offer the investor a better hedge against inflation.

(c) In the 1970s the rate of inflation overtook the anticipated rate of earnings and with the added confusion of the imputation system of corporation tax in 1973, investors' attention turned to the following.

(*i*) *Liquidity ratios.* The very high cost of money meant that companies should be self-financing as far as possible. Alternatively, trade credit should be used when cheaper than loans. Consequently, the current and quick ratios and stocks to creditors ratio became more widely used.

(*ii*) *Dividend and earning yields.* With the very high yields on fixed-interest stock (15 per cent in May 1974) attention once more reverted to comparative yields on equities.

(*iii*) *Prospective P/E.* Many investment analyses replaced the historical P/E, which uses past earnings per share, with the prospective P/E, which uses estimates of future earnings per share.

40. Window dressing

While the published accounts represent the state of affairs of the company when they are drawn up, the reader should be aware that the company might carry out window-dressing operations to show its position in the best possible light. These operations might include the following:

(a) paying off overdrafts with money borrowed from subsidiaries;

(b) borrowing long-term money which is then maintained in liquid form;

(c) pressing debtors for cash at the end of the financial year.

It is argued that these measures do not materially change the company's balance sheet and are perhaps endorsed by management in order to present the information in the best possible light. However, measures that do alter the real financial position, e.g. revaluation of stocks, unwarranted changes in bad-debt provisions, capitalization of expenditure and manipulation of intercompany transactions that are contrary to best accounting practice, are inexcusable and may be fraudulent.

41. Comparability of ROCE

This key financial ratio is invaluable in monitoring managements' performance over a period of time. Furthermore, it may be used to compare performance between different companies and the divisions of a company when the numerator and denominator are measured in identical ways. However, in practice the definition of profits and capital employed often differs between companies.

Example:

	Company A	Company B
Sales revenue	£150m	£150m
Operating profit	20	10
Net assets	100	40

$$\text{ROCE} = \frac{£20m}{£100m} \times 100 = 20\% \quad \frac{£10m}{£40m} \times 100 = 25\%$$

Company B is apparently more efficient: both companies have equal sized markets judged by sales revenue, yet Company B earns a higher return than Company A. However, closer examination may reveal that:

(a) Company A's performance is better because Company B is using antiquated equipment which must be replaced, possibly in the near future.

(b) Company B's performance is better because:

(*i*) the management recognizes that it is the use and not the ownership of the asset that generates profit. Consequently it leases fixed assets which reduces the fixed assets employed in Company B's balance sheet and thereby enhances the ROCE percentage. Admittedly, such an arrangement means that leasing expenses are incurred and tends to reduce profits as well.

(*ii*) The company has a policy of buying inexpensive second-hand plant and equipment which tends to reduce the investment base in the ROCE calculation.

42. Residual income
In recognition of ROCE problems some organizations try to assess divisional performance by using residual income. This is defined as the surplus of net earnings over the cost of capital.

43. Advantages of residual income as a yardstick of managerial success
Suppose there are two divisions in an organization as follows:

	Division X [£000]	Division Y [£000]
Assets employed	1000	4000
Net profit	150	500

	Division X	Division Y
ROCE	15%	12.5%
(a) Cost of capital at 11%	110	440
Residual income	40	60
(b) Cost of capital at 13%	130	520
Residual income	20	(20)

The calculations show that Division X has a higher profitability percentage but that either X or Y may be preferable in terms of residual income, depending on the cost of capital. This example provides sufficient information to illustrate the advantages of this concept as a measurement of management performance.

(a) Divisional and organizational interest coincide. If senior management measure divisional success by ROCE then Division X is superior: its management will endeavour to improve the percentage and thereby perhaps their career development. However, this means that they will only implement expansion schemes earning in excess of 15 per cent. On the other hand, any surplus over and above the cost of capital benefits the organization as a whole: hence the encouragement given to divisional managers in companies using this method to maximize their residual income.

(b) It overcomes the problems of measuring ROCE. By comparison the cost of capital is established quite simply and accurately and particularly for new projects where it is the cost of, say, the bank loan earmarked for this purpose. True, residual income is either a positive or negative figure (the difference between net revenue and cost of capital) and thereby as an absolute number like profit may be criticized as not measuring relative performance. However, there is nothing to stop senior management setting targets on residual income by adjusting upwards the cost of capital to reflect the risk interest in each division's activities. Thus, while the cost of capital is 11 per cent, Division X might be expected to earn more, say, at least £50 000, while Y's target is maintained at £60 000 as a reasonable trade-off between the risk interest in both divisions' activities.

44. Added value
This is defined by the **CIMA** as: 'The increase in market value resulting from an alteration in the form, location or availability of a product or service, excluding the cost of bought out materials or services.'

45. Added-value statements
Profits figures and profitability percentages have long been used as

indicators of company performance. However, there is an opinion that profit represents only part of the wealth created by the collective efforts of capital, labour and management and a more complete picture of performance and activity is provided by a statement of added value. This statement emphasizes the interdependence of labour, managers and investors, and provides a basis for measuring performance when added value is related to employees, or capital employed.

Statement of added value for X Company

	Year to Dec. 31		Previous year	
	£000	%	£000	%
Sales turnover	210		180	
Less bought in materials and services	100		100	
Added value	110	100	80	100

Applied in the following way:

(*a*) To pay employees' wages, salaries and pension contributions	23			21	
PAYE and Social Security contributions	10	33	30	10	31	38
(*b*) Interest paid on borrowed money	6			6	
Dividend paid to shareholders	5	11	10	—	6	8
(*c*) Customs and Excise duty paid	25			15	
Corporation tax paid	20			10	
Local rates paid	10	55	50	10	35	44
(*d*) To retain in the business Depreciation	5			5	
Retained profit	6	11	10	3	8	10
Added value	110	100		80	100

46. Added-value ratios

Added value may be used to indicate the efficiency of different groups of workers within the organization or for comparison with others in different companies. Let us imagine that the following information is known about the X company.

	Current year to Dec. 31	Previous year to Dec. 31
Wages of direct labour	£25 000	£24 000
Administration salaries	8 000	7 000
Capital employed	60 000	50 000

By comparing the added value with these figures we have the following ratios:

	£000	£000
Added value/£1 of direct labour	$= \dfrac{£110}{£25} = £4.4$	$\dfrac{£80}{£24} = £3.3$
Added value/£1 of administration salary	$= \dfrac{£110}{£8} = £13.75$	$\dfrac{£80}{£7} = £11.4$
Added value/£1 of capital employed	$= \dfrac{£110}{£60} = £1.8$	$\dfrac{£80}{£50} = £1.6$

The advantage of these ratios is that the effect of input costs, which are beyond the control of management and workers, is excluded, and they show that for reasons of better organization, greater efforts on the part of employees and improved utilization of capital employed, direct and indirect works were more productive in the second year.

Progress test 10

1. (a) What is the purpose of the balance sheet? **(1)**
   (b) Who is interested in its contents? **(2)**

2. Describe the main indicators (contained in company reports) of company performance, in terms of the following:
   (a) Profitability. **(6–9)**
   (b) Activity. **(10–18)**
   (c) Solvency. **(19–27)**
   (d) Gearing and capital structure. **(28–32)**
   (e) Ownership and control. **(33–36)**

3. Examine the meanings of profit and profitability. **(6–7)**

4. State three ways of measuring profitability. **(7–8)**

5. Distinguish between comparative and trend analysis. **(38–39)**

6. Explain what is meant by the term 'window dressing'. Give examples. **(40)**

7. Explain what is meant by added-value statements. **(44–45)**

8. Explain how added-value ratios may be usefully employed to measure productivity. **(46)**

9. Compare profitability and residual income as measures of managerial performance. **(41–43)**

11

Controlling profitability

How to improve profitability

1. Profitability
Company profits are expressed in pounds: profitability is the relation-ship (expressed as a percentage) between this profit figure and the capital used to generate these profits and is a more useful indicator of how efficiently management is using total company funds.

$$\text{Profitability} = \frac{\text{Profits}}{\text{Assets}} \times 100.$$

This is the product of two separate ratios: profit margin and asset turnover:

$$(i) \text{ Profit margin \%} \times (ii) \text{ Asset turnover}$$

$$= \frac{\text{Profits}}{\text{Sales}} \times 100 \times \frac{\text{Sales}}{\text{Assets}}$$

Thus, if profitability is measured by return on capital employed (ROCE; *see* Chapter 10) and sales revenue is £2000, profits before interest and tax are £100 and total assets are £1000, then the whole relationship between ratios (*i*) and (*ii*) can be visualized from the following:

$$\frac{\text{Profit before tax and interest}}{\text{Sales}} = \frac{£100}{£2000} \times 100 \times \frac{\text{Sales}}{\text{Assets}} \frac{£2000}{£1000}$$

$$= 5\% \times 2$$

$$= 10\%.$$

Furthermore, the sales values cancel out so that we are left with the profitability formula (ROCE):

$$\frac{\text{Profit before tax and interest}}{\text{Assets}} = \frac{£100}{£1000}$$

$$= 10\%.$$

2. Ways to improve profitability
A closer examination of the above relationship reveals that profitability

can be improved by either increasing the numerator (profits) or reducing the denominator (assets). Consequently, management has four variables under its influence or control that directly affect company profitability.

1. Price
2. Cost.
3. Sales volume.
4. Assets.

(a) *Increase selling price.* If price is raised while costs remain unchanged or rise proportionally less than the price increase, then the profit margin is obviously increased. However, in practice there is a real danger of reaction by customers who may turn to alternative suppliers; ideally, management should predetermine the elasticity or responsiveness of demand to price changes before taking any action in this respect.

(b) *Reduce costs.* The problems and uncertainties of **(a)** may be overcome by approaching profit from the viewpoint of costs. In comparison with selling price, costs are more predictable and more easily controlled by managers, so that a more positive way of improving profit margins is to cut costs rather than to increase price. This is clearly seen in the following example:

Profit		= Sales price	–	Cost of sales
£10	=	£100	–	£90
£15	=	£100	–	£85

A comprehensive cost-reduction exercise covering the areas of purchasing, production, selling and distribution, administration and research and development could well produce significant savings in costs, and consequently a corresponding improvement in profit and the profit margin.

(c) *Increase sales volume.* Thirdly, profitability can be increased by generating a higher sales turnover from the same value of assets, i.e. a better utilization of assets.

(d) *Reduce capital employed.* Finally, it may be possible to reduce capital employed in the business. If sales are maintained from a smaller value of capital employed, then the more efficient utilization of assets raises the asset-turnover figure and directly contributes to a higher profitability percentage.

3. Example of profitability analysis
Consider the following information supplied by a small manufacturing company for the year 19–2.

| | 19–2 |
	£
Profit	2 700
Sales revenue	37 000
Production costs of sales	27 380
Establishment costs	1 000
Administration costs	4 000
General expenses	1 924
Assets	
Motor van	1 000
Plant and equipment	3 000
Land	10 000
Stock and work-in-progress	3 000
Debtors	4 000
Cash	1 000

This data can now be analysed by means of ratios (*see* Fig. 11.1 for a worked example of simple profitability analysis).

The left-hand side of Fig. 11.1 deals with the costs/sales percentages. Since profits are 7.3 per cent of sales, costs must be 92.7 per cent of sales which are further analysed as follows: production costs 74 per cent, establishment 2.7 per cent, administration 10.8 per cent and general costs 5.2 per cent.

The right-hand side deals with asset turnover. However, this is more clearly visualized if $\frac{\text{Sales revenue}}{\text{Assets}}$ fractions are reversed so that $\frac{\text{Motor van}}{\text{Sales}} = 0.27$, which means that 2.7p worth of investment in a motor van is required to generate £1 of sales revenue. Similarly, 8.1p of plant, 27.02p of land and in total 37.8p of fixed assets is needed to produce £1's worth of sales revenue. The corresponding figure for total current assets is 21.61p.

However, the corresponding ratios for 19–3 (figures in brackets) reveal that the ROCE is down to 7.6 per cent (the product of a lower profit margin of 3.8 per cent and a slightly higher asset turnover of 2.0) and clearly show the usefulness of ratios as a control technique. Obviously, higher costs have caused the deterioration in the profit margin. In particular, production costs/sales have increased from 74 per cent to 76.6 per cent so that if we assume that the 19–2 ratios are the norm or standard for the organization, management should immediately examine the production area to establish the reason for the unfavourable variance of 2.6 per cent. This may reveal the following (on p. 191):

$$\text{ROCE} = \frac{£2\,700}{£22\,000} \times 100$$
$$= 12.2\% \ (7.6\%)$$

$$\text{Profit margin} = \frac{£2\,700}{£37\,000} \times 100 \quad \times \quad \text{Asset turnover} = \frac{£37\,000}{£22\,000}$$
$$= 7.3\% \ (3.8\%) \quad \times \quad \quad = 1.68 \ (2.0)$$

$$\text{Profit} = \text{Sales} - \text{Cost}$$
$$7.3\% = 100\% - 92.7\% \ (96.2\%)$$

$$\frac{\text{Production costs}}{\text{Sales}} = \frac{£27\,380}{£37\,000} \times 100 = 74.0\% \ (76.6\%)$$

$$\frac{\text{Establishment costs}}{\text{Sales}} = \frac{£1\,000}{£37\,000} \times 100 = 2.7\% \ (2.6\%)$$

$$\frac{\text{Administration costs}}{\text{Sales}} = \frac{£4\,000}{£37\,000} \times 100 = 10.8\% \ (11.9\%)$$

$$\frac{\text{General costs}}{\text{Sales}} = \frac{£1\,924}{£37\,000} \times 100 = 5.2\% \ (5.1\%)$$
$$= 92.7\% \ (96.2\%)$$

Now turn the fraction upside down $\dfrac{\text{Sales}}{\text{Assets}}$

$$\frac{\text{Motor van}}{\text{Sales}} = \frac{£1\,000}{£37\,000} = 2.70\text{p} \ (1.00\text{p})$$

$$\frac{\text{Plant}}{\text{Sales}} = \frac{£3\,000}{£37\,000} = 8.10\text{p} \ (6.20\text{p})$$

$$\frac{\text{Land}}{\text{Sales}} = \frac{£10\,000}{£37\,000} = \frac{27.02\text{p} \ (25.00\text{p})}{37.82\text{p} \ (32.20\text{p})}$$

$$\frac{\text{Stocks}}{\text{Sales}} = \frac{£3\,000}{£37\,000} = 8.10\text{p} \ (8.00\text{p})$$

$$\frac{\text{Debtors}}{\text{Sales}} = \frac{£4\,000}{£37\,000} = 10.81\text{p} \ (9.75\text{p})$$

$$\frac{\text{Cash}}{\text{Sales}} = \frac{£1\,000}{£37\,000} = \frac{2.70\text{p} \ (2.50\text{p})}{21.61\text{p} \ (20.25\text{p})}$$

Figure 11.1 *Example of profitability analysis (a Dupont chart)*

		19–2	19–3
$\dfrac{\text{Labour costs}}{\text{Sales revenue}}$	× 100	36.6%	37.7%
$\dfrac{\text{Material costs}}{\text{Sales revenue}}$	× 100	37.4%	38.9%
$\dfrac{\text{Production costs}}{\text{Sales revenue}}$	× 100	74%	76.6%

The explanation may lie in higher wage-rates or overtime working and higher prices of materials, which, if controllable, demand immediate remedial action in the area of work schedules to avoid costly overtime payments and in the buying department to obtain cheaper supplies.

Similarly, the higher administration costs should be investigated. Fortunately, small economies in establishment costs and general costs have been made, which partly offset the diseconomies within production and administration.

Furthermore, the right-hand side of Fig. 11.1 reveals a more efficient use of both fixed and current assets in 19–3. Asset turnover is higher so that in total 52.45p of assets are needed to produce £1 of sales revenue compared with 59.43p in 19–2. Dealing firstly with fixed assets, we see that although a lower value of motor vans is required to support the sales revenue (1.00p compared with 2.7p in 19–2), relatively less capital per £1 of sales revenue is tied up in plant and land, i.e. 6.20p and 25.00p respectively compared with 8.10p and 27.02p in 19–2. Furthermore, less money is tied up in all current assets, so that only 20.25p is required in 19–3 (21.61p in 19–2).

Controlling working capital

4. Working capital

Working capital is the capital required to finance a company's sales. An examination of the following simplified balance sheet shows that the fixed assets (£70) are financed entirely by shareholders' funds (£80) and the long-term loan (£20) and that the surplus of these funds (£30) spills over into the area of current assets. This surplus capital is referred to as the company's working capital (£30).

Alternatively, one can derive the working-capital figure, £30, from a comparison of short-term sources and short-term uses of funds. These sources, trade creditors and tax payable totalling £40, are used to finance the stocks, debtors and cash that total £70. Clearly the balance of £30 must be financed by other funds, i.e. shareholders and longer-term loans.

Balance Sheet of X Ltd

Sources of Funds	£	£	Assets	£	£
Shareholders' funds		80	Fixed assets		70
Long-term loan		20	Current assets		
Current liabilities			Stocks	20	
Trade creditors	30		Debtors	40	
Tax payable	10	40	Cash	10	70
		140			140

Thus working capital (or net current assets) is defined as current assets minus current liabilities.

5. Control of working capital

Time is the common feature of all items making up working capital. Clearly the longer stocks and work in progress are held and debtors remain outstanding, the more capital needs to be found to finance them. Consequently an effective working capital control should concentrate on minimizing the time stocks are held, work in progress is processed, debtors pay up, but on the other hand extending the time in which creditors are paid.

6. Calculation of working capital

Assume that a company's expected annual trading figures are as follows:

Sales turnover	£1 800 000
Direct material cost	400 000
Direct labour cost	500 000
Overhead costs, variable	100 000
fixed	200 000
Selling and distribution expenses	50 000

On the average the company takes credit as follows: direct materials 5 weeks; direct labour 1 week; overheads (fixed) 4 weeks; overheads (variable) 5 weeks; selling and distribution 3 weeks. On average debtors pay in 8 weeks; pending use, the stocks of raw materials are held for 5 weeks; finished goods are held for 5 weeks; finished goods and work in progress are valued as materials, labour and variable overheads and take 4 weeks to process.

Working capital required:

	Materials	Labour	Variable overheads	Fixed overheads	Selling and distribution
Raw materials	5	—	—	—	—
Work in progress:					
Materials	4	—	—	—	—
Labour	—	2^1	—	—	—
Variable overheads	—	—	2^1	—	—
Finished goods	5	5	5	—	—
Debtors	8	8	8	8	8
	22	15	15	8	8
Less creditors	5	1	5	4	3
No. of weeks that finance is required	17	14	10	4	5

Raw materials
17 weeks of annual material cost $= 17 \div 52 \times £400\,000 = £130\,769$

Direct labour
14 weeks of annual labour cost $= 14 \div 52 \times £500\,000 = £134\,615$

Overheads variable
10 weeks of annual variable overheads $= 10 \div 52 \times £100\,000 = £19\,230$

Overheads fixed
4 weeks of annual fixed overheads $= 4 \div 52 \times £200\,000 = £15\,384$

Selling and distribution
5 weeks of annual selling costs $= 5 \div 52 \times £50\,000 = £4\,807$
                                                     $= £304\,805$

Note: (^{1}) Wages and variable overheads accrue evenly over the production process from zero at the start of week 1 to their maximum at the end of week 4; therefore, the effective times over which they are incurred is 2 weeks.

This company requires working capital of £304 805 to support its expected sales turnover of £1 800 000 or 16.9p per £1 of sales revenue.

The implications on company policy are:

(a) If funds are insufficient to support these sales then either sales must be limited or the length of the working-capital cycle reduced. Failure to do either could cause overtrading and possibly insolvency.

(b) A reduction in the length of the working-capital cycle is effected by:

    (*i*) Reducing the times of stocks.

    (*ii*) Speeding up the production process.

    (*iii*) Reducing debtor days.

    (*iv*) Increasing creditor days.

(c) A reduction in the working-capital cycle releases scarce resources that can be used either for investment in fixed assets or to support additional sales.

Controlling current assets: stock-in-trade

7. Introduction

Ceteris paribus, any improvement in the asset-turnover ratio produces a corresponding improvement in the profitability percentage. Thus in this section, we concentrate our attention on the analysis and control of stocks consisting of raw materials, WIP and finished goods, to investigate possible ways of improving the asset turnover by maintaining a given sales revenue from a smaller value of stocks.

8. Factors influencing stock levels

There are basically two factors influencing the optimum level of stocks to be held by an organization:

(a) *Demand*. There must be sufficient stocks to satisfy:
   (*i*) normal production demands determined by the production cycle,
   (*ii*) anticipated growth in sales and production,
   (*iii*) abnormal demands, i.e. buffer stocks to allow for the unexpected.
These variables may be illustrated by reference to Fig. 11.2 which indicates a hypothetical re-order level, bearing in mind the assumed lead time, i.e. the time taken to order, receive and inspect stocks ready for use.

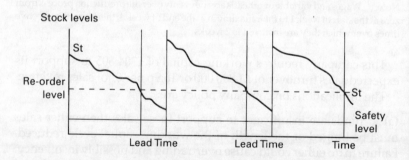

Figure 11.2 *Demand for stocks and re-order levels*

The line St–St represents irregularity and abnormality in sales and hence production demands over time; the required safety stock level or buffer stocks and the lead time determine the stock level when re-ordering must take place.

(b) Economic quantities. Orders should be made bearing in mind the following:

(*i*) costs involved in ordering and carrying stocks (naturally, any saving in this respect is of benefit to the organization and directly improves the stock-turnover ratio, but any decision to place small orders must be made by reference to **(a)** above), and

(*ii*) economies of bulk purchases.

9. The re-order level
This is calculated as follows:

Re-order level (ROL) = Average consumption rate × Lead time.

However, if materials already ordered are awaiting delivery when further re-orders are being considered, then the ROL will have to be adjusted accordingly.

ROL = (Average consumption rate × Lead time) – Goods in transit.

10. The cost of carrying stocks
There are three elements in the costs of carrying stocks.

(a) Costs of holding stocks,[1] e.g.:
  (*i*) cost of tied-up capital;
  (*ii*) storage costs;
  (*iii*) insurance;
  (*iv*) spoilage costs, etc.
(b) Out-of-stock costs, e.g.:
  (*i*) lost revenue from being out of stock;
  (*ii*) lost future sales because of damaged goodwill;
  (*iii*) spoilage, damage caused by hold-ups in production.
(c) Administrative and financial costs:
  (*i*) costs of placing, processing orders;
  (*ii*) handling costs;
  (*iii*) cost of forgoing bulk purchase discounts;
  (*iv*) cost of failing to anticipate price increases.

Note:([1]) Managers should resist the temptation of issuing an instruction to cut all stocks by, say, 10 per cent as an economy measure. Instead they should first analyse stocks by value to find that some 80 per cent of the total stock value is tied up in about 20 per cent of certain stocks; consequently, tighter control on these particular items alone is likely to produce substantial savings without the interruptions to production caused by being out of stock of less valuable but essential items.

11. The optimum order quantity
An alternative way of classifying these costs is to express them according to how they behave in relation to order size and stock levels.

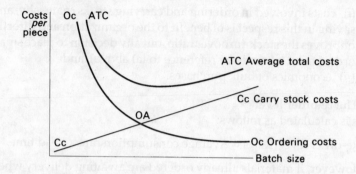

Figure 11.3 *Costs per piece for different batch sizes and optimum order sizes*

Clearly, certain costs rise (perhaps directly) with the amount of stocks, e.g. cost of capital tied up, storage, spoilage, etc.; on the other hand, some costs will vary inversely, e.g. costs of being out of stock, the costs of ordering and processing through the operation of economies of large-scale buying. If we now graph these relationships then we have Fig. 11.3 that contains the hypothetical curve ATC–ATC which is the sum of the two curves (Cc and Oc) representing these increasing and decreasing costs. The slopes of the two curves Cc–Cc and Oc–Oc are identical at OA, where the marginal increasing costs and the marginal decreasing costs are equal. At this unique point, average total costs are at a minimum value. At stock levels below OA, marginal decreasing costs exceed marginal increasing costs so that average total costs (ATC) are falling. Above OA, marginal increasing costs are greater, so that ATC rises. Thus total costs are neither increasing nor decreasing and at their lowest value at OA, which represents the optimum or Economic Ordering Quantity (EOQ) or Economic Batch Quantity (EBQ) if the goods are produced within the organization's production department.

A formula for the EOQ for a single independent inventory is as follows:

$$EOQ = \sqrt{\frac{2SD}{CI}}$$

where D = consumption rate per annum
S = ordering/handling costs per order
C = cost per unit
I = percentage stock carrying charge.

12. Examples
Problem 1

(*i*) If an organisation uses 300 units of the material at a cost of £1 per unit when carrying costs are 20 per cent of the stock value and ordering and preparation costs are £10, then:

$$EOQ = \sqrt{\frac{2SD}{CI}}$$

$$= \sqrt{\frac{2 \times 300 \times 10}{0.2 \times 10}}$$

$$= \sqrt{\frac{6\ 000}{2}}$$

$$= 55 \text{ units}$$

(*ii*) If we now assume that sales are doubled, and all other assumptions are unchanged, then:

$$EOQ = \sqrt{\frac{2 \times 600 \times 10}{0.2 \times 10}}$$

$$= \sqrt{\frac{12\ 000}{2}}$$

$$= 77 \text{ units (note EOQ has not doubled)}$$

(*iii*) If we assume that sales treble, then:

$$EOQ = \sqrt{\frac{2 \times 900 \times 10}{0.2 \times 10}}$$

$$= \sqrt{\frac{18\ 000}{2}}$$

$$= 95 \text{ units (note EOQ has not trebled)}$$

Problem 2

If the assumptions are unchanged except that the cost of ordering/handling the order is doubled to £20, then the reworked examples for sales of (*i*) 300, (*ii*) 600 and (*iii*) 900 units are as follows:

(*i*)
$$EOQ = \sqrt{\frac{2 \times 300 \times 20}{0.2 \times 10}}$$

$$= 77 \text{ units}$$

(*ii*)
$$EOQ = \sqrt{\frac{2 \times 600 \times 20}{0.2 \times 10}}$$

$$= 110 \text{ units}$$

(iii)
$$EOQ = \sqrt{\frac{2 \times 900 \times 20}{0.2 \times 10}}$$
$$= 134 \text{ units}$$

Problem 3

Finally, if the stockholding charge is doubled to 40 per cent of the stock value, with the same assumptions, then:

(i)
$$EOQ = \sqrt{\frac{2 \times 300 \times 10}{0.4 \times 10}}$$
$$= 39 \text{ units}$$

(ii)
$$EOQ = \sqrt{\frac{2 \times 600 \times 10}{0.4 \times 10}}$$
$$= 55 \text{ units}$$

(iii)
$$EOQ = \sqrt{\frac{2 \times 900 \times 10}{0.4 \times 10}}$$
$$= 67 \text{ units}$$

Summary of problems 1, 2 and 3

		1 $S = £10$ $I = 20\%$ EOQs	2 $S = £20$ $I = 20\%$ EOQs	3 $S = £10$ $I = 40\%$ EOQs
Sales	300	54	77	39
	600	77	110	55
	900	95	134	67

This confirms one's intuitive judgment that EOQs are lower when stock-carrying costs are high (Problem 3) and that EOQs are higher when ordering/preparation costs are lower. Furthermore, these are clearly economies of scale, in that stock levels do not rise in proportion to sales whatever the assumptions for S or I.

13. Value of the EOQ

In practice, it is certainly more difficult to calculate the EOQ and re-order level than is demonstrated in these examples. Nevertheless, these illustrations show the nature of the variables in stock control and the different costs which need quantifying, and give an introduction to the principles that the stock controller must master if he is to implement an efficient inventory policy. A more ambitious treatment of stock control systems is outside the scope of this study and lies within the province of operations research.

14. Stocks and work-in-progress

The principles underlying EOQ and EBQ that we have discussed in relation to stocks apply equally to work-in-progress and finished goods. However, one aspect of efficient stock control that has not been mentioned is ratio analysis, i.e. comparison of the production cycle with the balance sheet stock-in-trade values. For instance, if stock-in-trade is as follows:

Raw materials	£6000
Work-in-progress	£5000
Finished goods	£9000

and we assume that the normal cycle is five days but that fifteen days' stocks are held, then clearly the business is overstocked (assuming readily available supplies of materials). Furthermore, assuming that WIP is valued halfway between raw-material and finished-goods values then on a fifteen-day cycle it is £7500; but on a five-day cycle it should be one-third, i.e. £2500, half of the actual WIP figure.

Ideally, for optimum stock-in-trade levels and for positive contributions towards profitability, a manufacturing company should employ ratio analysis to establish standards within the areas of working capital to monitor its performance and to compare its performance with similar companies in the industry. To this end, the following ratios are commonly employed.

(a) Number of days raw-materials stocks

$$= \frac{\text{raw–materials stocks} \times 365}{\text{raw materials consumed}}$$

(b) Number of days work in progress

$$= \frac{\text{work in progress} \times 365}{\text{cost of sales}}$$

(c) Number of days finished-goods stocks

$$\frac{\text{finished-goods stocks} \times 365}{\text{cost of sales}}$$

(d) Sales revenue ÷ stocks of raw materials (£)
(e) Sales revenue ÷ work in progress (£)
(f) Sales revenue ÷ stocks of finished goods (£)

The analysis may show a comparatively poor or deteriorative performance in stock and WIP utilization, which suggests that excessive stocks are building up. Close scrutiny may reveal that the company has dead money tied up in:

(a) obsolete stocks;
(b) slow-moving items;
(c) duplication of stocks;
(d) excess holdings of stocks.

Controlling current assets: debtors

15. Reasons for granting credit
The reasons for granting credit to customers are varied.

(a) *It is customary in the trade.* However, this may be argued to be a negative attitude. More positive reasons are:

(b) *To increase the company's market.* In fact, it may be the sole way to increase turnover if marginal customers are only attracted and secured by the prospect of buying on credit. Indeed, if fixed costs are already fully covered, then these marginal sales may be contemplated if they are expected to make only a small contribution to overall profit.

(c) *To increase profit.*

(d) *To realize funds earmarked for specific uses,* e.g. investment in new plant.

16. The cost of granting credit
There are basically three elements in the cost of granting credit.

(a) *The financial cost.*
   (*i*) To a borrower of funds, this is the interest charge on the loan or overdraft.
   (*ii*) Otherwise, it is the opportunity cost of the funds, i.e. the revenue the company could have earned by using it in some alternative investment.

(b) *The administration cost,* i.e. the cost of employing a credit control and collection department (covering staff salaries, accommodation expenses and other related costs).

(c) *The insurance cost,* which includes the expenses of factoring or invoice discounting or simply charging provisions for bad debts against profits.

17. Debtors and the growing firm
It is not uncommon for profitable, fast-growing companies to experience cash-flow problems: the amounts required for investment in raw materials, work in progress, finished goods, and debtors as well as for extra fixed assets may very well exceed available cash. An efficient debtor-control policy can alleviate the problem. Figure 11.4 illustrates

Month	Sales	Total payments	(i) Credit term two months			(ii) Credit term one month		
			Cash receipts	Cash flow Net	Cash flow To date	Cash receipts	Cash flow Net	Cash flow To date
	£	£	£	£	£	£	£	£
Jan.	20 000	18 000	—	(18 000)	(18 000)	—	(18 000)	(18 000)
Feb.	21 000	19 500	—	(19 500)	(37 500)	20 000	500	(17 000)
Mar.	22 000	21 000	20 000	(1 000)	(38 500)	21 000	—	(17 500)
Apr.	23 000	22 000	21 000	(1 000)	(39 500)	22 000	—	(17 500)
May	24 000	22 500	22 000	(500)	(40 000)	23 000	500	(17 000)
June	25 000	23 000	23 000	—	(40 000)	24 000	1 000	(16 000)
July	26 000	23 500	24 000	500	(39 500)	25 000	1 500	(14 500)
Aug.	29 000	24 000	25 000	1 000	(38 500)	26 000	2 000	(12 500)
Sept.	31 000	24 500	26 000	1 500	(37 000)	29 000	4 500	(8 000)
Oct.	34 000	25 000	29 000	4 000	(33 000)	31 000	6 000	(2 000)

Figure 11.4 *Anon Co.: cash flow and credit terms*

a typical cash-flow problem for a fast-growing company. Assuming that the firm pays for supplies within the month, that debtors are given two months' credit (Column (*i*) in Fig. 11.4) and that sales invoiced to debtors expand initially by some 5 per cent per month but that total payments increase faster because of the additional purchases of goods and services needed in order to gear up production to the higher anticipated levels, then the company must find considerable external funds to finance its day-to-day trade. Alternatively (Column (*ii*) in Fig. 11.4), by cutting down on the period of credit allowed to debtors, i.e. one month, it can reduce its borrowings dramatically and has excellent prospects of a positive cash flow for November. In summary, a shorter credit-period improves company liquidity.

18. How credit control improves profit and profitability

An efficient credit-control system reduces the costs of extending credit to customers outlined in **(16)** and improves the ROCE percentages. For example, we can construct a hypothetical balance sheet of Anon Co. as at 31 October (*see* Fig. 11.5) to illustrate these cost savings and the attendant improvement in profit and profitability by making certain assumptions.

(a) Profitability is defined as
   (*i*) the ratio of profits to total assets employed in the business and
   (*ii*) as profits as a percentage of the equity.
(b) Cash-in-hand and stock-in-trade are constant and total £25 000.
(c) Net fixed assets are £10 000.
(d) Profits are 15 per cent of sales.
(e) Debt collection costs are initially £500, and bad debts are 2 per cent of debtors.

Thus as a result of a more efficient credit control system whereby the credit period is reduced (situation 2 in Fig. 11.6), and where credit controllers carefully scrutinize debtors and thereby minimize bad debts (say 1 per cent of debtors) the following benefits accrue.

(a) The improved cash-flow reduces bank interest payable on the overdraft.
(b) If the company is self-financing, then the funds locked up in debtors may be released for profitable reinvestment.
(c) Careful selection of credit customers avoids bad debts.
(d) There are savings in management and staff time in pursuing and collecting debts.

Clearly profits are improved (in situation 2 in Fig. 11.6), as too is

	Situation 1		Situation 2	
Fixed assets		£10 000		£10 000
Current assets				
Debtors	£65 000		£34 000	
Other current assets	25 000		25 000	
Total current assets		90 000		59 000
Total assets		£100 000		£69 000
Financed by:				
Equity		£67 000		£67 000
Bank borrowing at 15%		33 000		2 000
		£100 000		£69 000
Sales turnover Jan.–Oct.		£255 000		£255 000

Figure 11.5 *Balance sheet of Anon Co. as at 31 October*

	Situation 1		Situation 2	
Profit 15% on turnover		£38 250		£38 350
Less Bad debts 2%				
of debtors	£1 300		(say, 1%) £340	
Bank interest	4 950		300	
Collection costs	500	6 750	250	890
Assumed profit attribut-				
able to the equity		£31 500		£37 460

Profitability (a) ROCE $= \dfrac{£31\,500}{£100\,000} \times 100$ $\dfrac{£37\,460}{£69\,000} \times 100$

$= 31.5\%$ $= 54.2\%$

(b) Return on equity $= \dfrac{£31\,500}{£67\,000} \times 100$ $\dfrac{£37\,360}{£67\,000} \times 100$

$= 47.0\%$ $= 55.9\%$

Figure 11.6 *Adjustments to Anon Co.'s profit and loss account*

profitability. In summary, a more efficient credit-control system increases profits and profitability, which is further improved by earlier settlement of debt. Indeed, this confirms our original conclusions on profitability that a smaller investment in debtors for a given value of sales improves the asset turnover and thereby the ROCE value.

19. Analysis of credit
A comprehensive credit-control system includes the following techniques.

(a) *Ratio analysis.*

(*i*) Debtors ÷ capital employed, i.e. the proportion of company capital tied up in debtors.

(*ii*) Debtors ÷ sales, i.e. the asset turnover.

(*iii*) Average debtor collection period, i.e. how quickly debtors pay.

Certainly trend analysis and preferably comparative analysis should be carried out, so that the credit department's performance can be compared over time and with other companies in similar industries.

(b) *Ageing analysis of debtors.* This involves the credit controller or responsible accountant preparing a schedule of debtor balances analysed by age groups. Fig. 11.7 contains a typical example of age analysis that conveys to the credit controller trends in age-debts that reflects in part the effectiveness of the credit control system in customer selection and in collecting debts. It is axiomatic that excess amounts of old debts deprive the organization of its most scarce resource, i.e. finance, and must be minimized.

(*i*) Marginally overdue accounts 31–45 days have increased from 12 to 16 per cent.

(*ii*) Debts aged 46–60 days have slightly improved, i.e. 2 per cent compared with 5 per cent in January.

The next step is to prepare a schedule that identifies the overdue accounts and summarizes remedial action on the part of the credit controller (*see* Fig. 11.8).

Thus in the case of Brown and Smith & Co., letters have been sent reminding them of the outstanding amounts and the terms of credit; Lord has had a second; Hogg and Slough Eng. have had their deliveries stopped following a letter threatening legal action and Horsebrass has all orders refused. Obviously, the next course of

		31 January		28 February	
		£k	%	£k	%
Age of debtor balances					
0–30 days		81	80	87	79
31–45 days ⎫	overdue between	12	12	18	16
46–60 days ⎬	1 and 2 months	5	5	2	2
61–90 days ⎫	at least 2	2	2	2	2
91– days ⎬	months overdue	1	1	1	1
		101	100	110	100

Figure 11.7 *Ageing analysis of debtors (normal term 30 days). (The percentage columns reveal the trends shown in Fig. 11.8)*

						Date: 1 Feb		
Days overdue: 40–60			*Days overdue: 61–90*			*Days overdue: 91+*		
Debtors	*£k*	*Action*	*Debtors*	*£k*	*Action*	*Debtors*	*£k*	*Action*
J. Brown	2.5	1 reminder	I.Hogg Eng.	1.7	Deliveries stopped	Horsebrass Co.	1.0	No new orders
B. Smith & Co.	0.5	1 reminder	Slough Eng.	0.3	Deliveries stopped			
I. Lord Ltd	2.0	2 reminders						
	5.0			2.0			1.0	

Figure 11.8 *Ageing analysis of debtors*

action, i.e. whether further reminders are sent or legal proceedings commenced, depends on the standing of the customer and the amounts involved in relation to the cost involved in recovering the debts (*see also* Fig. 11.9).

20. A credit control system
Figure 11.9 summarizes the relationships between the accountant, credit controller and sales manager and the procedures inherent in a typical credit-control system.

Firstly, once management has weighed the long-term trading consequences against the short-term effects on cash flow implicit in a tight or easy credit policy, the adopted policy and terms and conditions must be communicated to all interested parties.

Next, the credit-controller account and sales manager should set target figures for the credit-control department that reflect the agreed credit policy, the sales manager's expected level of business, and the accountant's judgment on the impact this will have on the general financial state of the company. These target figures may be bad debts as a percentage of sales turnover or the average number of days' worth of sales that are tied up in debtors at any one time, and serve as a yardstick against which the effectiveness of the credit-control department may be measured.

It is difficult to lay down hard and fast rules to suit every type of organization and trade. However, typical procedures for controlling credit are as follows.

(a) The credit controller should establish the credit-worthiness and a credit limit for new customers by means of:
   (*i*) two known trade references;
   (*ii*) a banker's reference for a specified amount;

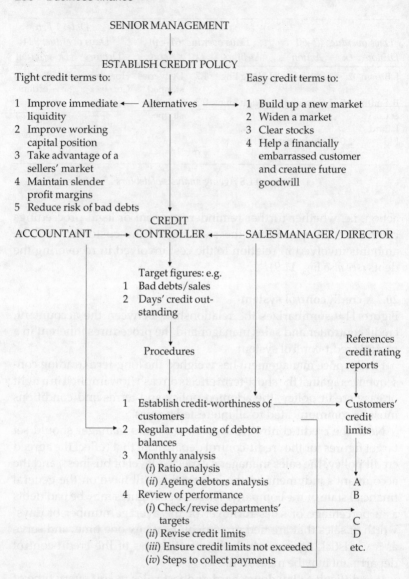

Figure 11.9 *Credit control policy/system relationships*

(*iii*) a credit-rating agency's report, e.g. Dun and Bradstreet;
(*iv*) reports by company representatives and salesmen; and
(*v*) analysis of the customer's latest report and accounts.

The credit limit and the credit term should be related to the degree of risk associated with the customer. Throughout, the purpose should not be to avoid all risks; some sales will fall into this classification and should be approved as long as the price compensates for this risk and the credit period being offered.

(b) All orders in excess of this limit should be reported to the controller for investigation and approval. Inflation may be to blame when it lifts sales values over credit limits that have not been reviewed; on the other hand a customer's order clearly in excess of a reviewed limit must be acted on quickly. Ideally the credit controller:

(*i*) places a stop on the order; or

(*ii*) requests the customer to reduce outstanding debts; or

(*iii*) contacts the customer for first-hand assessment; and

(*iv*) gives approval if satisfied.

(c) The accounts department should up-date the sales ledger continuously.

(d) Every month outstanding invoices should be 'aged' to find which customers have failed to observe the agreed credit terms.

(e) Consequently the credit controller should revise the credit limit upwards for reliable customers and downwards for poor payers and possibly put stops on further deliveries.

(f) In cases of outstanding debts the course of action should be:

(*i*) a statement of the account should be sent; then

(*ii*) a second statement and a letter; then

(*iii*) telephone calls to specific personnel; then

(*iv*) personal visits; then

(*v*) legal action to recover the debt.

(g) The monthly analysis will indicate the credit department's performance which may be compared with the target standards. Next, variances should be investigated and remedial action taken either to control performance to plan or to revise the standards to more realistic levels.

21. Controlling cash flow

The prerequisite for efficient control of cash flow is accurate forecasting of receipts. A system to forecast and control receipts is as follows.

(a) Assign the responsibility for cash control to a specific individual or team.

(b) Analyse the pattern of sales receipts over the last few months to establish the average delay period and how receipts typically flow in during the month. A company might discover that cash receipts average 90 days after invoice and tend to be received towards the end of each month. A receipts profile of a company and worksheet for daily control of cash receipts follows.

Working days	Jan. Credit sales £60 000	Feb. £70 000	Mar. £80 8000	Apr. £80 000	May £90 000		
		Forecast receipts			£60 000		£70 000
	Cumulative % receipts: Standard			Actual	Amount	Actual	Amount
1		1		1	£600	1	£700
2		3		5	3 000	2	1 400
3		7		10	6 000	5	3 500
4		10		15	9 000	7	4 900
5		12		20	12 000	etc.	
6		17		25	15 000		
7		20		30	18 000		
8		22		35	21 000		
9		25		40	24 000		
10		27		45	27 000		
11		30		50	30 000		
12		33		55	33 000		
13		35		60	36 000		
14		40		65	39 000		
15		45		70	42 000		
16		50		75	45 000		
17		55		80	48 000		
18		60		85	51 000		
19		65		90	54 000		
20		70		95	57 000		
21		80		97	58 200		
22		90		100%	60 000		
23		100%					

(c) Use the receipts profile as a standard to control daily receipts during the current month. Thus, if credit sales in January, February and March were £60 000, £70 000 and £80 000 respectively then receipts can be forecast from April onwards and checked on a working-day basis against the norm of the previous few months. Above in (b) we see a 'standard' cumulative per cent receipts and actuals for April and May. April receipts represent credit sales for January and are received earlier than standard: May receipts of February's sales lag behind the standard on the fourth working day when only 7 per cent of receipts are in compared with the expected 10 per cent.

Admittedly the example has been simplified by assuming that all of January's sales are received in April. In practice experience may show that cash receipts are spread over several months as shown opposite.

In this situation the forecast cash receipt figure for April is 5 per cent of April credit (£4000), 25 per cent of March (£20 000), 30 per cent of February (£21 000), 35 per cent of January (£21 000) and 5 per cent of December credit sales of, say, £50 000 (£2500), which total £68 500.

(d) Use current cash-receipt data to update the standard if necessary.

Months in which credit sales are invoiced	% of monthly credit sales received as cash in April
(Dec.)	5
(Jan.)	25
(Feb.)	30
(Mar.)	35
(Apr.)	5
Total	100%

Controlling current assets: cash

22. Motives for holding cash and bank balances

The reasons or motives why individuals hold funds in liquid form proposed by John Maynard Keynes, the eminent economist, apply equally to corporations. Keynes's reasons for 'liquidity preference', i.e. a certain proportion of savings kept in liquid form, were

(a) In order to meet current commitments, i.e. the transactionary motive. For example:
 (*i*) to buy materials;
 (*ii*) to pay staff and indirect expenses.

(b) To guard against future contingencies, i.e. the precautionary motive. For example:
 (*i*) to finance promotional schemes in order to match competitors' actions;
 (*ii*) to settle legal actions;
 (*iii*) to minimize risk in uncertain financial and trading periods.

(c) To exploit profitable opportunities that may arise, i.e. the speculative motive. For example:
 (*i*) to accomplish a takeover;
 (*ii*) to exploit an innovation.

In addition to these general motives, we may add specific reasons why corporations, as profit-dependent organizations, hold cash.

(a) To take advantage of cash discounts which may represent significant savings. (*See* 6:3)

(b) To maintain credit-worthiness and goodwill.

It is of paramount importance to maintain adequate liquid assets and thereby satisfactory liquidity ratios, since these are increasingly regarded by suppliers as the yardstick of credit-worthiness. Furthermore, criticism regarding liquidity on the part of analysts or city editors would certainly damage the organization's financial standing and goodwill in the eyes of the investing public, which would cause a fall in the share price (e.g. secondary banks, property and insurance companies in July–August 1974) and difficulties if acquiring additional external funds is contemplated.

Accepting the need for adequate liquid funds, we now turn our attention to the employment of such assets.

Clearly, the disposition of funds will vary between companies and certainly between industries because of their special characteristics, e.g. the very nature of financial institutions as custodians of depositors' funds demands that they maintain a far larger proportion of assets in a highly liquid form in order to meet withdrawal demands than, say, manufacturing companies, whose short-term liabilities are slight by comparison. Moreover, liquidity preference will vary over time and is certainly influenced by rates of interest and the company's expectations regarding future sales, e.g. transferring more cash into short-term investments when rates of interest are high. However, we can conclude that the profit-dependent organization should try to achieve a compromise between the conflicting needs to hold non-earning cash for the reasons advanced above and the need to invest cash in profitable opportunities (*see* Chapter 7). Indeed, from a viewpoint of pure profitability the less cash held the better, because of the higher cash/asset turnover ratio, i.e. a higher sales/cash balance ratio multiplied by the company's profit margin magnifies the ROCE percentage.

23. Liquidity in British industry

It is interesting to examine the liquidity pattern of all large UK industrial and commercial companies. Figures are those which can be realised or have to be paid within one year (and are seasonally adjusted). Their measure of liquidity does not summarize the whole financial position of companies but concentrates on monetary current assets and liabilities:

$$\frac{\text{Monetary current assets}}{\text{Monetary current liabilities}} \times 100 = \text{Liquidity ratio}.$$

Where current assets are cash, bank, finance company and building society deposits, local and central government securities and current liabilities are loans and advances from financial institutions. This ratio in effect measures the real cash position:

| | *Liquidity ratios of larger companies* | |
	Non-manuf. (%)	*Manufacturing (%)*
1989	81	120
1990	100	120
1991	115	118
1992	148	122

The reaction of companies to the recession, in particular the repayment of debt, suggests that having borrowed heavily in the 1980s, companies have recently sought to restructure their balance sheets. At the same time they have continued to acquire liquid assets. Although still historically high, capital gearing has declined, and the improvement in liquidity has allowed companies to reduce income gearing levels.

24. What determines company liquidity?

Basically the factors determining company liquidity are:

(a) *Management's success in controlling stocks and debtors.* Failure to control these inevitably means more funds tied up.

(b) *The level of trade.* Sales require financing by way of additional raw materials, work-in-progress and finished stock and debtors if customers take credit. Although extra sales may be profitable, they do not necessarily generate cash and thereby contribute to liquidity. An understanding of the distinction between cash flow and profitability is fundamental – ask any one of the many businessmen who owned quite profitable firms that went into liquidation in the severe economic freeze following devaluation because they were unable to pay their way and meet immediate debts!

Example _____

Assume that a company is established with a capital of £10 000. During the first year's operations sales total £20 000, purchases £15 000 and administrative and selling costs £2000. Fixed assets are purchased for £6000, which are to be depreciated at 20 per cent p.a.[1] Over the year £19 000 is received from customers, while payments to creditors total £12 000. Stocks are valued at £1000 at the year end. Cash flow from the enterprise is:

Note: [1] Reducing balance method.

Total receipts from debtors		£19 000
Less Payments:		
Fixed assets	£6 000	
Purchases	12 000	
Expenses	2 000	
		£20 000
Cash flow		(1 000)

The profit from the enterprise is:

Total sales		20 000
Less Cost of sales		
Purchases	15 000	
Less Stock at end	1 000	14 000
Gross profit		6 000
Less Expenses	2 000	
Depreciation	1 200	3 200
Net profit		2 800

In year 2, sales total £20 000, purchases £16 000 and expenses £2000. Total receipts from debtors are £20 000 while payments to creditors total £14 000. Year-end stocks are £2000. Cash flow for the second year is:

Total receipts from debtors		£20 000
Less Total payments		
Purchases	£14 000	
Expenses	2 000	16 000
Cash flow		4 000

Profits for the second year are:

Sales		20 000
Less Cost of sales		
Stock at beginning	1 000	
Purchases	16 000	
	17 000	
Less Stock at end	£2 000	£15 000
Gross profit		5 000
Less Expenses	2 000	
Depreciation	960	2 960
Net profit		2 040

This clearly shows that there is a fundamental distinction between cash and profits in the short term (since they vary inversely over these two years) although over the long term profit is eventually made equal to a net inflow of cash when debtors pay up and creditors are satisfied.

(c) *The relationship between movements in fixed and current assets* with long- and short-term sources of funds. If additional funds invested in fixed assets are in excess of new long-term funds received, then the shortfall must necessarily be drawn out of working capital. New investments in fixed assets on a large scale can spell illiquidity for the company. On the other hand, a surplus of long-term funds over new fixed-asset investment spills over into current assets, which improves the liquidity ratios.

25. Source and use of funds statement

Public companies include in their published accounts, a source and use of funds statement. It is one of the most useful methods to give shareholders an idea of where company funds have come from and how they are being employed. If sufficiently detailed, it will highlight company progress and problems.

Alternatively, it explains why working capital changes between two dates, or if based on a future date provides a cash forecast and is useful in financial planning, showing how much surplus cash is likely to be available to meet capital expenditure requirements.

Basically, one is comparing the balance sheets of a company at two different dates and noting the changes that have occurred over the period. For example, if an examination reveals that the value of an asset has fallen, then less money is now tied up so it must represent a source of funds. Similarly, if a liability has increased then money or money's worth has been received by the company and again it is a source of funds. Conversely, an increase in an asset or decrease in a liability represents a use of funds. This is summarized below.

Source of funds:

(a) decrease in an asset;
(b) increase in a liability

Use of funds:

(a) increase in an asset;
(b) decrease in a liability.

26. Source and use of funds statement: an example

Veneered Tabletops Ltd is an expanding company which has completed its second year of trading. The balance sheets as at 31.12.–1 and 31.12.–2 (*see* Exhibit 1) and extracts from the profit and loss account for the year ended 31.12.–2 (Exhibit 2) are summarized overleaf. You are required by a senior company executive to produce a movement of funds statement for 19–2.

Exhibit 1

Balance sheets of Veneered Tabletops Ltd as at 31.12.–1 and 31.12.–2

	19–1	19–2		19–1	19–2
	£000	£000		£000	£000
Share capital			Fixed assets at cost	300	360
Ordinary shares	250	250	Less Depreciation	50	70
				250	290
			Current assets		
			Work in progress	5	20
Profit and loss			Stock of finished goods	50	55
account	10	15	Debtors	95	85
Debentures 10%	170	180	Bank	70	25
Current liabilities					
Trade creditors	40	30			
	470	475		470	475

Exhibit 2

	£
Balance at 31.12.–1	10 000
Less Dividend	5 000
	5 000
Net profit for year[1]	10 000
Balance at 31.12.–2	15 000

Note: ([1])Depreciation for the year was £20 000.

Veneered Tabletops Ltd

Statement of sources and application of funds for the year ended 31 December 19–2.

Source of funds	£000	£000
Profit		10
Depreciation		20
Total generated from operations		30
Funds from other sources		
Issue of debentures		10
Total sources		40
Application of funds		
Addition to plant	(60)	
Dividend paid	(5)	(65)
Increase (decrease) in working capital		(25)
Increase in work in progress	15	

Application of funds	£000	£000
Increase in stocks of finished goods	5	
Decrease in creditors	10	
Decrease in debtors	(10)	
Movement in net liquid funds:		
Decrease in cash at bank	(45)	
		(25)

27. The cash forecast

The cash forecast is an integral part of efficient corporate financial planning. Management needs to forecast the cash position at a future date, say, in one year's time, divided into monthly or even weekly intervals to find out how the money is coming in. More specifically, the purpose is to:

(a) Ensure that the company's working capital and cash are *sufficient to carry out day-to-day transactions*. If growth is envisaged, then sufficient funds must be made available to finance it. Extra stocks are needed to service increasing production and the higher sales turnover.

(b) Confirm that adequate cash is *available to the corporate financial plan*, e.g. projected capital investments for expansion or replacement.

(c) indicate whether *surplus cash exists*.

(d) Indicate *deficiencies in cash balances* which might necessitate a reappraisal of the financial plan. Calling in debts, using bank facilities and running down stocks may alleviate the cash-flow problem, although if it persists a serious reconsideration of the planned expenditure is called for or more permanent funds must be raised to meet the shortfall.

Methods of cash forecasting

(a) *Receipts/payments forecast*. Figure 11.11 illustrates a typical cash forecast layout, in which are inserted monthly cash receipts and payments.

(b) *The balance sheet cash forecast*. The balance sheet (Fig. 11.12) is forecast as at the end of the period under consideration and serves as a check on the cumulative receipts-payments forecast. Naturally, it does not indicate the cash-balance situation in the interim.

The balance-sheet items are prepared from the various operating and financial budgets and the cash balance inserted as the balancing figure.

(c) *Profit-cash forecast*. This third method of forecasting the cash balance at a predetermined date also serves as a check on the accuracy

Electron Minor Co. Ltd
Balance sheet as at 1.1.–3

	Forecast			Forecast	
	1.1.–3	28.2.–3		1.1.–3	28.2.–3
Share capital 90 000 £1 ordinary			Fixed assets		
shares	£90 000	£90 000	Land and buildings	£35 000	£35 000
Reserves	30 000	30 000	Plant and machinery	£50 000	
Profit and loss			Less Deprec.	10 000	
balance	10 000	84 000		£40 000	£44 200
	£130 000	£204 000	Vehicles	20 000	
Deferred taxation	20 000	20 000	Less Deprec.	5 000	
				15 000	14 800
Current liabilities					
Trade creditors	70 000	75 000	Current assets		
Current tax	10 000	10 000	Stocks	60 000	70 000
Dividends	20 000	—	Debtors	80 000	75 000
			Cash	20 000	70 000
	£250 000	£309 000		£250 000	£309 000

Notes: (*i*) Depreciation for the two-month period is as follows:

Plant and machinery	£800
Vehicles	£200

(*ii*) Tax payable is paid on 1 Jan. 19–3
(*iii*) Dividends payable are paid in Feb. 19–3
(*iv*) Stocks at 28 Feb. are expected to be £70 000
(*v*) Tax reserve against profits for the period is £10 000.

	1.1.–3	28.2.–3
Information from budgets		
Receipts:		
Cash sales	£25 000	£40 000
Debtor receipts	70 000	90 000
Payments:		
Materials	£25 000	£50 000
Wages	25 000	30 000
Salaries	5 000	5 000
Plant and machinery	—	5 000
Debtor balances	80 000	75 000
Creditor balances	70 000	75 000

Figure 11.10 *Balance sheet as at 1.1.–3*

Cash forecast for two months ending 28.2.–3

	31 Jan.	28 Feb.	Total
Cash receipts			
Cash sales	£25 000	£40 000	£65 000
Credit sales	70 000	90 000	160 000
Total receipts	£95 000	£130 000	£225 000
Cash payments			
Materials	£25 000	£50 000	£75 000
Wages	25 000	30 000	55 000
Salaries	5 000	5 000	10 000
Plant and machinery	5 000	—	5 000
Dividends	—	20 000	20 000
Taxation	10 000	—	10 000
Total payments	£70 000	£105 000	£175 000
Surplus/(Deficit)	£25 000	£25 000	
Cash balance at beginning of month	20 000	45 000	
Cash balance at end of month	45 000	70 000	

Figure 11.11 *Receipts/payment method*

of the first method's cumulative total (Fig. 11.13). First, the profit figure for the period under consideration is forecast. Next, adjustments are made; depreciation is added back since it is a non-cash charge against profits; similarly, the reduction in debtors and increase in creditors are added back, increases in stocks are deducted, as are appropriations of profits and capital expenditures. The net effect of these adjustments is to convert the profit figure into cash receipts, which when added to the opening cash balance gives the balance at the end of the period.

Figures 11.10–13 illustrate the principles underlying the cash forecast using these three methods. The balance sheet of the Electron Minor Co. Ltd as at 1 January 19–3 (Fig. 11.10) is supplied with information from operating and financial budgets. Clearly, the accuracy of the cash forecast depends on the accuracy of these budgets and in particular the sales forecast. In view of the importance of sales, methods of demand estimation are dealt with in the following sections **(28–30)**.

Improving profit margins

28. Introduction
In this section we turn our attention to techniques to improve the

profit margin which may be effected by reducing costs and/or raising price as a means of raising profitability. However, we confine our examination to pricing and assume that the company under consideration has discretion as to the selling price for its product; either it is a price-fixer or if in a market dominated by a price leader it has some degree of control over its volume of sales by altering price.

Profits anticipated for January and February 19–3

Credit Sales Invoiced		£160 000
Less Opening Dr balance	£80 000	
Plus Closing Dr balance	75 000	5 000
Receipts in January and February		155 000
Cash sales for January and February		65 000
Total sales		£220 000
Cash costs for the period		£140 000
Less Opening Cr balance	£70 000	
Plus Closing Cr balance	75 000	5 000
Cost of goods produced		145 000
Plus Stock level at 1 Jan.	60 000	
Less Stock level at 28 Feb.	70 000	10 000
Cost of sales		£135 000
Profit on sales		85 000
Less Depreciation		
Plant and machinery	£800	
Vehicles	200	1 000
		84 000
Tax reserve		10 000
		74 000
Balance on a/c b/f		10 000
Profit and loss balance 28.2.–3		84 000

Figure 11.12 *Balance sheet method of cash forecasting*

29. Optimum price/sales combination

Below is a hypothetical demand schedule for a product.

Hypothetical demand schedule

Price (p)	Quantity demanded
125	2000
100	2800
75	3300
50	4000
25	4500

Moreover, fixed costs identifiable with this product are assumed to be £1000 and variable costs per unit 25p. We can now graph the cost information showing the relationship between volume and total costs (*see* Fig. 11.15). Furthermore, by graphing total revenues assuming the selling price to be 25, 50, 75, 100 and 125p, we have the familiar break-even graph which shows that break-even occurs at:

> 1000 units at a selling price of 125p
> 1300 units at a selling price of 100p
> 2000 units at a selling price of 75p
> 4000 units at a selling price of 50p

Obviously at no point can sales break even at a selling price of 25p or less, since this exactly covers average variable costs and therefore makes no provision for fixed costs.

Finally, we plot the anticipated demand at the various prices to arrive at the curve DD. Comparison of the total revenue and total cost curve at a particular price–output combination indicates the profit or loss; in particular, the vertical distance between a location on the total cost curve and the corresponding point on the demand curve DD represents profit. Thus, if selling price is 75p, total revenue is £2475, total costs £1825 and profit £650.

	125p	100p	75p, etc.
Selling price			
Marginal cost (variable)	25p	25p	25p
Contribution	100	75	50
Anticipated sales	2 000	2 800	3 300
Total contribution	£2 000	£2 100	£1 650
Less Fixed costs	£1 000	£1 000	£1 650
Profit	£1 000	£1 100	£650

Estimating the cash figure at 28 February 19–3		
Profit at 28 February 19–3		£84 000
Plus Sources		
Plus depreciation	£1 000	
fall in debtors	5 000	
increase in creditors	5 000	11 000
		95 000
Less Uses		
capital investment	5 000	
increase in stocks	10 000	
dividend paid	20 000	
taxation paid	10 000	45 000
Cash balance		50 000
Plus Balance at Jan. 1 19–3		20 000
Cash balance at Feb. 28 19–3		70 000

Figure 11.13 *Profit-cash forecast*

	Pessimistic estimate		Most likely estimate			Optimistic estimate	
Price (p)	125	100	125	100	75	125	100
Marginal cost (p)	25	25	25	25	25	25	25
Contribution (p)	100	75	100	75	50	100	75
Quantity	1 800	2 500	2 000	2 800	3 300	2 100	3 000
Total contribution (£)	1 800	1 875	2 000	2 100	1 650	2 100	2 250

Figure 11.14 *Hypothetical market research results*

30. Establishing demand

The foregoing presupposes an accurate demand schedule. However, although precision is impossible, in practice it is possible to achieve significantly accurate results.

(a) Market research has a proven success record adopting quantitative and scientific methods, e.g. probability analysis.

(b) Surveys may be adjusted to take account of the marketing staff's experience of the industry and their intuitive judgment.

(c) To reduce error, the 'demand curve' or contribution curve may be drawn as a band to allow for the more optimistic, most pessimistic and most likely estimates of demand. Thus for any one price there may be several output, revenues and profits or contributions (*see* Fig. 11.14).

If the company currently sells 3300 units at a price of 75p and contemplates a price increase to 100p, marketing staff and accountants should feel confident on the basis of the market suitably amended to take account of experts' intuitive judgment (*see* Fig. 11.14). There is the highest probability that total contribution will increase to £2100 and even to £2250 if the market is underestimated. Even the most pessimistic estimate of a contribution of £1875 is a significant improvement on the current level of contribution of £1650.

Moreover, assuming that the objective is to maximize profit, the marketing strategy will be to sell 2800 units at a price of 100p where the corresponding point on the curve DD in Fig. 11.15 is furthest away from the total cost line.

The method has clear advantages over the conventional approach of the economist to cost-demand analysis.

(a) It represents virtually the whole relationship between price, costs, profit and volume in total terms, which is immediately more meaningful to the business person who is probably unfamiliar with marginal analysis.

(b) It facilitates understanding of the marketing or product manager's difficulties of efficient pricing. Certainly cost-plus pricing is unlikely to arrive at the unique profit-maximizing price-output combination except by accident.

(c) It is an approach readily appreciated by marketing people and accountants and should provide the basis for discussion of the financial implications of marketing.

(d) It may be adapted to express the contributions made by the product towards fixed costs. Indeed, there is a very powerful argument that managers should be forward-looking, concerning

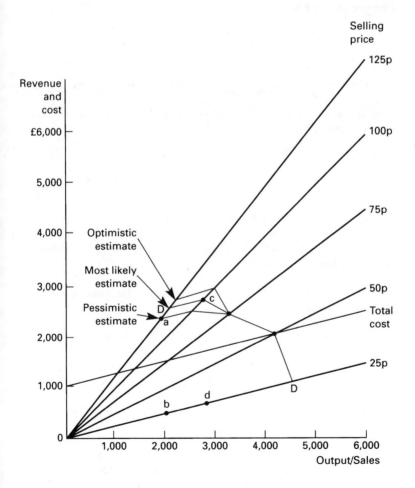

Figure 11.15 *Total revenue, cost and demand curves*

themselves with future marginal costs and revenues rather than total costs that include fixed costs which are sunk and unavoidable in the short run.

Thus the 25p revenue line becomes the variable-cost line (since average variable cost is also 25p) and contributions towards fixed costs of £1000 can be read off for given selling prices, i.e. a contribution of a–b at a price of 125p, c–d at a price of 100p, etc. These values may be confirmed by calculation.

Progress test 11

1. Explain the nature of the factors that directly affect company profitability. **(1–2)**

2. Describe the structure of the pyramid of ratios. **(3)**

3. How can working capital be controlled in order to make an organisation more efficient? **(4–6)**

4. Explain the following:
(a) ROL,
(b) EOQ. **(8–13)**

5. Why is credit important to firms and what are its costs? **(15–16)**

6. Using hypothetical data, show how an efficient credit control policy improves profitability. **(17–19)**

7. Define 'liquidity preference' and its relevance to the business organization. **(22)**

8. Explain the essential difference between profit and cash flow. **(24)**

9. 'A source and use of funds statement if sufficiently detailed can highlight company progress and problems.' Discuss. **(25–26)**

10. Examine three methods of forecasting the cash position. **(28)**

11. 'The profit margin may be improved either by raising price or by lowering costs. Admittedly the former is the least reliable method but may be used in conjunction with demand analysis.' Discuss. **(28–30)**

12. *CD Products*

Balance sheet as at 31 March

	£000			£000		£000	
	19–2	19–3	*Fixed assets*			19–2	19–3
Issued capital							
Ordinary shares	160	160	Cost 160			120	—
			Cost 220			—	164
P. and L. account	36	80					
	196	240					
			Current assets				
			Stock			20	28
			Debtors			100	120
			Bank			40	8
			Preliminary expenses not written off			2	—
Reserve for tax	24	20					
Creditors	62	60					
	282	320				282	320

P. and L. Account Extract – Appropriation Section – for 19–3

	£		£
Tax reserve, on current profit	20 000	Net profit for year[1]	70 600
		Balance b/f	36 000
Net dividend (ordinary)	6 600		
Balance c/f	80 000		
	106 600		106 600

Note :([1]) Net profit is after providing for depreciation and writing off the preliminary expenses.

Prepare a source and use of funds statement from the information provided.

13. Explain how a demand curve is useful in estimating the sales of a particular product. **(30)**

12

Controlling fixed assets

Financial planning

1. Financial planning

Financial planning – generally regarded as the means whereby the company ensures immediate and future solvency and liquidity and adequate finance generated internally or externally at the best possible terms for revenue and capital commitments – forms an essential part of the overall company plan. In other words, predetermined and quantified company objectives are the prerequisites for an effective corporate plan or strategy in which the quality of the integral financial plan plays a vital role. Obviously a strategy formulated without consideration for the sources and availability of finance is nonsense; funds must be matched against expenditure, both in amount and timing, if strategy and objectives are to be met.

Furthermore, the relationship between strategy and the financial plan implies a dialogue: a two-way relationship. For instance, in addition to the 'requests' that financial planners provide adequate funds at appropriate times, feedback responses, as for example when funds are unavailable or available only at unacceptably high cost, may necessitate compensatory adjustments to corporate strategy.

2. Finance a scarce resource

Finance is an economic resource both in the macro-economic sense (hence its price, or rate of interest it commands in the financial markets) and at the micro or company level because of its limited supply in relation to the competing uses the company may put it to. In general terms, this scarcity of finance is influenced by a number of factors.

(a) *Company performance.* Clearly the supply of funds generated internally depends on how successful the company is at present and in the future in employing its capital.

(b) *The company's financial plan.* This may act as a constraint on the company's potential supply of finance.

(*i*) Company controllers may adopt a high pay-out policy.
(*ii*) Planners may be reluctant to increase capital gearing beyond a certain level because of the extra risk.

3. Adjustments to the financial plan

In the event of a shortfall between planned expenditure and actual funds, financial managers may resort to predetermined contingency plans designed to secure the corporate objectives by other means. Alternatively it may mean:

(a) capital rationing, where projects are selected by comparison of:
   (*i*) risk, or
   (*ii*) return on investment, or
   (*iii*) payback;
(b) postponement of investment;
(c) review of strategy to see whether alternative courses of action are consistent with the selected objectives, e.g. securing use of equipment by means of HP instead of buying, or buying parts from subcontractors as a short-term solution.

4. Generation of investment projects

The process of selecting investment projects can be analysed into the following stages.

(a) The project is conceived, i.e.:
   (*i*) internally generated in response to company strategy or from opportunities created by company activities;
   (*ii*) externally generated by environmental forces.
(b) The proposal for specific expenditure. (*See* Fig.12.1.)
(c) Appraisal of the proposal on the basis of the following:
   (*i*) Specifications of project.
   (*ii*) Estimate of costs. In particular, accurate investment appraisal depends on the reliability of these estimates, and correct forecasts of capital.
      (1) Capital expenditure required.
      (2) The life of the project.
      (3) Working capital required.
      (4) Residual value of the equipment.
      (5) Tax rates and allowances.
   (*iii*) Estimates of revenues generated by the investment.
      (1) The selling price of the article.
      (2) The volume of sales.
      (3) The operating costs.

INVESTMENT PROPOSAL

Replacement/New projects*　　　　　　　　Proposal No: _____

Company name: _____　　Date submitted: _____

Location: _____

	Amount (£)
A. *Description and purpose of project* Gear testing machine. Provides a means of measuring and inspecting the teeth of a wide range of involute gear wheels	15 000

　　Estimated life: 14 years
　　Year of initial outlay 19–1
　　Year of start up 19–2

B. *Class of expenditure*　　　　(1) *Productive/Other**　　　*Country of purchase*: UK

C. (1) *Details of expenditure*

	Year (1)	Budget £ (2)	Amount of investment anticipated £ (3)
(a) Capital expenditure 　　(as section A)		16 000	15 000
(b) Ancillary expenditure		500	500
(c) Permanent increase in 　　working capital			
		16 500	15 500
LESS:			
(d) Investment credits		(say)	5 000
(e) Disposal value			200
			10 300

If capital expenditure varies from budget, state why: If project not included in budget, state why omitted:

(2) *Return on investment*
　　(a) *First year gain*　　　　　　　　　Expected £2 000
　　　　Savings in operating costs plus
　　　　additional earnings from higher output
　　(b) *Pay back period*　　　　　　　　Expected 3 years
　　(c) *% return on investment*　　　　　Expected 12%

D. *Recommendations and approval/rejection**
　　recommendations

　　　　　　　　　　　　　　　　Initial　　*Date*
　　*Approval/Rejection**

*Delete as necessary

Figure 12.1 *Example of investment appraisal form*

(*iv*) Consistency with corporate and appropriate departmental strategy.

(*v*) Availability of funds.

(d) Testing using investment appraisal techniques.

(*i*) Payback.

(*ii*) Rate of return.

(*iii*) Discounted cash flow (DCF).

(e) Selected projects introduced into capital budget.

(f) Authorization.

(g) Implementation.

(h) Feedback to check actual against anticipated performance.

5. Investment appraisal and approval procedure

Investment appraisal and approval procedures differ in detail between organizations. However, a sound appraisal and approval system contains the following:

(a) Authority levels. Managers have authority to purchase items of equipment up to a predetermined level against provisions within the current budget. However, all expenditure proposals in excess of this level are submitted through senior management for examination by a validation panel and are subject to an investment panel for final approval before the budget is compiled for the next period.

(b) Validation panel. This is in effect a filter and consists of the financial controller, company planner and managers with the appropriate specialized knowledge. The panel examines the proposal with the sponsors to establish that:

(*i*) it is consistent with the corporate plan;

(*ii*) the assumptions and calculations are correct, e.g. in production, marketing and finance;

(*iii*) the financial and resource implications are quantified;

(*iv*) the effect on employees is considered;

(*v*) the risks involved in the project are assessed.

If it is satisfied that the proposal is sound then it reports to the investment panel.

(c) Investment panel. This consists of the most senior management who have the final word whether to proceed or not and representatives of the validation panel. The sponsors present their case, which is considered with the validation panel's report in relation to:

(*i*) the stated object of the investment;

(*ii*) alternative options to achieve this objective;

(*iii*) the company strategy;

(*iv*) the effect on company financial resources;

(*v*) the availability of management resources;

(*vi*) any side-effects on competition, labour relations and the environment.

6. Nature of investment

Investment in this context may be defined generally as 'the commitment of company resources in the expectation that this will realize a profit or gain'. Clearly investment decisions must never be made lightly, but only after rigorous appraisal of the alternative project, because investment once made is often irreversible and thus commits management to a fixed policy in the future. Furthermore, it introduces risk since the anticipated profit or gain cannot be guaranteed at the outset. In summary the nature of company investment is such that:

(a) A decision is often irreversible since abandonment would probably involve considerable financial loss if the asset is resold.

(b) It introduces inflexibility into future company policy.

(c) It means that the expenditure is at risk because future incomes cannot be forecast exactly.

With the need for cost-consciousness on the part of management and increasing capital intensiveness in industry, it is vital that managers should understand the principles underlying the various techniques of capital appraisal to secure the optimum use of company and departmental resources. The principal investment-appraisal techniques available to managers are now considered in detail.

Methods of measuring the profitability of capital projects

7. Pay-back method

This method measures the length of time it takes to recoup the capital outlay out of the expected earnings, usually defined as pre-tax profit plus depreciation (note that in 1964–5 96 per cent of companies used pay-back gross of tax (source: A. J. Merret and A. Sykes). It is a simple concept to operate and can be illustrated by way of example.

Assume that a company is about to launch a new product which is thought by the marketing manager to have a reasonably long product life cycle. He illustrates this by means of Fig. 12.2.

The marketing manager explains this typical product life cycle curve as follows:

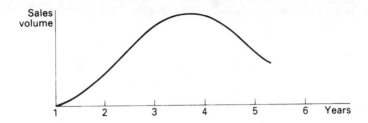

Figure 12.2 *Product life-cycle of Swallow brand cassette tape recorder*

Year 1 – *Period of product innovation when sales increase slowly.* Development and launching costs are being incurred so that profits are low.

Year 2 – *Period of maximum growth in sales.* The public quickly appreciate the novelty of the product and a high sales volume generates high profits.

Year 3 – *Period of maturity of the product.* In a competitive market rivals are launching similar goods which slows down the growth in sales. Higher marketing costs to counteract rival products tend to reduce profits.

Year 4 – *Period of decline.* Profits fall rapidly as customers prefer competitors' products instead as they are newer and probably incorporate technological improvements.

8. Pay-back: example

In the light of the Swallow brand's product life cycle let us imagine that the initial capital outlay, column *(ii)* of Table 12A on manufacturing equipment is £200 000 and net profits from sales are as shown in column *(i)*.

Table 12A *Pay-back calculations*

Year	(i) Net annual earnings (inflow)	(ii) Investment (outflow)	(iii) Cumulative net inflow
1	£10 000	£200 000	–£190 000
2	100 000	—	–90 000
3	70 000	—	–20 000
4	50 000	—	+30 000
5	40 000	—	+70 000

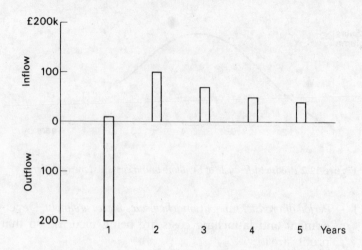

Figure 12.3 *Cash flows for Swallow cassette tape recorder*

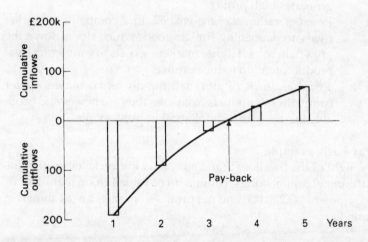

Figure 12.4 *Cumulative net cash flows and pay-back period for Swallow cassette tape recorder*

Here the project pays for itself during Year 4, when the net revenue balances with the capital outlay. This is shown graphically in Figs. 12.3 and 12.4.

9. Advantages of the pay-back method
The main advantages of this method are:

(a) It is simple to calculate.
(b) It recognizes the timing of cash flow.
(c) It is particularly appropriate and informative for a company short of liquid assets, in which case projects with short pay-back periods are preferred.
(d) It is valuable as a method for investment decisions for companies operating in high-risk markets. Companies whose products tend to be overtaken by changing technology or fashion and therefore have short product life cycles, will prefer short pay-back periods to lessen risk.

10. Disadvantages of the pay-back method
The chief disadvantages are:

(a) It ignores the value of receipts after the point of recovery of original capital outlay (pay-back).
(b) It fails to consider the timing of receipts beyond this break-even point.
(c) It ignores the profitability of the project, since it is preoccupied with speed of repayment.
(d) If the company is concerned with liquidity, then pay-back measured gross of tax overstates the true cash flow and is therefore inaccurate.

11. Compound interest
The investment appraisal methods that we next consider have one thing in common. They are all based on the concept of 'present value', i.e. they overcome the objections raised against pay-back by considering the 'time value of money', which means that more weight is given to immediate cash flows than to future cash flows. To appreciate the real significance of this concept, let us look first at compound interest.

If an investor deposits £100 in a deposit account of a bank that pays 10 per cent interest then the total investment will grow as follows:

	Initial deposit	Interest 10%	Total deposit
at start of year 1	£100	—	£100.00
at end of year 1	—	£10.00	110.00
at end of year 2	—	11.00	121.00
at end of year 3	—	12.10	133.10
at end of year 4	—	13.31	146.41

A visual presentation, as in Fig. 12.5, may help the reader to appreciate the nature of compound interest.

Of course in practice it is unnecessary to go through this tedious process; instead we use a formula. The formula for calculating compound interest per unit of principal is

$$(1 + i)^n$$

where i is the rate of interest and n is the number of years that the principal sum is invested.

Thus to calculate the interest that £1 will earn at 10 per cent over four years so as to check the above table, we substitute the values of i and n in the formula.

$$
\begin{aligned}
\text{Compound interest} &= (1 + i)^4 \\
&= (1 + .10)^4 \\
&= 1.1 \times 1.1 \times 1.1 \times 1.1 \\
&= 1.4641.
\end{aligned}
$$

If we extend the formula to include the initial sum invested (principal) then the total sum invested at the end of the period if calculated by the formula:

$$
\begin{aligned}
&P(1 + i)^n \\
&= £100(1 + i)^n \\
&= £146.41 \text{ This is the sum invested} \\
&\qquad\qquad\quad \text{at the end of fourth year.}
\end{aligned}
$$

In conclusion of this brief analysis of compounding, it is worth stating two principles, which, if appreciated at the outset of the examination of discounting that follows, will avoid difficulties that might arise.

(a) £1 now is worth more than £1 in the future because the present £1 can be invested and will in time be equal to £1 plus interest.

(b) We are interested only in the monetary value of £s and not the real or economic value. Consequently, the analysis is not intended to compensate for the depreciation in the value of future money caused by inflation. However, this does not mean that inflation is not taken into account: under conditions of inflation interest rates tend to rise and the stream of expected receipts and payments expected to arise from a project are adjusted upwards for the anticipated rate of inflation.

12. Discounting

Discounting is essentially compound interest in reverse, and tells us the present value of a future sum of money. For example, if an investor

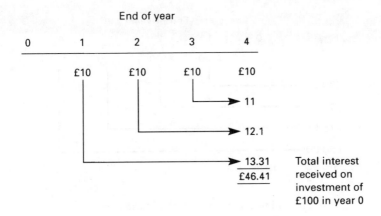

Figure 12.5 *Compound interest calculations*

wants exactly £100 at the end of Year 1 when the rate of interest is 10 per cent then he or she must invest £90.91 now. The reader is probably wondering where this figure of £90.91 came from. The answer is simple. We know that £100 with interest of 10 per cent will grow to £110 at the end of one year, and £121 at the end of year two. Then if we divide

£100 by £110, then we obtain 0.9091 for Year 1
and £100 by £121, then we obtain 0.8264 for Year 2.

These figures are called discount factors, and inform us that:

£1.00 at the end of Year 1 is worth £0.9091 now at 10 per cent
and £1.00 at the end of Year 2 is worth £0.8264 now at 10 per cent.

Using these factors we can reduce any future sum of money back to present-day value: at 10 per cent interest £127 at the end of Year 1 has a present value of £115.45 (£127 × 0.9091); £147 500 at the end of Year 2 has a present value of £121 894 (£147 500 × 0.8264).

Returning to a visual presentation, if £100 is received at the end of each year for four years then in present-value terms the total cash flow discounted at 10 per cent is worth £316.98 (*see* Fig. 12.6).

A formula for calculating the discount factor is

$$\frac{1}{(1+i)^n}$$

so that if we substitute the information for Year 1 in this example as a check on the above calculation we have:

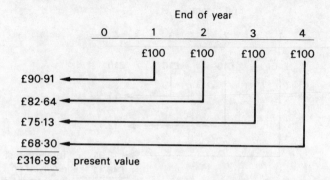

Figure 12.6 *Present-value calculations*

$$\left(\frac{1}{1+0.10}\right)^1 = \frac{1}{1.1} = 0.9091,$$

i.e. £1 at the end of Year 1 is worth £0.9091 now: the investor is indifferent between receiving £0.9091 immediately or £1.00 at the end of one year.

13. What the discount rate means

Let us assume that Ivor Hogg borrows £200 from a building society at 11 per cent and repays the loan over two years. The transactions are as follows:

		(i)	*(ii)*
		£	
Start of Year 1	Capital outstanding	200	
	Interest on this capital (11%)	22	
		£222	11% discount factors
			£
End of Year 1	Repayments	117 × 0.9009 = 105.4	
Start of Year 2	Capital outstanding	105	
	Interest on this capital (11%)	12	
		117	

End of Year 2 Repayments $\underline{117} \times 0.8116 = \underline{94.9}$
   Capital
      outstanding   —   200.3 (£200)

Ivor has repaid a total of £117 + £117 = £234 which represents a repayment of the loan of £200 plus interest payments of 11 per cent on the capital balance outstanding at the start of each year. Column *(ii)* confirms that the repayments repay the £200 capital when brought back to present values. This relationship between compounding and discounting can be clarified and the full implications of the DCF percentage used in capital appraisals appreciated if the above example is explained in a different way, i.e. a business person borrowing £200 for investment can just afford to pay compound interest on this sum of 11 per cent if it generates an equal return of 11 per cent because the actual cost of the investment equals the present value of the investment, measuring the time value of money as 11 per cent. However, an 11 per cent return does not make any allowance for risk; the business person might expect a return of 13–14 per cent to compensate for slight risk and correspondingly higher returns over 11 per cent for more risky investments.

14. Present-value tables
If one is to have a sound grasp of the concept of discounting, it is crucial to understand the meaning of discount rates and how the discount factors are determined. Indeed this has been the purpose behind these numerous examples. Fortunately, however, the chore of calculating individual discount factors is unnecessary in practice because they are already calculated and available in present-value tables which can be found in most books on management accounting and capital budgeting (*see* Appendix II).

15. Present value of future earnings
So far, we have applied discounting to investment income resulting from a deposit of money at compound interest, but in fact it has a far wider application. If we now reconsider the financial data set out in Table 12A we can apply this discounting technique to future earnings arising from a company's investment, that are unlike bank deposit interest in that they are positively skewed (i.e. earnings are highest in the early years) as reflected by the product life-cycle diagram. By assuming that the time value of money is 10 per cent we discount future earnings at 10 per cent and thereby give greater weighting to earnings achieved in the immediate periods. The result is a new

Year	Net annual earnings £	Discount factor (10%)	Discounted net annual earnings £	Cumulative net inflow (discounted) £
1	10,000	0.9091	9,090	−190,910
2	100,000	0.8264	82,640	−108,270
3	70,000	0.7513	52,590	−55,680
4	50,000	0.6830	34,150	−21,530
5	40,000	0.6209	24,830	+ 3,300
			£203,300	

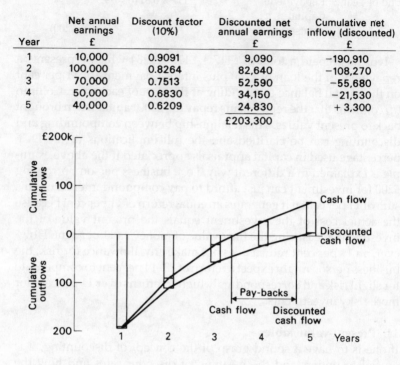

Figure 12.7 *Effect of discounting cash flow on pay-back*

break-even point: pay-back is put back one year and now occurs during Year 5 (*see* Fig.12.7).

16. Discounted cash flow (yield) method

The next method of capital appraisal, known as the yield, internal rate of return or discounted cash flow (DCF) method, is defined as the annual return on the outstanding capital balance at the end of each year. This internal rate of return is unique because it is that rate that makes the present-day value of future cash flow equal in aggregate to the present-day capital cost of the project.

We can illustrate its operation by using the estimated annual sales, costs and capital outlay of the Swallow brand cassette recorder set out in Table 12A. In **(15)** we discounted the net earnings at 10 per cent to arrive at total net earnings measured at present-day values of £203 300 which exceed the present-day value of the cost of the project (£200 000) by £3300 (called net present-day value). Therefore a 10 per cent discount factor is too low; the return must be greater than 10 per cent. A little thought will show that this must be so since the cash flow pays for the original investment and earns a 10 per cent return on this outlay with an additional surplus of £3300 over and above this return. The next step, therefore, is to discount the earnings at a higher rate of interest.

Let us now discount the earnings at 11 per cent:

Year	Net annual earnings	Discount factor 11%	Discounted net earnings
1	£10 000	0.9009	£9 000
2	100 000	0.8116	81 160
3	70 000	0.7319	51 180
4	50 000	0.6587	32 930
5	40 000	0.5935	23 740
			£198 010

In comparison with the previous calculation, this calculation produces a negative balance (or net present value) of £1990 and shows that an 11 per cent discount rate is too high, so that the true rate lies between 10 per cent and 11 per cent where the discounted cash flow exactly equals the cost of the investment. In summary:

(a) The DCF rate is too high if the present value of future earnings is less than the cost of the original investment.
(b) The DCF rate is too low if the present value of future earnings is more than the cost of the original investment.
(c) The true DCF rate is that when the present value of future earnings equals the cost of the original investment.

17. DCF rate by interpolation
The method (shown in **15** and **16**), is appropriately known as the 'trial and error' method, since at least two calculations must be made that straddle the true rate. This rate is then found by interpolation, i.e.:

Net present value of earnings at 10%	=	+£3300
Net present value of earnings at 11%	=	−£1990
Overall difference		£5290

Therefore the true discount is found by interpolation; it lies at a point $\frac{3300}{5290}$ of the difference between 10 per cent and 11 per cent, i.e. 10 per cent + 0.62 per cent or 10.62 per cent.

Thus the profits from the project are sufficient to repay the cost of the investment and earn a rate of interest on the capital of 10.62 per annum. However, one note of caution regarding interpolation to establish the internal rate of return. This method assumes a linear trend (in fact it is non-linear) in net present values between 10 and 11 per cent and therefore tends to overestimate the true return. Although the error is too small to worry about in the above example, it would produce less accurate results if we were to interpolate between extreme values of, say 10–15 per cent or more. This is apparent from the example in Fig.12.8.

In the first situation, the error is insignificant, but not in the second case; the answer is to avoid large extremes in the rates of returns straddling the true return when interpolating with the trial-and-error method.

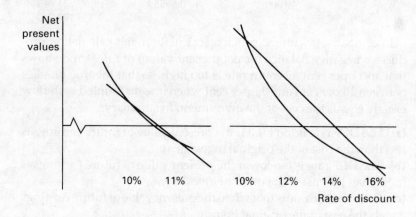

Figure 12.8 *Interpolation to establish the internal rate of return*

18. Net present value (NPV) method

This method also makes use of discount factors, but is less onerous than the previous trial-and-error method where several calculations are needed. Here, one simply discounts the cash flows at a stipulated rate of discount to find their present-day values, selecting the project showing the largest surplus of earnings at present-day values. An example serves to illustrate this technique.

Assume that a company can borrow sufficient funds at 10 per cent to finance one or two projects it has under consideration: the minimum acceptable return on capital for the company is 12 per cent.

The difference of 2 per cent represents the return to compensate for the risk inherent in the project, discussed in **(15)**. The capital expenditure required for projects A or B is £25 000 and net cash flow is as follows:

	Project A	Project B
	£	£
Net cash flow		
Year 1	7 000	12 000
2	12 000	10 000
3	15 000	8 000
Total net cash flow	£34 000	£30 000

Calculations of net present values at discount rate of 10 per cent p.a.:

	Project A			Project B		
	Net cash flow	Discount factor	Discounted net present value	Net cash flow	Discount factor	Discounted net present value
Year						
	£		£	£		£
1	7 000	0.9091	6 363	12 000	0.9091	10 909
2	12 000	0.8264	9 916	10 000	0.8264	8 264
3	15 000	0.7513	11 269	8 000	0.7513	6 010
	£34 000		£27 548	£30 000		£25 183

		Less Capital cost	25 000		*Less* Capital cost	25 000
		NPV =	2 548		NPV =	183

Calculations of net present values at discount rate of 12 per cent:

Year	£		£	£		£
1	7 000	0.8929	6 250	12 000	0.8929	10 714
2	12 000	0.7972	9 566	10 000	0.7972	7 972
3	15 000	0.7118	10 677	8 000	0.7118	5 694
	£34 000		£26 493	£30 000		£24 380

		Less Capital cost	25 000		*Less* Capital cost	25 000
		NPV =	1 493		NPV =	(620)

The calculation shows that both projects achieve a return in excess of the 10 per cent, the cost of capital, but only Project A passes the threshold return of 12 per cent and is therefore preferable to B. In other words, the size of the net present value indicates that the project earns a true return in excess of the discount percentage selected for the exercise; the larger the NPV, the larger the rate of return.

19. The choice of discount rate

(a) The stipulated rate of interest may be the organization's ROCE percentage. Possible projects that fail to meet this test should be disregarded; projects whose profitability exceeds this figure will tend to improve the organization's overall profitability.

(b) It may be the company's cost of capital. It goes without saying that a profit-dependent organization should never invest funds if the expected return is lower than the cost of the capital.

Let us assume that a hypothetical company has the following capital structure (column (*i*).

	(*i*)	(*ii*) Post-tax cost	(*iii*) Cost
Ordinary shares	£100 000	20%	£20 000
Undistributed profits	25 000	20%	5 000
8% Debenture	75 000	4%	3 000
6% Loan Stock	50 000	3%	1 500
	£250 000		£29 500

Average cost of capital = 11.8% (£29 500 ÷ £250 000 × 100)

Column (*ii*) indicates the post-tax cost of the various categories of capital employed by the company. The loan capital needs no further mention except that the interest is tax-deductible where tax is assumed to be 50 per cent. The cost of the equity capital, however, does require comment; here, the opportunity cost of investment is used on the basis that the shareholders expect a return consistent with the yield on similar equity shares and given the opportunity would transfer their investments if company returns failed to match these alternative returns. Thus, assuming that ordinary shareholders traditionally expect, say, 7 per cent, and with a rate of inflation of 13 per cent, a total cost of 20 per cent is required.

Thus, the weighted cost of capital is 11.8 per cent, which should be the minimum acceptable rate of return figure for projects. Preferably returns should exceed this figure if the organization is to grow, but should never be lower on the grounds that the debt capital is very low-cost capital (*see* **(d)**).

(c) It may be based on the cost of capital plus a percentage for uncertainty or the degree of risk.

(d) Certain projects or capital expenditure produce a nil return, as for example expenditure on safety installations. Naturally they cannot be rejected merely on profitability grounds.

20. Ranking projects and DCF

A company possessing limited resources and faced with several projects, each competing for funds, may select projects by ranking them in order of:

(a) Pay-back.
(b) Net present value.
(c) Profitability index, which is the net present value of net earnings divided by the present value of the capital outlay. Thus at 10 per cent discount rate the profitability indices for projects **A** and **B** described in **(18)** are:

$$\begin{array}{cc} A & B \end{array}$$

$$\frac{\text{Net present earnings}}{\text{Capital outlay}} \ \frac{£27\ 548}{£25\ 000} = 1.01 : \ \frac{£25\ 183}{£25\ 000} = 1.007$$

This confirms our conclusions reached in **(18)** that at a 10 per cent discount rate both projects succeed, but if they are mutually exclusive then **A** is preferred to **B** on the basis of its higher profitability index number.

Perhaps the reader will have noticed that the DCF method does not appear above as a means of ranking investment projects. This is because, unlike the other methods, it fails to take into account the cost of the capital expenditure. However, this is not a serious obstacle and in view of DCF's significant overall advantages (*see* **21**) should not appear to be deficient in this respect. Consequently, a ranking procedure for DCF follows.

Assume that management has two alternative projects under consideration. A requires a capital outlay of £120 000 but B needs £180 000. Both are estimated to provide a cash flow for five years; A £40 000 per year and B £58 000 per year. The cost of capital is 10 per cent:

		A			B	
Year	*Net earnings*	*Discount 10%*	*Discounted net earnings*	*Net earnings*	*Discount 10%*	*Discounted net earnings*
1	£40 000	0.9090	£36 360	£58 000	0.9090	£52 722
2	40 000	0.8265	33 060	58 000	0.8265	47 937
3	40 000	0.7513	30 052	58 000	0.7513	43 575
4	40 000	0.6830	27 320	58 000	0.6830	39 614
5	40 000	0.6209	24 836	58 000	0.6209	36 012
			151 628			219 860
	Less Capital outlay		120 000	*Less* Capital outlay		180 000
		NPV	31 628		NPV	£39 860
	By trial and error DCF = 19.8%				DCF = 18.5%	

Calculation would show that A is preferable, in that it earns a higher DCF rate, but it must be remembered that the two projects require different capital investments. Thus we are not comparing like with like.

However, we may usefully employ the economist's concept of the margin, and by comparing the two projects calculate the marginal or incremental capital outlay and marginal net earnings:

	Capital outlay	Annual net earnings
A	£120 000	£40 000
B	180 000	58 000

Marginal
investment = £60 000

Marginal
earnings = £18 000
DCF   = 15.7%

Thus the marginal capital of £60 000 invested in project B generates marginal earnings of £18 000 p.a. which earns a DCF rate of 15.7 per cent.

To conclude, the second project performs as well as project A, but the incremental investment of £60 000 generates additional earnings that yield 15.7 per cent, which is to be preferred bearing in mind that the cost of the capital is only 10 per cent.

21. Advantages of yield method
The yield method has certain advantages over other capital appraisal techniques:

(a) It is expressed as a percentage.
(b) As a percentage it is easily understood by managers who conventionally measure profitability and yields in this way.
(c) It can be readily compared with the cost of capital, which is also expressed as a percentage.

22. Determination of annual rentals
Goggle Box Services Limited wish to rent out a black-and-white TV set to a new customer. Their policy is to charge an annual rental that within four years pays for the set (£300) and in addition generates a 15 per cent return. The rental is determined as follows (ignore tax and capital allowances).

Year	Discount factor 15%
0	1.0000
1	0.8695
2	0.7561
3	0.6575
	3.2831 total factors

$$\frac{\text{Capital investment}}{\text{Total factors}} = \text{Rental/year}$$

$$\frac{£300}{3.2831} = £91.37 \text{ p. a.}$$

23. Lease or buy

The owner-manager of the Wayside Garage is interested in installing a diagnostic-tuning system and establishes that such a machine can be bought for £4000 or rented for £600 p.a. In both cases operating costs and maintenance are borne by the garage. The anticipated life of the equipment is ten years. Obviously the running costs and sales revenue are identical, whether the equipment is bought or leased, so the decision rests on the relative capital costs of acquiring the system. The garage at present earns 16 per cent return on capital. (Tax and capital allowances are ignored.)

Cost of purchase		*Cost of rental*	
Cost	= £4000	Rental cost	= £600 p.a.
Present value	= £4000	Present value of £1	
		for 10 years at 16%	= 4.833
		Present value of £600	= 4.833
			£2 899

Therefore, on these comparative costs the rental agreement is preferable as it produces the lower present value.

Note:
In this example the rental agreement requires the garage to pay a regular fixed sum of £600 p.a. for ten years (which is like an annuity). We could employ the same method as in (22), but this would be tedious considering the life of the project. Fortunately there is a short cut. We look therefore in a compound-interest table called 'Present Value of an Annuity of £1' for the appropriate term (ten years), and at the appropriate rate of interest, in this case 16 per cent; this gives an answer of 4.833.

Taxation

24. Taxation considerations

Throughout this chapter we have ignored taxation in the capital-appraisal calculations in order to clarify understanding of the essential principles underlying the different methods. However, we are now in a position to introduce taxation and capital allowances and consider the effect on a typical investment decision. The basic rules for dealing with taxation are:

(a) The net earnings before depreciation arising from the capital outlay should be adjusted for corporation tax liability.
(b) Any capital allowances must be set off against tax liability.

The reader is advised to study thoroughly the following example, which is self-explanatory as long as he remembers that the 100 per cent capital allowance reduces tax liability in the year of purchase (1993) and that a capital charge is made against the receipts from the sale of the plant.

25. Example
PP Refrigeration is considering the purchase of a machine to make pressings for its domestic refrigerators. It is estimated that the machine, which costs £40 000 will have a life of five years, at the end of which it will have a scrap value of £6000. In addition, the project involves an investment in working capital of £2000 at the commencement of operations and an additional £4000 one year later, all of which is released at the end of the project's life. Overheads and commissioning expenses are expected to be £2000 payable at the end of the first year. This is summarized in the profit and tax calculation sheet shown in Fig.12.9.

It is assumed that corporation tax is 50 per cent and that the project qualifies for a 100 per cent capital allowance for 1993 which is applied to the operating profit of that year to calculate the tax *which is payable the following January*. The company carried on other manufacturing activities from which it derives taxable profits.

Capital appraisal and risk

26. Introduction
So far in this chapter we have examined the principles of investment-appraisal techniques and the relative pros and cons of each method. Perhaps the precision with which estimated costs and revenues, and therefore cash flow, were stated caused readers to wonder at the remarkable confidence of the forecasts! However, let us now introduce a degree of realism into the calculations by considering the risks and uncertainties that underlie investment appraisal.

27. Risk and uncertainty
It is axiomatic that in a dynamic situation no forecast, however accurate, can precisely predict future events; nor can a company completely avoid the risks and uncertainties present in an unpredictable world.

(a) Risk in this context is defined as the situation where events can to some extent be quantified so that the probability that a specific

Year ending	1993	1994	1995	1996	1997	1998	1999
					Project:	Machine Press	
Sales revenue	—	£20 000	£40 000	£50 000	£60 000	£60 000	—
Cost							
Variable costs	—	£15 000	£30 000	£35 000	£40 000	£40 000	—
Fixed-costs	—	500	500	500	500	500	—
Other overheads	—	2 000	—	—	—	—	—
Cost of project	—	£17 500	£30 500	£35 500	£40 500	£40 500	—
Profit before depreciation	—	£2 500	£9 500	£14 500	£19 500	£19 500	—
Capital allowances	£40 000	—	—	—	—	—	(£6 000)
Taxable profits	—	2 500	9 500	14 500	19 500	19 500	—
Taxation at 50%	(£20 000)	1 250	4 750	7 250	9 750	9 750	(£3 000)

Note: Outflow ( )

(a) Profit and tax calculations

Year	Fixed assets	Working capital	Operating profit	Corporation tax	Net	Project: Machine Press Cumulative total
1993	(40 000)	(42 000)	—	—	(42 000)	(42 000)
1994	—	(£4 000)	£2 500	£20 000	18 500	(23 500)
1995	—	—	9 500	(1 250)	8 250	(15 250)
1996	—	—	14 500	(4 750)	9 750	(5 500)
1997	—	—	19 500	(7 250)	12 250	6 750
1998	—	—	19 500	(9 750)	9 750	16 500
1999	6 000	6 000	—	(9 750)	2 250	18 750
2000	—	—	—	(3 000)	(3 000)	15 750

(b) Cash flow summary

Net cash flow out

					Project:	Machine Press
	0%		10%		20%	
Year	Actual cash	Factor	Present value	Factor	Present value	
1993	£42 000	1.0	£42 000	1.0	£42 000	
1994	—		—		—	
1995	—		—		—	
Total	£42 000		£42 000		£42 000	

Net cash flow in

	£		£		£	
1993	—	1.000	—	1.000	—	
1994	18 500	0.909	16 816	0.833	15 410	
1995	8 250	0.826	6 814	0.694	5 725	
1996	9 750	0.751	7 322	0.579	5 645	
1997	12 250	0.683	8 367	0.482	5 904	
1998	9 750	0.621	6 055	0.402	3 919	
1999	2 250	0.564	1 269	0.335	754	
2000	(3 000)	0.513	(1 539)	0.279	(837)	
Totals			£45 104		£36 520	
Profitability index			1.07		.86	
Net present value			+£3 104		+£5 480	

Yield by interpolation:

$$+ \ 10\% + \frac{3104}{3104 + 5480} \times 10\%$$
$$= 13.6\%$$

(c) Discounted cash flows

Figure 2.9 *Profit and tax calculations for a machine press object* investment will yield a certain return can be calculated.

(b) Uncertainty on the other hand is the situation where no probability estimates are possible.

28. Analysis of risk

Let us imagine that a company has sufficient surplus management, staff and productive capacity to produce one additional product and must decide which one of two new restyled products (A and B) to select. As a first step in evaluating the products it conducts extensive research to obtain objective judgments supported by expert opinion on the expected sales revenue in the first year if sales are made at a predetermined price. Admittedly, this assumes certain subjective judgments, as must any situation involving the sale of a product, because the data needed to calculate probabilities cannot be obtained with the same precision as when a sample of electric-light bulbs are life-tested, and the results used to calculate the probability of one bulb selected at random failing at x hours. Nevertheless, we can assume that the product has a very short life-cycle of one year, that the experts are well experienced in selling similar products and that there are no changes in Government economic policy or in competitors' reactions within this time span.

Once the estimated sales are known they can be recorded and presented in the form of normal curves and the standard deviations and coefficients of variation for A and B compared.

Figure 12.10 represents a typical normal curve and the relationship between σ, the standard deviation, and the area beneath the curve. Thus 68.2 per cent of the total area lies inside the 1 standard deviation limit so that two out of three events lie within 1 standard deviation of the mean. If this figure relates to product A, showing the anticipated sales revenues on the horizontal axis against recorded frequencies (i.e. how often each sales revenue figure was selected) on the vertical axis, then we can directly compare the standard deviations of anticipated sales revenues for products A and B, as in Fig. 12.11. It appears that on the grounds of risk, product A is superior (i.e. less risky) in that the majority of the sales values are more concentrated around the average observation, compared with B's which are more variable (although this must be confirmed by comparing their coefficients of variation) (*see* **29**) and therefore more risky. On the other hand, product B is judged to perform better on the average in terms of returns and whether management proceeds with A or B depends on their relative attitudes to risk.

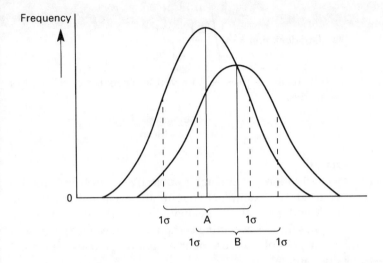

Figure 12.10 *Risk and standard deviation. Area under the normal curve*

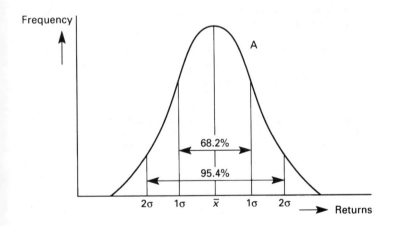

Figure 12.11 *Risk and standard deviation*

29. Formula for comparing risk

(a) The standard deviation provides a comparison of risk between projects, i.e. a lower standard deviation indicates lower risk when return is expressed in percentage terms. Its formula is:

$$\text{Standard deviation} = \sqrt{\left(\frac{\Sigma \int (x - \bar{x})^2}{\Sigma \int}\right)}$$

(b) Where returns are expressed in revenue terms the coefficient of variation is needed:

$$\text{Coefficient of variation} = \frac{\text{Standard deviation}}{\text{Mean}} \times 100.$$

30. Uncertainty

There may be situations where highly subjective or arbitrary weighting must be used. For example, two mutually exclusive projects are considered (X and Y); both are evaluated scientifically on accurate costing and sales figures assuming certain rates of economic growth resulting from possible Government economic policies. Their net present values are:

	Project X	*Project Y*
(a) Pessimistic forecast (nil growth)	£15 000	£18 000
(b) 'Neutral' forecast (2% growth)	27 000	25 000
(c) Optimistic forecast (4% growth)	40 000	38 000

If the weight of probability of any one forecast of proving correct is assumed equal (i.e. ⅓), then the weighted average for project X is £27 060 and that for project Y £26 730.

X		Y	
0.33 × £15 000 =	£4 950	0.33 × £18 000 =	£5 940
0.33 × 27 000 =	8 910	0.33 × 25 000 =	8 250
0.33 × 40 000 =	13 200	0.33 × 38 000 =	12 540
	£27 060		£26 730

Thus project X shows a marginally better return.

However, if the economic situation deteriorates and remedial government economic controls are expected then additional weighting can be applied to the pessimistic forecast. Assuming the following subjective weightings for situations (*i*), (*ii*) and (*iii*) to be 0.5, 0.3 and 0.2 respectively, then we have

Project X		*Project Y*	
(*i*) 0.5 × £15 000 =	£7 500	0.5 × £18 000 =	£9 000
(*ii*) 0.3 × 27 000 =	8 100	0.3 × 25 000 =	7 500
(*iii*) 0.2 × 40 000 =	8 000	0.2 × 38 000 =	7 600
	£23 600		£24 100

Consequently the position is reversed, and project Y is selected.

For a different approach to uncertainty let us reconsider the earlier example of the cassette tape recorder. Thus if the forecasts of profits from their sales are thought to be realistic, in that they are based on the most accurate costing and sales figures and on the probable growth in the economy, then we can regard the figures as the most likely to occur. However, we may estimate that there is a likely range within which actual profits may fall. The most optimistic level of profits may lie 5 per cent above the expected level; the most pessimistic level may lie, say, 10 per cent below the most likely level.

The profits or cash flows can then be calculated for these two extreme levels and DCF or net present values calculated to see in particular whether the most pessimistic level meets the investment criterion. If the minimum acceptable return for the organization is 10 per cent and the return at the least favourable level is, say, 8 per cent, then the capital may be invested elsewhere for higher returns at less risk. If, however, it suggests a minimum return of 12 per cent then the project is viable, since it satisfies the minimum requirement and stands a very high chance of exceeding this most pessimistic figure. Figure 12.12 illustrates the three assumptions of expected cash flows.

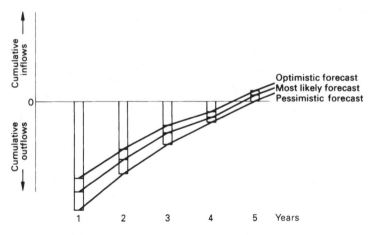

Figure 12.12 *Forecasts and discounted cash flows*

31. Decision trees
Decision tree analysis is particularly appropriate to capital budgeting problems where the pattern of complex quantifiable relationships between decisions, e.g. investments, and chance events, e.g. change

in demand, and their conditional consequences, e.g. sales revenues, can be illustrated visually and thereby simplified.

The decision tree is so called because of its resemblance to a tree, the branches representing a decision or outcome each with symbols indicating whether the branch is due to a possible alternative outcome or an alternative decision becoming available. Conventionally, decision points are represented by ○ and chance outcomes by □.

In order to illustrate the construction and nature of a decision tree and its utility in capital budgeting the data contained in **(30)** are reproduced in Fig. 12.13 in the form of a decision tree.

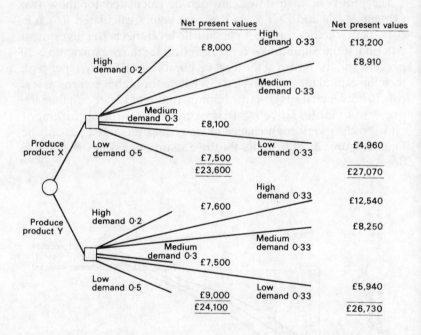

Figure 12.13 *Application of simple decision tree to investment analysis*

32. Dealing with risk
There are a number of ways of dealing with one risk inherent in a particular investment decision.

(a) *Rule of thumb.* After the evaluations regarding costs, revenues, life of project, etc. have been undertaken, and the calculations made to establish the return on the investment, there still remains the decision whether to proceed in preference to alternative investments. In contrast to the scientific methods of appraising capital projects, this is often done by rule of thumb whereby mutually exclusive projects are listed in order of priority on the basis of an unquantified trade-off between profitability or pay-back and the degree of risk associated with each one. Some projects are considered 'too risky' and given low priority regardless of the anticipated return, others carrying an 'acceptable risk' will eventually be ranked according to relative performance, while 'low-risk' projects may be afforded highest priority, assuming the return exceeds the cost of capital. Clearly, this basis is highly subjective and therefore makes any analysis of the way risk is dealt with very difficult.

(b) *Necessity/postponability.* A company starved of capital may be forced to employ all funds becoming available to service existing investments coming up for replacement or repair.

(c) *Discounting for risk.* The decision-maker may well add a premium on to the accepted rate of discount for low-risk projects in order to compensate for the degree of extra risk associated with a particular investment. For example, if the cost of capital is, say, 12 per cent, this same figure may be used for risk-free investments, but 3 per cent may be added for marginally risky ventures, 8 per cent for moderately risky ones and, say, 18 per cent for high-risk ones. Naturally the choice of these risk premium values depends on the subjective attitude of the individual risk-averter towards risk and his or her evaluation of the degree of risk inherent in each project.

(d) *Sensitivity analysis.* This is a complex computer-based exercise. Briefly, it involves the following:

(*i*) identification of the variables;

(*ii*) evaluation of probabilities for these variables;

(*iii*) selection and combination of variables to calculate net present value or rate of return of the project;

(*iv*) substituting different values for each variable in turn while holding all others constant to discover the effect on the rate of return;

(*v*) comparison of original rate of return with this adjusted rate to indicate the degree of sensitivity of the rate to changes in the variable;

(*vi*) subjective evaluation of the risk involved in the project, e.g. chance of unfortunate change of a key factor causing deterioration of a highly sensitive rate of return.

Control of investment expenditure

33. Need for recording and controlling expenditure

Once the investment project has been approved, it is important to record and control all expenditure to ensure that it is maintained within budget. Furthermore, the manager-sponsor should be held accountable for the data contained within the proposal and asked to explain any serious variances between budgeted and actual expenditure. Failure to do so will tend to encourage other proposals that understate the true cost of projects which if sanctioned will play havoc with the company's capital expenditure plans.

An investment control system. The system for control used in industry varies between companies and according to the nature of the project. For instance, the one-off purchase of a piece of equipment is straightforward, i.e. entry in the plant and machinery register. On the other hand a large-scale project, e.g. commissioning a new factory overseas, requires a detailed recording system for all aspects of expenditure. Typically a project is controlled as follows:

(a) The project is entered on to a project record sheet with details of start dates, department responsible, authorized cost by item, etc.
(b) Expenditures incurred on the project are entered. These will result from analysis of material requisitions and customers' invoices for goods and services and job sheets for man-hours incurred.
(c) Actual performance is compared against budget as the project proceeds. Variances are identified and reported to senior management for action.
(d) Possibly costs can be brought back to plan or, as a last resort where the authorized sum underprovides for the actual costs, a supplementary authorization is applied for.

Progress test 12

1. Carefully explain the nature of financial planning, its purpose and advantages. (1–3)

2. How do capital investment proposals arise? (4)

3. Discuss the pros and cons of the method of investment appraisal. (5)

4. How do you account for the widespread use of 'pay-back' in investment decision-making? (7–10)

5. Compare and contrast compounding and discounting, using examples. **(11–15)**

6. Explain the following terms:
DCF. **(16)**
Interpolation. **(17)**
NPV. **(18)**
Trial-and-error method. **(17)**
Profitability index. **(19)**
Decision trees. **(31)**

7. Distinguish between risk and uncertainty and explain how the decision-taker achieves a trade-off between risk and return. **(27–32)**

8. The PP Refrigeration Co. are considering the purchase of a new moulding machine which will cost £40 000. It is estimated that the machine will have a life of seven years, at the end of which it will have a scrap value of £1000. This will involve an investment in working capital of £10 000. The net pre-tax cash inflows which this will produce are:

Year 1   £8 000
  2   10 000
  3   14 000
  4   13 000
  5   11 000
  6   12 000
  7   10 000

This company has a target return on capital (after tax) of 12 per cent and on this basis you are required to prepare a statement evaluating the above project.

Taxation: Assume the following:
1. Corporation tax 50 per cent.
2. Full allowance of 100 per cent in first year.

The company carries on other trading activities from which it derives taxable profits.

13

Mergers and takeovers

Motivation and terms of mergers

1. Company environment
Companies operate in a dynamic environment created and influenced by a variety of forces. These influences on industrial and company environment are:

(a) *political*, e.g. uncertainty over timing of general election, tax policy;

(b) *economics*, e.g. shortage of labour, power crisis, inflation, actions and reactions of competitors;

(c) *social*, e.g. changes in income, demand;

(d) *technological*, e.g. innovation, new energy-saving processes.

2. Company strengths and weaknesses
These changes in a dynamic environment, while creating uncertainty and risk, also create opportunities for management to exploit the situation for profit objectives or whatever their criterion of success, e.g. Wilkinson Sword's innovation of the revolutionary stainless steel razor blade. However, success cannot be guaranteed and there are many instances in recent history where companies have recognized opportunity but failed to exploit it, sometimes at considerable expense, by reacting too slowly to change so that they are overtaken by new and different market forces or by failing to interpret correctly the nature of their environment, e.g. the Sinclair C5.

In view of the risk inherent in a dynamic market, it is vital that management correctly appraises the industry, its prospects and relative strengths and weaknesses of the organization in relation to its competitors. Ideally, management should first ensure that there is a current and future demand for the product, that production is generally viable in terms of supplies of materials, labour and capacity, and that it is potentially profitable. Thereafter, assured by the above, management should draw up a list of company strengths and weaknesses to establish its competitive position by asking such questions as:

(a) What is the company's general standing in the eyes of customers?
(b) Are there competitors who dominate?
(c) How efficient is production?
(d) Has the company sufficient financial resources to finance sales?
(e) Is management up to the task?

3. Company strategy

Finally, management devises a plan of campaign, a strategy to exploit the opportunity (*see* Fig. 13.1).

(a) Products are selected, e.g. innovative products such as a new efficient fuel-injection system for internal combustion engines.
(b) Production methods are decided, e.g. make rather than buy because of the need for secrecy and in view of the shortage of sub-contracting capacity.
(c) Timetable of operations agreed.

(i) Acquire the knowhow, and productive capacity, by merging with the company developing the system.

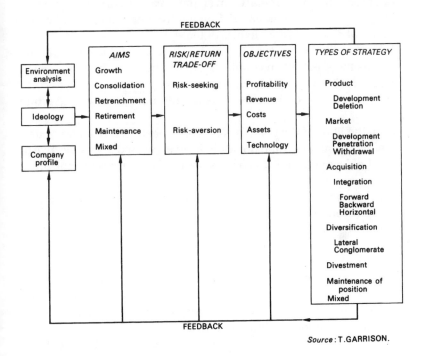

Figure 13.1 *Strategy determination*

(*ii*) Decide on and implement the terms of the merger.

(*iii*) Set up the organization and detail production and marketing plans to achieve the anticipated benefits.

4. A model of strategy determination

It is appropriate at this stage to extend our thoughts on company strategy beyond the takeover situation to consider a model of how companies generally determine their strategy. Figure 13.1 provides a valuable insight into this process and facilitates understanding of this complex subject.

(a) The company's board of management has an ideology either implicit or explicit. If implicit, the ideology is expressed in the form of appropriate objectives. On the other hand, if the ideology is explicit, perhaps formulated in the manner described by the Cyert and March behavioural theory of the firm, and influenced by its analysis of the company's environment and company strengths and weaknesses, then the board has definite aims.

(b) These aims in summary cover the areas of corporate growth, consolidation, retrenchment, retirement from operations, and maintenance of position, or a mixture of these.

(c) Next is the risk/return trade-off. The board adopts an attitude towards the risk/return conflict. At one extreme is the risk-seeking board which for the prospect of high returns is prepared to accept high risks; at the other extreme is the ultra-cautious, risk-averting board.

(d) In the light of the board's compromise between risk and return, the aims are qualified and quantified and expressed as an objective or mix of objectives. Specific targets or standards are set in the areas of:

(*i*) profitability;

(*ii*) revenue;

(*iii*) costs;

(*iv*) assets;

(*v*) technology.

(e) Next a strategy is formulated to achieve these objectives. In particular, plans are drawn up in the areas of products, markets, acquisitions, diversification and divestment, for the maintenance of the company's position or for a mixture of these.

(f) Finally, strategic actions cause reactions. The environment and company strengths and weaknesses are affected and perhaps ideology changes. Clearly the board should then review its aims; its attitude towards risk/return; its objective and type of strategy. However, the feedback may call only for a reconsideration of objectives (if ideology, aims and attitude towards risk are unchanged) when for instance company profit targets are not met or if the latest technology proves to be too expensive.

A hypothetical example will illustrate the steps in the model.

Step 1

The management of Economy Propulsion Ltd believe that shareholders will leave management to pursue a policy that satisfies their monetary, authority and reputation aspirations if their demands for above-average payments of dividends and capital growth are met. Moreover, they believe that workers will accept the organization's objectives for the price that satisfies their monetary demands, i.e. above-average pay.

Moreover, the energy crisis creates a demand for a low-fuel-consumption propulsion unit which Economy Propulsion might exploit. Management's view is that the organization has substantial financial resources, capable management, efficient though limited production facilities and a good reputation among customers. However, it lacks the know-how to develop a suitable unit within the near future.

Step 2

Management decides to consolidate its position as a leader in the field of economy motors and to expand its share of the total market.

Step 3

Management may have an aversion to risk and prefer a course of action whose worst possible outcome provides the highest payoff. Thus, faced with two alternatives A and B,

	Returns to Economy Propulsion	
Alternatives	*(i) Maximum*	*(ii) Minimum*
A. Buy out competitor who possesses the technology and modify for own use	£2 000 000	£2 000 000
B. Develop technology independently	£5 000 000	£5 000 000

Management will prefer project A.

Step 4
Management formulates objectives to:

(a) Acquire the technology.
(b) Achieve a target on capital employed based on sales revenue of £x and costs of £y which satisfy the explicit ideology, aims and attitude to risk.

Step 5
Strategy is determined.

(a) Acquisition of the company possessing the know-how, i.e. horizontal integration.
(b) Penetration of the market.
(c) Development of the fuel-saving motor, i.e. product development.

Feedback

(a) A successful strategy may cause management to revise their profitability objective upwards.
(b) Management's success may cause them to be slightly less cautious and accept a slightly higher risk for greater returns. Consequently, profitability objectives are again revised.
(c) On the other hand, an adverse feedback, when for instance competitors react by introducing similar or superior products, or when unforeseen teething troubles cause costs to rise, may cause management to amend its ideology. Perhaps retirement becomes the general aim, conservation of assets the objective and divestment of the product and productive facilities the new strategy.

5. Definitions

(a) *Takeover*. This is where a party gains control over a company by acquiring a controlling interest in its voting share capital.
(b) *Merger*. This is an arrangement where the assets of two companies are placed under the control of a single company which is owned jointly by the shareholders of the original companies.

The distinction between these is not clear-cut, as in the past offerors would bid for control without reference to the board of directors and perhaps successfully take over the company against their wishes.

6. Possible methods

Takeovers and mergers may be brought about by the following means.

(a) An agreement between the parties, especially when the shares are held by a small number of persons.

(b) Buying up shares on the Stock Exchange.

(c) A takeover bid, i.e. a general offer to the body of shareholders which may be against the wishes of the offeree's directors.

It takes the following forms:

(*i*) An offer to buy shares for cash.

(*ii*) An offer to exchange shares for shares.

(*iii*) A combination of these.

7. Valuation of the business

To effect a purchase or amalgamation the parties must first establish the value of the undertaking's shares, quoted, unquoted or controlling.

8. Valuation of quoted shares

The Stock Exchange price of the shares is a useful guide to their valuation. This will be determined by investors' attitudes towards security, yield and the marketability of the securities.

Naturally the offeror will bear in mind these same considerations, but will also pay regard to any voting rights, increasing his or her offer price accordingly to secure the benefits which control affords.

9. Valuation of unquoted shares

(a) The offeror wishing to value unquoted shares which are in a minority (i.e. control is exercised by others) uses as a criterion the company's true earning record compared with the opportunity cost of his or her capital. A yield comparable to other investments in similar fields will be expected, adjusted accordingly for reduced marketability of shares and the degree of risk associated with this investment.

For example, X Co. has an issued share capital of 50 000 £1 ordinary shares. Profits for distribution average £20 000 per annum. An offeror who has considered the above factors estimates a satisfactory rate of return on capital employed to be 25 per cent.

$$\text{Value of 50 000 ordinary shares} = \frac{£20\,000}{1} \times \frac{100}{25}$$

$$= £80\,000$$

$$\text{Value of one share} = \frac{£80\,000}{50\,000}$$

$$= £1.60$$

(b) The assets-valuation method is generally used to value shares that control the company.

Example

AA Co. Ltd

	£k	£k	£k
Fixed assets (at cost less depreciation)			
Freehold buildings		120	
Fixtures and equipment		20	
Vehicles		20	160
Goodwill			50
Net current assets			
Stocks		170	
Trade debtors		150	
Balance with bank		10	
		330	
Less			
Creditors	120		
Corporation tax	40		
Proposed dividend	40	200	130
			340
Financed by			
Ordinary shares of £1 each:			
Smith		220	
Jones		20	240
Revenue reserves			100
			340

Note: The freehold buildings have been revalued at £160 000. In order to value Smith's shares in the business it is necessary to calculate the net assets attributable to the shareholders and then make adjustments.

(a) The goodwill is eliminated since we do not know whether goodwill from the past still exists.

(b) The book value of assets must be revalued in line with current values, e.g. freehold buildings are worth £40 000 more than the book value.

	£k
Net assets in balance sheet	340
Add appreciation in buildings	40
	380
Less goodwill	50
Net tangible assets	330

Value of Mr Smith's holdings

$$\frac{£220\,000}{£240\,000} \times £330\,000 = £302\,500$$

(c) A third and popular method of valuing unquoted shares is to compare the earning ability of the unquoted company with an otherwise identical quoted company. The first step is to analyse thoroughly the financial performance of quoted companies engaged in the same activities, ideally companies which are similar in terms of balance sheet values, earnings and dividend policy, so as to develop a feel for the current climate of investment opinion regarding the industry.

The next stage is to apply the P/E ratio of the quoted company to the unquoted company. However, the P/E to be used should be halved to reflect the unquoted shares' low marketability.

Example _____

CC Co. Ltd

Balance sheet at 31 December 19–6

	£k
Fixed assets	500
Goodwill	50
Net current assets	150
	700
Financed by:	
Share capital:	
1 000 000 ordinary shares of 50p each	500
100 000 7% preference shares of £1 each	100
Reserves	100
	700

The P/E ratio for comparable listed companies in the industry is approximately 14:1.

The following additional information is supplied:

(a) Included in fixed assets are premises shown at cost at £300 000. They are now worth £400 000.

(b) An examination of current assets suggests that provisions for doubtful debts of £10 000 should be made, and obsolete stocks of £12 000, written off.

(c) Profits before taxation have been:

	£k
19–3	160
19–4	40
19–5	100
19–6	120

and the forecast profit before taxation for 19–7 is £180 000

The next step is to make the necessary adjustments to the valuation of fixed assets, debtors and stocks to provide an assets-valuation of the shares.

	£k	£k
Fixed assets	500	
Add property appreciation	100	600
Net current assets		
150 000 – (10 000 + 12 000)		128
		728
Deduct preference shareholders' capital		100
Net assets value		628

Net assets value per ordinary share $= \dfrac{£628\ 000}{1\ 000\ 000} = 63\text{p}$

Finally, the earnings should be weighted to give more emphasis to the most recent profits, and the resulting average earnings figure capitalized using the adjusted P/E ratio.

Earnings		Weighted average £k
19–3	160 × 1	160
19–4	40 × 2	80
19–5	100 × 3	300
19–6	140 × 4	560
19–7	180 × 5	900
	15	2 000

Average per annum = £2 000 000 ÷ 15 = £133 333
Taxation, at say, 35%   46 666
Preference dividend   7 000
Net earnings   79 667
Capitalized at P/E ratio of 7.0   £557 669

$$\text{Value per share} = \frac{£557\ 669}{1\ 000\ 000} = 55.7p$$

The above calculations show how different nettings produce different share values, and demonstrate that there is no exact value of a share. The method selected depends on the purpose of the valuation: whether, for instance, the viewpoint is asset values, or capitalization of the company's earnings.

10. Determination of the consideration price
The selling price, which must be acceptable to both the offeror and offeree, is based on their evaluation of the company's earning power, adjusted according to their attitudes to other factors, as follows.

(a) Offerees will naturally not accept a bid price which differs greatly from the market price of the shares, although they may demand a premium in the following circumstances:
(*i*) if other bids are expected;
(*ii*) if higher returns are anticipated from future investment projects;
(*iii*) if the offeree is a controlling shareholder, in which case he or she may expect compensation for giving up the benefits which control affords (e.g. determining the company's distribution or trading policy).
(b) Offerors will naturally wish to pay the lowest price to acquire the company, but may be prepared to exceed the financial evaluation in the following circumstances:
(*i*) the offeree's company has products which will complement the offeror's product range;
(*ii*) the offeree possesses new processes;
(*iii*) the offeree possesses competent management;
(*iv*) the offeree has assets which are inefficiently used;
(*v*) the offeree has efficient R & D, marketing, advertising and promotion departments;
(*vi*) self-development by the offeror of these could incur considerable efforts, costs and time. It might be easier to buy them instead.

On the other hand, the offeror may offer a lower price for a highly specialized organization or one whose shares are less readily marketable.

11. Factors determining the basis of a share for shares amalgamation

(a) The pre-offer market values of the offerors' and offerees' shares when they are unaffected by amalgamation hopes or fears.
(b) The cover and dividend records of the two companies. If the offeror's record is unattractive to offeree shareholders, they may be induced to exchange their shares by:

 (*i*) preference shares and their guaranteed dividends;
 (*ii*) debentures and their guaranteed interests;
 (*iii*) convertible debentures. These may be included as part of the consideration of the exchange transaction.

(c) The value of the assets of the companies. Offerees will expect a consideration which at least equals the break-up value of assets owned by their company.
(d) The growth potential of the two companies.
(e) The capital-gearing factors of the two companies. A shareholder in the offeree company might refuse shares in a lower-geared company on the grounds that earnings are diluted.
(f) The vote-gearing factors of the two companies. Shareholders in the offeree company will not readily accept a situation where they exercise reduced voting powers in an enlarged company, although some compensation may persuade them to accept.

12. Acquisitions in practice: a checklist

The first problem facing a company which sets out on a policy of acquisition is the direction of the diversification. There may be several potential markets that the company could expand into, but as a first step each market should be evaluated and a short list drawn up of those markets that appear to satisfy the company's acquisition criteria of say, sales growth, profitability, stability of sales, etc. The second problem once the company has decided to enter a market, is how to decide which companies to pursue within that market.

One way of tackling these problems is to use:

(a) a checklist to evaluate the markets;
(b) a checklist to evaluate companies.

13. Checklists to evaluate markets and companies

A checklist to evaluate the markets:

Market characteristics

(a) What is the size (sales value) of the market this year?
(b) What is its ten-year growth rate?
(c) Can it maintain its growth rate?
(d) Is it subject to a trade cycle effect?

Market size and growth (overseas)

(e) What is the size of world market this year?
(f) What is its ten-year growth rate?
(g) What is the growth potential in
    (*i*) developing nations?
    (*ii*) developed nations?
(h) How much competition is there in the UK market?
(i) What is the average profitability of the market leaders?
(j) What proportion of turnover do they export?

Relationship between the market and the offeror

(k) What is the likely reaction by shareholders and press to the offeror's move into this market?
(l) Is there a good relationship between the offeror and firms in this market as supplier/distributor/customer?
(m) Would the offeror's production techniques and technology be sympathetic with the markets?

    A checklist for evaluating companies:

Company characteristics

(a) What is the sales value of this company this year?
(b) What is its ten-year growth rate?
(c) Can it maintain its growth rate?
(d) What is its ten-year growth rate in profits?
(e) How stable are its profits?
(f) What is its current market share?
(g) How concentrated/diversified is this company in markets and products?
(h) What is the trend in return on investment?
(i) What is the trend in profit margins?

(j) What is the trend in borrowing to equity?
(k) What is the calibre of its management?

Compatibility of the company with offeror

(l) What is the level of potential synergy arising from the acquisition?
(m) What is the potential for improvement through reorganization?
(n) How do the company's and offeror's reputations compare?
(o) How will shareholders react?

While many of these questions are quantitative and can be answered precisely, others require opinions. Nevertheless, all require interpretation and qualification by somebody expert in company affairs, who may have to apply subjective valuations or weightings to the analysis, to establish which markets and acquisitions seem to be in the offeror's best interest. This final decision whether to acquire or not should only be made after a thorough investigation into the finance, marketing, manufacturing, technology, management and administration areas confirms this intention and provides information on which to base an offer.

14. Arithmetic of a takeover
Let us now consider the situation where a purchaser acquires assets at a discount because assets are under-utilized and management is poor (*see* Fig. 13.2). The intention is to sell surplus assets and install new management to raise profits significantly.

Clearly the purchaser is keen to buy in the region of 540p per share although prepared to go higher on the basis of the anticipated higher earnings and the profit on the sale of surplus assets, but obviously no higher than the total cash flow he or she believes the investment can generate.

Another way of calculating the maximum purchase price for an income maximizer, assuming that the accurate forecasts of profits are available for the next four years, is to use DCF analysis. Thus, assuming that the surplus assets are sold at the end of Year 1, and the profit distributed, that forecast profits distributed to the purchaser are as shown below, that the cost of capital to the company is 15 per cent, then by discounting this cash flow to present values, we have the cash payment needed to secure a post-tax return of 15 per cent on the purchaser's investment which he or she regards are the minimum acceptable return to justify the acquisition.

Victim Co. balance sheet

Fixed Assets			
Land and buildings			£100 000
Plant and machinery			200 000
			£300 000
Current Assets			
Stocks		£150 000	
Debtors		100 000	
Cash		50 000	
		£300 000	
Less Current liabilities			
Creditors	£130 000		
Current taxation	30 000		
Current dividend	20 000		
		180 000	
Net current assets			£120 000
Net assets			420 000
Represented by:			
Ordinary £1 shares			200 000
Preference shares £1 @ 6%			200 000
Deferred liabilities			20 000
			£420 000

Notes: (*i*) Market value of land is £460 000.
      (*ii*) Earnings currently £60 000 can be raised to £240 000 by Year 4.
           Current earnings ÷ share = £60 000 ÷ 200 000 = 30p
      (*iii*) Ordinary shares are selling at 10 times earnings, i.e. 300p

(a) Net assets attributable to equity

Net assets		£420 000
Less Deferred liabilities	£20 000	
Preference shares	200 000	220 000
		£200 000
Plus Increase in value of land	360 000	
Less Potential tax liability 50%	180 000	
Net increase in value		180 000
Net assets		£380 000

(b) Market valuation of shares at a P/E of 10

Earnings forecast	£240 000
Less Tax, say 50%	120 000
	£120 000
Less preference dividend	12 000
	£108 000*
EPS (£108 000 ÷ 200 000)	54p
Share value	540p

(c) Range of bid prices:

(i) On earnings forecast	540p
(ii) On basis of higher earnings and higher land valuation i.e. 9p per share × 10 P/E	540p 90 630p

Note: ([1])£180 000 ÷ 200 000 = 9p/share × 10 P/E

Figure 13.2 *Victim Co. balance sheet*

Thus in Year 0, the income maximizer interested in a minimum return of 15 per cent would fix the maximum price at £865 551, or 433p per share (i.e. present value of all receipts).

Year	Sales of assets	Distributed profits (assumed)	Total receipts	Discount factors 15%	Present values
0	£40 000				
1	£180 000	£40 000	£220 000	0.8696	£191 312
2		60 000	60 000	0.7561	45 366
3		80 000	80 000	0.6575	52 600
4		$\left\{ \begin{array}{l} 108\ 000^* \\ 900\ 000 \end{array} \right.$	1 008 000	0.5717	576 273
					£865 551

Note: (*) Reorganization completed and £108 000 of the anticipated profit of £240 000 distributed. Thereafter, dividends are expected to grow by 3 per cent p.a.: at this time, year 4, these future profits are valued at £108 000 discounted at 15 per cent, *less* the anticipated growth rate of 3 per cent i.e. £108 000 ÷ 0.12 = £900 000.

Reasons for mergers and takeovers

15. Defensive motives
There are three varieties of amalgamations undertaken for defensive reasons. They are as follows:

(a) horizontal integration;
(b) lateral integration;
(c) vertical integration.

16. Horizontal integration
Firms may integrate horizontally by means of takeovers and mergers for a number of defensive reasons, as follows.

(a) *Trading difficulties.* The rationalization schemes of the 1920s and 1930s, where firms merged to remove excess capacity and to maintain prices can also be seen in the record industry and breweries.
(b) *Economies of scale.*
(c) *The desire to eliminate competitors.* A firm may react to competition or potential competitors by eliminating them by means of takeovers.

17. Lateral integration
Possible defensive motives are:

(a) to counter competition by extending the product range;
(b) to secure economies of scale;
(c) to solve a financial problem, e.g. Bats' acquisition of Pricerite and International Stores to augment earnings to offset advance corporation tax;
(d) to acquire new potentially profitable products when present products are at the maturity stage in their life cycle (*see* Fig. 13.3).

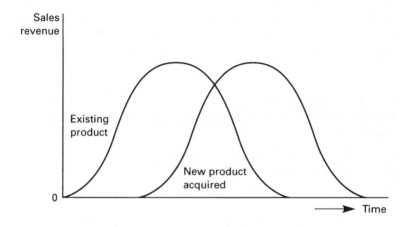

Figure 13.3 *Acquisition of new product to compensate for declining sales revenue*

18. The reverse takeover
This a rare type of bid which may be used by a firm to get a Stock Exchange quotation. For example, an unquoted company, X, wishing to acquire Y, a quoted company, may arrange with Y's directors that they offer a share-for-share exchange of equity so that X becomes Y's subsidiary. The motive is defensive, to avoid the costs of formal quotation and the exacting disclosures demanded by the Stock Exchange Council and the possibility of an unfavourable reaction in the capital market. But success is by no means guaranteed, for the Council may now suspend quotation where a takeover materially alters the style of the company, until information regarding its new form is forthcoming.

19. Vertical integration

Firms may attempt to integrate vertically through mergers and take-overs of firms at different stages of the production process to secure the following.

(a) *Source of supplies.* These may be endangered if competitors are integrating backwards or if a monopoly situation already exists.

(b) *Marketing outlets.* These may be especially desirable if competition is severe. The firm may feel that it needs to protect its retailing outlets, increase its selling points or deal directly and perhaps more effectively with consumers.

(c) *Trading advantages.* These may be secured when the manufac-turers/retailers have control over their products' prices. They may prefer stable prices to price competition which aggravates the diffi-culties of production planning.

20. Offensive motives

There are three main groups of causes for takeovers and mergers for offensive motives:

(a) the acquisition of assets at a discount (*see* **21**);

(b) trading advantages (*see* **24**);

(c) personal reasons (*see* **25**).

21. Acquisition of assets at a discount (reduced value)

A frequently cited reason for takeovers is that the offeror finds available cash or other liquid assets in the offeree to finance the transaction. Alternatively, speculators sell fixed assets, usually land, to realize the cash and then arrange for the company to lease them back. In the past, balance sheets and share prices have often under-stated the true value of the business in order to produce the classical takeover situation.

22. Reasons for this discount

Assets may be available at a discount for various reasons, as follows.

(a) *Dividend restraint.* The offeree retains a larger than normal propor-tion of profits, which tends to depress the share price. This may be due to the following factors.

(*i*) Government tax policy. Up to 1957 and with corporation tax since 1965, high taxation on distributed profits makes for conser-vative distribution policies.

(*ii*) Company controllers may determine the company's

distribution policy to suit their own tax position, e.g. high-rate tax payers will prefer profit retention.

(*iii*) Company controllers may aim at complete ownership and control. A low-dividend policy will affect the share price to their advantage as buyers.

(b) *Inefficient management.* The offeror may feel that his or her management can realize the asset's full potential, e.g. public houses have been acquired and redeveloped profitably by breweries.

(c) *Inefficient capital structure.* When the return on assets is high, it is to the advantage of shareholders to finance long-term capital requirements by means of lower fixed-interest securities, i.e. debentures or preference shares. (Although, since corporation tax, debentures are preferred, since the interest is allowable against taxation.) Consequently a company which is low-geared and has issued preference shares would be attractive to a bidder who can profitably reorganize the company's capital structure.

(d) *Unrealistic valuation of assets.* The balance sheet may understate the true value of assets because:

(*i*) fixed assets may be valued at original cost less an over-generous adjustment for depreciation; or

(*ii*) the company may fail to appreciate the true worth of its land and the effect of inflation since 1945.

This places the company in the classic takeover situation.

(e) *'Tax-loss' companies.* Companies may set off accumulated losses against taxation due on future profits, so that a company having insufficient capital or ability to restore profitability may find itself taken over by another company in the same trade. The offeror may take over control cheaply, run the company profitably without 'discontinuing' the business and offset the past losses against profits, thereby increasing the effective return on capital.

23. Capital reconstructions

The offeror may carry out, with the members' agreement and the Court's sanction, an internal capital reconstruction which alters the rights of members as set out in the articles of association. They may do so for the following reasons.

(a) Additional share capital is required and it can only be attracted by offering securities on advantageous terms to prospective investors.

(b) Circumstances may demand a change in capital gearing.

(c) The existing structure may be unnecessarily complex and can be simplified, e.g. by reducing the number of share classes.

(d) Circumstances may demand a 'reduction in capital'. For example, a company might be in a weak financial position, dividends may be passed over or assets may have fallen below book values. One solution might be to reduce the nominal value of ordinary shares and the dividend on preference shares. This will reduce the prior charges on profits and give the company a better chance of paying dividends out of current earnings and improve its standing in the eyes of investors. However, it is the ordinary and not the preference shareholders who are expected to bear the main burden of the capital reduction. Any loss of income on the latter's part should be made good by giving them ordinary shares or allowing them to participate in profits. The exact form which the scheme takes will depend on the respective rights of share classes (e.g. participating preference shares bear a greater burden than fixed dividend preference shares).

24. Trading advantages
Firms may amalgamate to improve their competitive position to secure the following advantage.

(a) *Economies of scale.* The synergy principle explains why companies make offers for others operating in the same industry. The enlarged company may be worth more than the sum of the two companies (in effect $1 + 1 = 3$) and these economies, reflected in lower unit costs, should improve its competitiveness (e.g. Tate & Lyle's bid for Manbré on the grounds that they needed a strong, efficient unit to face European competition).

(b) *Diversification.* It is argued that multi-product firms are able to stabilize their overall trade and spread the risk of demand variations, so that a decline in one sector may be compensated for by increases in others. Obviously profit opportunities are relevant too. For example, Unilever is a company which has diversified its interests to a remarkable extent, producing a variety of branded goods varying from soap powders and perfumes to frozen foods.

Diversification may be an answer for industries whose traditional trade has been overtaken by modern technology. Textiles and tobaccos are good examples: Courtaulds has moved into nylon and paint, Imperial Tobaccos into confectionery and cosmetics.

(c) *Purchasing management.* An expanding company may acquire 'new blood' for its top management with the new company.

25. Personal motives
There are people who strive to build and extend financial or industrial

empires for personal reasons of power, interest, achievement and satisfaction.

Advantages and disadvantages of takeovers and mergers

26. Introduction

It is no exaggeration to say that the majority of mergers and takeovers proceed smoothly with agreement on both sides. Not infrequently it is the offeree who takes the initiative. Its management may be ambitious yet growth may be restricted by insufficient capital or technical knowhow and it realizes that an amalgamation, preferably with a company whose operations are complementary, provides a solution. The offeror may fulfil these requirements and both may benefit from greater economies of scale. There are companies today which specialize in advising firms in the choice of partners, timing and negotiation and who will provide funds to realise the full potential of the amalgamation. An example is Investors in Industry.

27. Advantages to shareholders

(a) A takeover bid may cause the board to end a policy of 'dividend restraint' with the result that higher dividends are paid and share prices climb. Even if the bid succeeds, the shareholder will probably receive a premium over the pre-bid price. Either way, the shareholder gains.

(b) A bid reminds directors that the voting shareholders are important and it should make them pay greater attention to their interests.

(c) A merger by means of an exchange of shares may bring future financial rewards in the enlarged company.

(d) All are given an equal opportunity to sell.

28. Disadvantages to shareholders

(a) Minority shareholders may find themselves compelled to sell their shares if the bidder gains 90 per cent of the shares (*see* Companies Act 1948, s. 209).

(b) The offer may be a 'partial bid', in which case some shareholders will be unable to sell all their shares. The takeover code regards partial bids as generally undesirable.

(c) It is just conceivable that the offeror might prevent opposition to its policy through a reconstruction or by the issue of non-voting securities.

29. Advantages to directors

(a) If the offeror requires their services then there may be greater scope in the larger company for:

   (*i*) promotion,

   (*ii*) remuneration, and

   (*iii*) achievement in the field of management.

(b) They may relinquish control on favourable terms.

30. Disadvantages to directors

(a) The possibility of dismissal and the loss of future remuneration.

(b) The loss of power, status and other benefits which the position offered.

31. Advantages to bidders

Where the bid is successful bidders increase their scale of operations and secure trading or other benefits.

32. Disadvantages to bidders

(a) When the bid fails, bidders suffer heavy irrecoverable capital losses.

(b) Acquirors may themselves be vulnerable to bids from other sources.

(c) The amalgamation may be refused by the Department of Trade and the Monopolies Commission on the grounds that it is against the public interest. This acts as a control over irresponsible bids.

33. Advantages to the national economy

(a) Bidders who promote takeovers and mergers have frequently shown great ability in putting the group assets to the most profitable use.

(b) As a consequence new firms entering the industry must set a standard at least as high as that of the group in order to compete successfully.

(c) Larger-scale production, marketing, purchasing, financing and distribution may produce lower average costs and prices.

(d) Large firms tend to invest more heavily than small ones, which could set higher productivity standards for the industry.

(e) Large firms may be more willing to export and finance import-substitution projects in the national interest or for prestige purposes, even when the profit margins are low.

Thus amalgamations can be regarded as being in the national

interest if they result in more efficient production, and if this leads to a more efficient redeployment of the nation's resources, lower consumer prices or a better balance of payments.

34. Disadvantages to the national economy

(a) Increasing returns to scale are not assured in every takeover or merger. Technical economies may be exhausted, so that instead of lower prices, consumers may be faced with rising prices, especially if administration becomes less efficient in the larger organizations.

(b) Amalgamations may result in monopolies which exercise their potential power over suppliers, who are forced to enter into contracts favouring the monopolist, or over consumers who find that choice is restricted through reductions in quality, selection or the life of the product.

(c) Amalgamations may stifle competition and so check the stimulus for increased efficiency.

(d) Any deterioration in the performance of the enlarged company has a proportionally more significant effect on the economy.

Methods of avoiding a takeover position

35. Defences against takeovers

Ideally, companies should organize and conduct themselves so as to avoid situations which attract bids. The following measures make for a complete defence against takeover bids:

(a) *The issue of non-voting or 'A' shares.* This arrangement allows companies to raise capital from the general public without affecting corporate control.

(b) *The issue of shares to a friendly partner.* It is possible to do this by:
> (*i*) exchanging shares with another company, so making it difficult for an outsider to acquire a controlling interest; or
> (*ii*) issuing a block of shares to a company which is uninterested in control, e.g. **EDITH**.

(c) *The defensive merger.* An amalgamation may make companies more secure from outside interference because a controlling interest of the enlarged share capital may be beyond the financial resources of many bidders.

36. Countering takeover bids

There are a number of measures management can take when faced with a takeover bid, although at this stage it is frequently a case of too little being done too late.

(a) The board may remove the object of the bid by:
  (*i*) revaluing fixed assets to current values; or
  (*ii*) capitalizing reserves to bring share capital into line with current values.

(b) The board might announce a higher dividend to improve the attractiveness of shares to their owners. It might also raise the share price, thereby making the bid more expensive.

(c) It may recommend rejection of the bid with reasons and promise projects expected to improve future earnings. Consequently, shareholders may consider the shares and the board more favourably.

(d) A capital reconstruction may frustrate a bid, based on an inefficient capital structure. Higher gearing might benefit ordinary shareholders, while a substitution of debentures for preference shares would improve post-tax profits.

(e) The board may improve earnings by disposing of unprofitable assets and reinvesting the proceeds for a higher return.

(f) The board may plead to the present directors for loyalty or for patriotism in the case of an overseas bid.

More drastic action may be possible.

(g) The board may resort to the sale and leaseback of assets. Although Savoy Hotel Ltd (1953) was not a legal precedent, it showed how courts might judge similar issues (i.e. unfavourably).

(h) The board may introduce restrictive clauses into the company's articles to modify voting rights or to limit the transferability of shares, all of which may or may not be valid. However, company law, *ultra vires,* and directors' responsibilities towards shareholders, all severely limit the scope for such desperate actions in the face of a bid.

37. Arguments against 'A' shares

(a) They are undemocratic in that some ordinary shareholders are not given voting rights in return for risk-bearing.

(b) They are against the national interest if they check takeovers which create more efficient industrial structures.

38. Arguments for 'A' shares

(a) Company controllers secure from outside interference can concentrate on developing and running the business.

(b) Investors, even when aware of their non-voting features, may be prepared to buy them as they are generally cheaper than shares with full voting rights.

(c) Some individuals, on balance, tolerate 'A' shares on the following grounds:

(*i*) prohibitive legislation is unjustified as only a handful of shareholders are affected;

(*ii*) legislation is undesirable because it would unnecessarily restrict and complicate company law;

(*iii*) shareholders are not forced to buy these shares;

(*iv*) shareholders tend to be apathetic whether they have votes or not;

(*v*) 'A' shares are now less common, for many companies, respecting either public opinion or the financial power of institutions, have granted voting rights to these shares or exchanged them for shares with rights.

Progress test 13

1.(a) Describe how you think companies arrive at a company strategy. **(1–4)**

(b) Draw up a strategy for a company with which you are familiar. **(1–4)**

2. Why do some companies develop strategy to acquire other companies? **(4)**

3. Discuss the advantages and disadvantages of the various purchase considerations used in company amalgamations. **(5–8)**

4. Compare the takeover and merger as a means of amalgamation and the possible methods by which each may be accomplished. **(5–8)**

5. How is the consideration price determined in amalgamation negotiations? **(5–14)**

6. You are asked to advise an investor on the valuation of three classes of shares in which he is interested. They are the following:

(a) ordinary shares in a quoted company;

(b) ordinary shares in an unquoted company;

(c) ordinary shares (in a minority) in an unquoted company.

Outline the nature of your recommendations. **(9–10)**

7. 'Firms expand horizontally, laterally or vertically for defensive motives.' Discuss this claim. **(15–19)**

8.(a) Indicate the main reasons why firms expand by acquisitions and mergers for offensive motives. **(20–24)**
(b) How important do you think 'personal motives' are to the functioning of an aggressive company? **(25)**

9. A frequently cited reason for takeovers is 'acquisition of assets at a discount'. Explain this term, giving reasons for this discount. **(21–22)**

10. What is the economic justification for a 'takeover bid'? Illustrate your answer by reference to any recent case. **(26–38)**

11. Discuss the pros and cons of takeovers from the viewpoint of:
(a) shareholders;
(b) directors; and
(c) bidders. **(26–32)**

12. Consider the advantages and disadvantages of takeovers from the viewpoint of the national economy. **(33–34)**

13. What measures can a company adopt to avoid a takeover situation? **(35–38)**

14

Financial decision-making techniques

Nature of break-even analysis

1. Introduction

Throughout this chapter, we examine the various financial aids that can be used in decision-making: in particular break-even and marginal analysis, the two most widely used techniques, will be the focus of our attention. In fact, we have already referred to break-even in Chapter 7 in connection with the economist's approach to revenue, costs and profit and the firm's typical revenue-cost-volume relationship: however, we now regard it from the accountant's or manager's viewpoint to consider its value as a practical tool.

2. Definition of break-even

Break-even is defined as the level of activity where no profits are made or losses incurred. In other words, that level of operations where total costs equal total revenue.

3. Break-even: the accountant's viewpoint

In contrast with the economist, who analyses the behaviour of continuous total costs and revenue over the company's entire output/sales range, the accountant is directly concerned with supplying management with past and future information of costs and revenue for a limited range of activities. Furthermore, since the accountant is primarily interested in the operational range, he or she considers the nature of costs and revenue at very low and high levels of activities to be irrelevant to immediate management decisions.

Consequently, the accountant uses break-even analysis suitably modified in the following ways.

(a) Total costs are represented by a straight line which tends to approximate to the actual values over the narrow sales/production range.

(b) Total revenue is represented by a straight line, on the assumption that moderate percentage increases in sales may be achieved without price cutting.

(c) These curves may be extended outside the narrow operational range and may illustrate the approximate cost/revenue/volume relationship as long as the limitations are remembered, i.e. revenue and costs are, in fact, non-linear over the entire range of activities.

Figure 14.1 illustrates a typical break-even diagram.

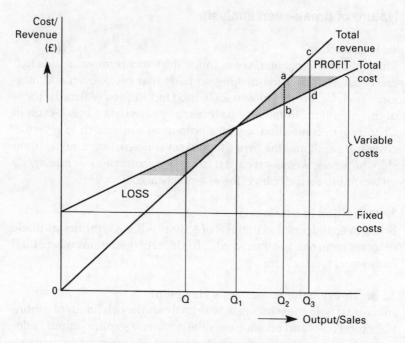

Figure 14.1 *Straight line break-even graph*

(*i*) Assumed normal operational range of output is Q–Q_2.

(*ii*) Profit at an output of OQ_2, is £a, b.

(*iii*) The graph shows that if output could be increased to OQ_3 then profit could be increased to £c, d.

(*iv*) Any level of output beyond OQ_1 (the break-even) is profitable.

(*v*) It shows the revenue-cost relationship at different levels of output, and not that the company initially makes losses and profits later in the year. Time is ignored and does not appear on the horizontal axis.

4. Calculation of break-even
The break-even level of activity can be calculated by formulae as a check on the accuracy of the graph. The formulae are as follows.

(a) Break-even sales revenue $= \dfrac{\text{Fixed cost}}{1 - \dfrac{\text{Variable cost}}{\text{Selling price}}}$

(b) Break-even sales volume $= \dfrac{\text{Fixed cost}}{\text{Selling price} - \text{Variable cost}}$

5. Limitations of straight-line break-even
Before we examine the application of break-even graphs to decision-making, it is important to remember that the graphs are a simplification of a complex relationship and are subject to several limitations which, if appreciated, are less likely to result in faulty diagnosis and poor decisions. These limitations can be summarized as follows.

(a) In practice, the cost–volume relationship is not necessarily linear.

(b) In practice, the revenue–volume relationship is not necessarily linear. In other words, it is dangerous to extrapolate the curves outside the normal range of activity. To resist this temptation, one should be aware of the economist's analysis on the behaviour of cost, revenue and volume and the relationship between each.

(c) Profits are not necessarily maximized at maximum output (OQ_3) since in practice:

(*i*) the revenue curve may be lower than shown because of discounts and price cuts to achieve this high level of sales;

(*ii*) the cost curve may be higher than shown, because of disproportionate increases in variable costs, e.g. overtime, shift work payments, to achieve this high output.

(d) It is a static illustration of a dynamic situation and therefore must be updated regularly.

(e) It assumes that sales and output are in balance, i.e. all that is produced is sold within the same time period.

(f) Fixed costs may in fact change. For example, to obtain high levels of output, additional machines or staff may be taken on. Thus the fixed-cost curve is not perfectly horizontal but is 'stepped' (*see* Fig. 14.2); the total-cost curve is similarly stepped.

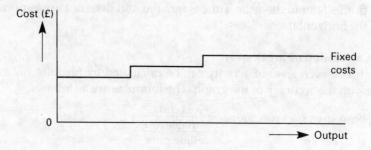

Figure 14.2 *'Stepped' fixed-cost curve*

Applications of break-even

6. Contribution break-even graph

Contribution is simply the difference between selling price and variable costs, consisting of direct wages, materials and other direct expenses. Thus if selling price is £6.00 and variable costs amount to £3.00,

Contribution	=	Selling price	–	Variable costs
£3.00	=	£6.00	–	£3.00

This £3.00 along with other contributions go into a fund which is used to meet the fixed costs and to provide a profit. For example, if fixed costs amount to £10 000 and 7000 units are sold, then

Total contribution	–	Fixed cost	=	Profit
£3.00 × 7000	–	£10 000	=	£11 000

The contribution break-even is graphed (*see* Fig. 14.3) in the following steps.

(a) Draw in the variable-cost curve.
(b) Add fixed costs to the variable-cost curve. This line represents total costs (TC = FC + VC).
(c) Draw in the sales revenue line.

7. Analysis of contribution break-even graph

(a) Examination of the graph shows that break-even is 3333 units and sales value of £20 000. The accuracy of the graph is checked by calculation (*see* **4**).

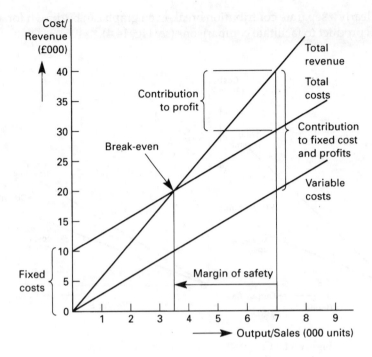

Figure 14.3 *Contribution break-even for Product A*

(*i*) Break-even (sales revenue) $= \dfrac{\text{Fixed cost}}{1 - \dfrac{\text{Variable cost}}{\text{Selling price}}}$

$$= \dfrac{\text{£10 000}}{1 - \dfrac{3}{6}}$$

$$= \text{£20 000}$$

(*ii*) Break-even (sales volume) $= \dfrac{\text{Fixed cost}}{\text{Selling price} - \text{Variable cost}}$

$$= \dfrac{\text{£10 000}}{\text{£6} - \text{£3}}$$

$$= 3333 \text{ units}$$

(b) Furthermore, the contribution towards fixed costs can be read off for a given level of activity. Thus the contribution measured by the vertical distance between the variable-cost line and the revenue line is:

£6000 at output and sales of 2000 units, and

£15 000 at output and sales of 5000 units, etc.

Clearly a separate contribution break-even graph can be drawn for each product to facilitate comparisons (*see* Fig. 14.4).

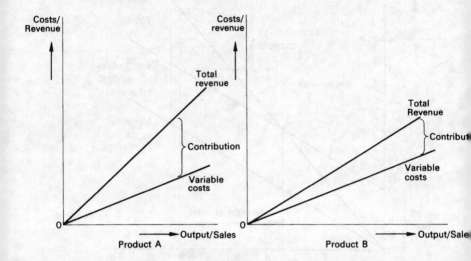

Figure 14.4 *Comparative contributions for two products*

8. Need for caution

These graphs present the cost-revenue-volume relationship simply, providing data that, if used wisely, allow a more flexible approach to decision-making, particularly in the pricing area. However, they should not be used independently as an absolute measure. For example, consider Figs. 14.3 and 14.5 and the respective contributions of products A and B.

Both product A and B make a contribution of £21 000 at a level of sales of 7000. However, further investigation of both charts reveals that product A possesses significant advantages over product B.

(a) Product A's profit is £11 000; B's is only £6000 because the contribution must cover higher fixed costs (£15 000 as opposed to £10 000 for A).

(b) Product A's superior profits are confirmed by the fact that it has a broader profit wedge than B.

(c) Product A has a lower break-even level than B. This means that if

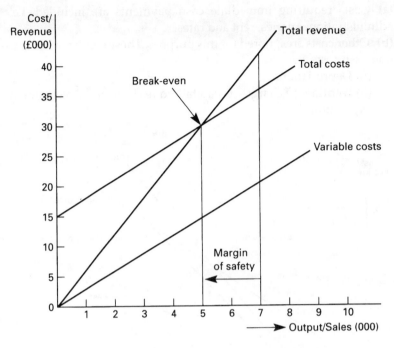

Figure 14.5 *Contribution break-even for Product B*

the level of activity is 7000 units for both products then sales of A can fall significantly before losses are incurred. This is termed the 'margin of safety'.

(*i*) The margin of safety of product A is 3667 units, £22 002 sales value or 52 per cent.

(*ii*) The margin of safety of product B is 2000 units, £12 000 sales value or 28 per cent.

9. Cash break-even
Today, inflation and anti-inflationary policies, with attendant high interest rates, have increased the cost of cash and made it more important than ever before to control cash effectively. Success in this respect demands a full appreciation of the probable values of cash inflows and outflows in relation to the level of business activity: a relationship that is clarified by means of a cash break-even graph. The only difference between this graph and the normal break-even graph is in the treatment of fixed costs. They are distinguished as follows.

(a) Costs requiring immediate cash payments are included, i.e. administration, salaries, rent and rates.

(b) Other costs are ignored for this purpose. These consist of book or non-cash costs, i.e.:

(*i*) Depreciation.

(*ii*) Writing-off charges on capitalised research and development expenditure.

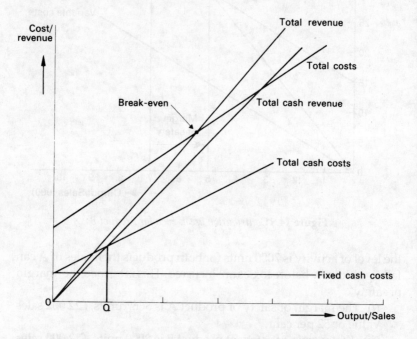

Figure 14.6 *Cash break-even point and comparison with ordinary break-even point*

(*iii*) Nominal depreciation charges on fully depreciated assets.

Figure 14.6 illustrates a typical cash break-even graph.

Note:

(*i*) Only immediate cash payments are included.

(*ii*) Variable costs are assumed to be cash. Where credit is taken such purchases should be eliminated.

(*iii*) Sales revenue is assumed to be for cash. Credit sales should be eliminated. The figure shows that at a level of output-sales of OQ, sufficient cash revenue is generated to pay immediate cash expenses.

Marginal analysis: definitions

10. Marginal costs

Marginal cost or incremental cost is the additional cost of producing one extra unit. Thus if 100 units are produced for a total cost of £250 and 101 units for £252, then the marginal cost is £2. In fact, marginal cost is the same as variable cost, which can be seen from the following:

Fixed cost	+	Variable costs	=	Total costs
£50	+	£200	=	£250 (for 100 units)
£50	+	£202	=	£252 (For 101 units).

Clearly the additional cost is £2 (£252 – £250) and results directly from the extra wages and material costs involved in producing the extra unit (since fixed costs are constant).

Marginal revenue. This is the additional revenue gained from the sale of one extra unit, i.e. the selling price of the goods.

11. Contributions

Contribution is the difference between selling price and marginal (variable) cost:

Contribution = Selling price – Marginal cost or variable cost per unit.

But contribution to what? To answer this, we must consider the special treatment of fixed costs in marginal costing. They are not apportioned to units of output as in full-cost pricing, but are set aside and eventually covered by a fund of contributions realized by the sale of individual units of output. Clearly, if total contributions exceed fixed costs (say £12 000), then profits are made.

Product A
Sales revenue	– Variable costs	= Contribution	
(price × sales volume)			
£5.00 × 4 000	– £6 000	=	£14 000

Product B
Sales revenue	– Variable costs	= Contribution	
£3.00 × 3 000	– £7 000	=	£2 000

Product C, etc.
Sales revenue	– Variable costs	= Contribution	
£2.00 × 3 000	– £5 000	=	£1 000
		Total contributions	£17 000

Therefore

$$Profit = Total\ contribution - Fixed\ cost$$
$$= £17\ 000 \qquad\qquad - £12\ 000$$
$$= £5\ 000$$

12. Importance of marginal costing

Marginal costing and contribution analysis are extremely useful tools for management in decision-making and cost control, providing the decision-maker with a very high degree of flexibility and scope for application in the areas of pricing, costing and resource allocation generally.

Application of marginal analysis

13. Range of application

Examples of areas where this may be applied are:

(a) pricing;
(b) marketing;
(c) allocation of scarce resources between competing uses;
(d) make or buy analysis;
(e) close-down decisions;
(f) comparisons of production methods.

14. Pricing decisions

Marginal costing allows management greater flexibility in setting selling price than full-cost pricing permits. In fact, price may be set below total cost.

For instance, let us consider a hypothetical example. Marginal (variable) costs are £20 per unit and fixed costs are £40 000 and anticipated sales are 3900 units at £30 each: the total cost per unit is the sum of the average fixed and variable costs:

$$Total\ cost\ per\ unit = AFC \qquad\qquad + AVC$$
$$= £40\ 000 \div 3\ 900 + £20$$
$$= £30.25$$

Assuming that the company is working below capacity and is in the course of tendering for a contract for the supply of 300 units, it might base its tender price on a full-cost basis of £29.52, i.e.

$$Total\ cost\ per\ unit = £40\ 000 \div (3\ 900 + 300) + 20$$
$$= £9.52 \quad + £20$$
$$= £29.52$$

As one would intuitively expect, the total cost per unit has fallen because the fixed costs of £40 000 are now being spread over a larger output.

However, using marginal pricing, a lower price is possible: a price of £27 might be low enough to secure the contract and yet provide an overall profit of £1100.

*Example:*_____

(*i*) Anticipated sales 3900 units at £30.

Selling price	–	Variable cost	=	Contribution per unit	
£30	–	£20	=	£10	

Total contribution = £10 × 3 900 units   = £39 000

(*ii*) Tender sales 300 units at £27

£27 – £20 = £7/unit   £7 × 300 units   =   2 100

                                                                                  41 100

                                                   less Fixed costs =   40 000

                                                                  Profit   £1 100

_____

A good example of the application of marginal pricing is found in the travel industry. Package-tour operators who book hotels for the whole year earn sufficient revenue in the peak periods to cover fixed costs and to provide profit so that they can then offer off-season rates at marginal cost (the cost of travel, accommodation, food, etc.). Obviously this is preferable to closing down the hotels.

(a) Off-season rates of, say, £5 per day cover marginal costs and may make additional, if small, contributions to total profit.

(b) Overall profits are increased as long as peak bookings are maintained. However, this example illustrates the danger inherent in marginal pricing, for if holidaymakers substitute the cheaper off-peak holidays for peak-period holidays then fixed costs will not be covered, so that losses are incurred.

(c) Hotel services are maintained and hotel staff retained.

Similarly, air carriers offer cheaper charter rates based on the marginal cost of transport, which makes a contribution to the airlines' overheads.

15. Marketing decisions

Marginal contribution and break-even analysis can be useful in a variety of marketing situations. Two examples are (a) where a company considers increasing its marketing expenditure and (b) where it considers increasing the weight or volume of the product to boost sales.

(a) *Increase in marketing expenditure.* Let us assume that a product, X, sells for 100p, variable costs are 50p, so that the contribution is also 50p, and fixed costs are £2000.

	Per unit (p)	(i) Marketing expenses £2 000 unit sales 10 000	(ii) Marketing increased by £2 000 unit sales 10 000
Sales revenue	100	£10 000	£10 000
Variable costs	50	5 000	5 000
Contribution	50	5 000	5 000
Fixed costs		2 000	4 000
Net profit		3 000	1 000

If fixed costs are assumed to be marketing expenses of £2000 and in situation (*ii*) are increased by £2000 to total £4000, then the break-even point for the same level of profits increases by 40 per cent (*see* the graph for Product X, Fig. 14.7). This analysis is useful to the marketing manager.

(*i*) It is not worth spending the extra £2000 of marketing expenditure if sales volume is unlikely to increase by 40 per cent.

(*ii*) If sales increase by over 40 per cent, profits will increase.

(*iii*) Products with higher contribution-percentages of the selling

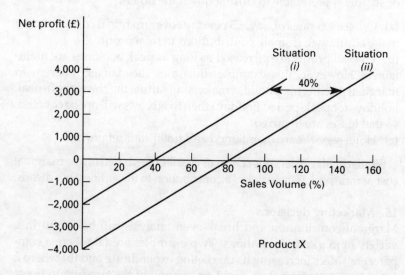

Figure 14.7 *Break-even point for additional marketing expenditure*

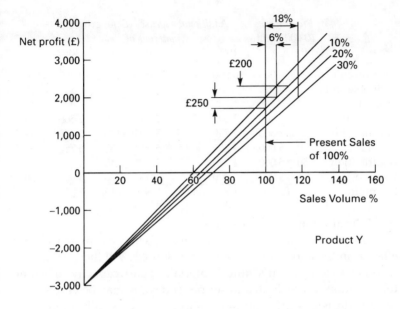

Figure 14.8 *Break-even points for additional expenses on raw materials*

price require smaller increases in sales volume to recoup the extra marketing expenditure.

(b) *Increase in the weight of the product for no increase in price.* Companies frequently give an extra free 10 or 20 per cent of the product. The justification for this can be seen in the following example. Let us assume that Product Y sells for 100p; variable costs total 50p, made up of costs that are proportional to sales revenue, e.g. commissions to salesmen of 25 per cent, and costs that are proportional to quantities, e.g. raw materials and packaging of 25 per cent fixed expenses are £3000.

This information is presented on the Product Y graph (Fig. 14.8) and provides the product manager with useful information.

(*i*) For an extra 10, 20 and 30 per cent of the product, profits will fall by £250, £500 and £750 respectively if sales are unchanged.

(*ii*) For the same level of profits of £2000, sales must increase by 6 per cent if an extra 10 per cent of the product is given away; by 18 per cent for an extra 30 per cent. If he believes that an extra '10 per cent free' will stimulate an extra, say, 10 per cent of sales, then net profits will be increased by £200.

		Present sales *10 000 units*		*Additional expenses (£) for extra* *materials of*				
	P	£	10%	P	20%	P	30%	P
Sales revenue	100	10 000	10 000	100	10 000	100	10 000	100
Variable costs proportional								
to revenue	25	2 500	2 500	25	2 500	25	2 500	25
to quantities	25	2 500	2 750	27.5	3 000	30	3 250	32.5
Total	50	5 000	5 250	52.5	5 500	55	5 750	57.5
Contribution	50	5 000	4 750	47.5	4 500	45	4 250	42.5
Fixed costs		3 000	3 000	30	3 000	30	3 000	30
Net profit		£2 000	1 750	17.5	1 500	15	1 250	12.5

16. Allocation of scarce resources

The second example where marginal analysis may be applied to good effect is in the allocation of company resources. All these resources, whether management's time, materials, plant capacity, machine time or money, are limited in supply and some may be very scarce, so that decisions affecting their allocation are vitally important. Bad decisions resulting in sub-optimal allocation between the competing uses directly contribute to poor performance and reduced profitability. Therefore, if management is faced with a scarcity of a factor of production (termed a limiting or key factor), it must ensure that these resources are used in such a way so that profits per unit of key factor are maximised. This is where contribution analysis comes in, for if fixed costs remain constant then maximum contributions per unit of this limiting factor automatically secure maximum profits.

17. Example

Veneered Table Tops Limited manufacture coffee and telephone table tops for the furniture industry. Costing details are as follows:

	Coffee table tops			*Telephone table tops*		
Variable costs						
Wood $0.2m^3$	@	£30.00/m^3 = 6.00		$0.225m^3$ @	£30.00	£6.75
Labour 2 hours	@	75p/h = 1.50		1½ hours @	75p	1.12
Expense 2 hours	@	50p/h = 1.00		1½ hours @	50p	0.75
Total variable costs per unit		8.50				8.62
Contribution: Selling price		10.00				10.00
Less Variable cost		8.50				8.62
		£1.50				£1.38

Note:

Management must organize output to take into account the following circumstances:

  (*i*) staff holidays in August, when labour hours will be the key or limiting factor, acting as a constraint on production;
  (*ii*) a shortage of wood in September due to a fire at the local wood stockist.

These problems can be solved by analysis of the contributions per unit of limiting factor.

(a) Contribution per unit of labour $= \dfrac{\text{Contribution}}{\text{Labour hours}}$

(*i*) Contribution per unit of labour (coffee table) $= \dfrac{£1.50}{2} = 75\text{p}$

(*ii*) Contribution per unit of labour (telephone table) $= \dfrac{£1.38}{1.5} = 92\text{p}$

(b) Contribution per unit of wood $= \dfrac{\text{Contribution}}{\text{m}^3 \text{ of wood}}$

(*i*) Contribution per unit of wood (coffee table) $= \dfrac{£1.50}{0.2} = £7.50$

(*ii*) Contribution per unit of wood (telephone table) $= \dfrac{£1.38}{0.225} = 6.10$

Thus, faced with this allocation problem, management should concentrate on telephone tables in August and coffee tables in September, which thereby maximises contributions and profits of these two limiting factors.

18. Make-or-buy analysis

The third application of marginal analysis is in the make-or-buy area, where managers may occasionally be faced with the problem of whether to continue to make a product or to buy it from an outside supplier. The decision obviously depends on the relative profitability of either source of action, which is measured by comparing the purchase price with the marginal cost of production. The justification of using only marginal costs in this calculation is that fixed costs exist in the short term, whether the goods are produced or not, and are therefore irrelevant to the analysis. Let us assume that the company producing two products, X and Y, has limited machine capacity and that the comparative cost data are as follows:

	Product X	*Product Y*
Marginal (variable) costs	£5	£7
Purchase price	£7	£10
Difference	£2	£3
Machine times	45 min	25 min
Difference per machine hour	£2.66	£7.20

This shows that to purchase products X and Y costs £2.66 and £7.20 per machine hour respectively, in excess of the cost of making them in the factory. Consequently, greater cost savings and perhaps higher profits would be secured if product X were purchased and the machine capacity so realized used for the production of Y.

19. Close-down decisions

A fourth example of marginal analysis is where management faces the problem of temporarily closing down a department or factory which is making losses. On cost grounds, there is a strong case for maintaining operations so long as sales revenue exceeds variable costs, since a contribution is made towards fixed costs, while to close down would not avoid the fixed costs; thus any contribution to fixed costs, however small, which reduces the amount of the trading loss, is preferred.

Figure 14.9 illustrates this point. Break-even occurs at a selling price of OP and output and sales of OQ, i.e. total revenue (price, OP × quantity, OQ = the area bounded by the points OPTQ) is equal to total cost (cost per unit, OP × quantity, OQ = OPTQ).

Whenever selling price is below OP, then total revenue is less than total cost, so that losses are incurred.

If price is OP_1 then total revenue is $OP_1 VQ$, total cost is OPTQ and the loss is $P_1 PTV$, which is equal to the fixed cost, i.e.:

$$\begin{aligned}
\text{Total cost} &= \text{Total variable cost} + \text{Fixed cost} \\
\text{OPTQ} &= \text{OP}_1\text{VQ} \qquad\qquad + \text{Fixed cost} \\
\text{Fixed cost} &= \text{Total cost} - \text{Total variable cost} \\
\text{Fixed cost} &= \text{OPTQ} \qquad - \text{OP}_1\text{VQ} \\
&= \text{P}_1\text{PTV}
\end{aligned}$$

It follows that:

(a) If selling price is below OP_1 then fixed cost and part of variable costs are not covered. On cost grounds, the firm should close down and minimize the size of the loss to the value of fixed costs.

(b) If price is above OP_1 but below OP, variable costs are covered and

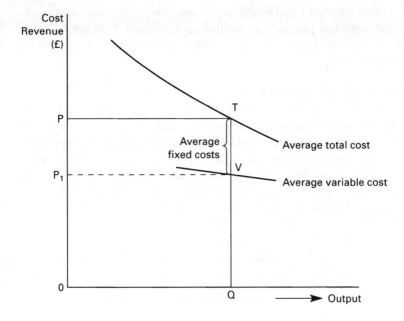

Figure 14.9 *Break-even graph*

a contribution is made to fixed costs. Here, losses are less than the value of fixed costs and are therefore minimized if the company continues to operate.

Non-cost considerations. However, non-cost factors must be considered in arriving at a closure decision.

(a) Suspension of activities may adversely affect customer goodwill and loss of business in the future.
(b) The firm may get a reputation as a bad employer, which will cause difficulties in the future when staff are recruited.

20. Comparisons of production methods

Management may have a choice between methods of production. For instance:

	Method 1		Method 2
Sales 1 000 units @ £20	£20 000		£20 000
Variable costs 1 000 units @ £10	10 000	@ £14	14 000
Contribution	£10 000		£6 000
Fixed costs per method	7 000		2 000
Contribution to factory overheads	£3 000		£4 000

Here, Method 1 makes the larger contribution to fixed costs associated with the production method, but Method 2 secures a larger overall contribution to factory overheads and is therefore preferable to Method 1.

21. Profit-volume (P/V) ratio

The value of the contribution concept has already been discussed in the previous section on break-even, where graphical comparisons were made between two products. However, this method compared absolute contributions only and made comparisons of relative contributions or profitability very difficult. Fortunately, this can be remedied by examining the profit/volume (P/V) ratio. This ratio, more accurately described as the contributions/sales ratio, measures contribution as a percentage of sales value.

$$P/V = \frac{\text{Contribution}}{\text{Selling price}} \times 100$$

$$= \frac{\text{Selling price} - \text{Variable cost}}{\text{Selling price}} \times 100$$

Table 14A *Applications of P/V Ratio*

Product	Selling price (£)	Variable cost (£)	Contri- bution (£)	P/V (%)	Sales value (£)	Total contribution (£)
A	10	5	5	50	80 000	40 000
B	8	3	5	62	70 000	43 400
C	7	2	5	71	60 000	42 600

Table 14A shows applications of the P/V ratio. Applying the formula, the P/V ratio for product A is 50 per cent $\frac{£10 - £5}{£10} \times 100$ and 62 per cent and 71 per cent for B and C respectively. The comparative profitabilities of these products are immediately revealed. For a given £1 of sales, A makes a contribution of 50p to fixed costs and profits, B 62p and C 71p. Furthermore, since contribution and sales are in direct proportion, total contributions can be calculated (P/V × Sales value) for a given amount of sales value. Clearly, product C is preferred to A and B on the grounds that it makes the highest unit contribution to overheads and profits and therefore management should try to either improve the ratios for A and B or transfer resources from A and B to the production of C. In other words, the P/V ratio enables management to rank products in terms of contributions, hence the preference for product C:

Product	P/V ratio	Ranking
A	50%	3
B	62%	2
C	71%	1

The P/V method of analysis may be usefully employed in any type of activity involving sales, and is a valuable complement to the contribution per unit of limiting factor methods of appraisal and ranking we have discussed. Thus, P/V analysis is particularly appropriate in the following areas:

(a) Product lines, as *above.*
(b) Divisions or factories, where the contributions to division sales or factory sales are calculated.
(c) Salesmen or sales areas.

22. Dangers of marginal costing
As shown by the foregoing example, marginal costing provides a technique for decision-making in a wide range of business situations. However, it must be applied with caution, for example in pricing decisions.

(a) One must not lose sight of the fact that in the longer term prices must be sufficient to cover total costs.
(b) Its usefulness is limited where a manufacturer makes a standard product that sells in a single market. Clearly there is no possibility of price discrimination in this situation: to base price on variable cost would mean disaster.
(c) Customers might react unfavourably to a price policy based on marginal costs that continually changes because of movements in labour and material costs.
(d) Additional sales secured through marginal costing must be justified, and not become an end in themselves. Thus, if sales have to be diverted from profitable markets in order to meet contracts priced on a marginal basis, overall contributions and profits are reduced.

Practical budgeting

23. Budgetary control
This is an effective management technique to plan, coordinate and control a business's activities and should be tailor-made to suit the organisation's particular needs and structure. The steps in setting and administering a budgetary control system are as follows:

(a) Set realistic, time-related targets for the business.
(b) Translate these into monetary terms to produce the budget.
(c) Compare actual figures against the budget.
(d) Analyse any variances and find the causes.
(e) Take action to bring performance back to budget.
(f) Apply the experience for better budget management in the future.

24. Financial skills for budget holders
The budget holder's objective is to perform to budget. Ideally, therefore, the budget holder should be involved in the setting of the budget and supplied with regular information showing how actual performance compares against budget. Some budget reports supplied to the budget holder are not 'user friendly' either because they show too little information or because they overwhelm the reader with detail. To help remedy this, the following steps are useful for the budget holder.

(a) Budget preparation.
    (*i*) Introduction.
    (*ii*) Key Performance Indicators.
    (*iii*) Dupont charts.
(b) Preparing the format of the budget report.
(c) Interpreting the budget report.
    (*i*) Z charts.

25. Introduction
The first steps in budget preparation are:

(a) Examine any costs and revenues for which you are responsible and identify those which you can control and those which are uncontrollable.
(b) Select a key measure of activity for the area for which you are responsible (these are termed Key Performance Indicators or KPIs), e.g. room occupancy for the hotel manager, sales revenue for the sales manager, units of output produced for the production manager, labour costs for the staff manager.

(c) Analyse all available information to find out how costs behave in relation to changes in levels of activity. The purpose is to identify costs that are fixed, variable or semi-variable.

(d) Use this knowledge to anticipate costs for varying levels of activity.

26. Key Performance Indicators

As the title suggests, KPIs are figures that are used to measure performance in key areas of the business. They can take several different forms:

(a) *Financial indicators*. These may be cost or revenue figures for a given operating period, e.g. weekly, monthly or annually.
   Examples are:
   (*i*) Sales revenue for Aylesbury branch for January 1993.
   (*ii*) Direct costs for the branch for January 1993.

(b) *Volume indicators*. These cover given time periods.
   Examples are:
   (*i*) Units of product X sold by Aylesbury branch in January 1993.
   (*ii*) Hours billed by the branch last week.
   (*iii*) Number of overtime hours worked last week.

(c) *Productivity indicators*. These are ratios designed to measure efficiency and must be compared with ideal standards of performance.
   Examples are:

   (*i*) $MPG = \dfrac{\text{miles travelled}}{\text{gallons of fuel used}}$

   (*ii*) Manning efficiency $= \dfrac{\text{number of overtime hours worked}}{\text{total number of hours worked}}$

(d) *Cost/Rate indicators*. These are average costs and revenues calculated from the financial and volume indicators and are the most important group of indicators because they provide data to
   (*i*) Calculate the cost of an activity.
   (*ii*) Set selling rates.
   (*iii*) Give warnings of any adverse trends.
   Examples are:

   (1) Wage cost per hour $= \dfrac{\text{Total wage bill}}{\text{Total hours paid}}$

   (2) Revenue per consignment $= \dfrac{\text{Total revenue}}{\text{No of consignments}}$

27. Standards

Realistic, attainable standards of performance must be set in terms of productivity and costs, if the products or services are to compete in the market place and generate a satisfactory profit.

28. Ideal qualities for KPIs

(a) They should be calculated so that they are useful for:
(*i*) Setting business targets.
(*ii*) Monitoring performance against the targets.
(*iii*) Monitoring trends in revenue, costs, productivity.
(b) They should be limited in number.
(*i*) Managers should only use those that measure their span of responsibility.
(*ii*) Too many will reduce focus.
(c) They should be the property of the manager.
(*i*) Imposed data will lack credibility.
(*ii*) Managers should be involved in the generation of KPIs.
(d) They should be shared with subordinates.
(*i*) This helps staff to understand targets and how to achieve them.
(*ii*) Visual representation makes it easier for staff to see how the business is faring.
(e) They should be used with a Dupont chart which will help to clarify the influences on profitability.

29. Dupont charts

Figure 14.10 is an example of a Dupont chart. It provides an effective method of planning and monitoring business activities for profit- and cost-centre managers. Its principal merit is that it forces the manager to analyse and understand the relationships between the many costs, revenues and resources in the business.

For example, suppose the manager of a security alarm business is expected to generate a return on assets figure of 20 per cent. His average assets per week are £4000 and he employs four engineers who make, on average, twenty service calls per week. Each engineer costs £300 per week in payroll, uses a van that costs £150 per week in running costs, and uses on average £15 of components per service call.

The revenue per call is £75 and the overheads on the business are £2500 per week.

The information is now included in a Dupont chart designed to accommodate this data. *See* Figure 14.10.

The result of the first input of the data (indicated by the notation '1'

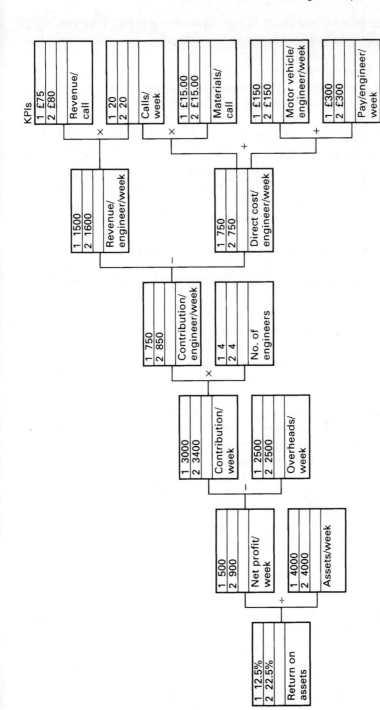

Figure 14.10 *Dupont chart*

in the boxes in the chart) is a profitability rate of 12.5 per cent which is below the required target.

The options available are:

1. Increase the revenue per call.
2. Increase the calls per engineer per week.
3. Increase the number of engineers.
4. Cut some direct costs.
5. Cut some overheads.
6. Cut some assets.

Suppose the revenue is increased to £80 per call. The outcome is shown at level 2 in the boxes. The profitability now exceeds the target of 20 per cent by 2.5 per cent.

Alternatively, if overheads are cut by £300 then the target is achieved.

30. Preparing the format of the budget report

The recommended layout is to use columns to show details of the items of revenues or costs as shown in Table 14B. Useful column headings are:

1. Budget figures for this month.
2. Actual figures for this month.
3. If revenue figures are contained in the budget then express the budget costs as percentages of the budget revenue and actual costs as percentages of actual revenue.
4. Variance figures for the month to show the difference between budget and actual figures. The variance can be expressed as the monetary difference or as a percentage of the budget figure.
5. Year to date budget figures.
6. Year to date actual figures.
7. Year to date variance figures.
8. Forecast performance figures for the next three months calculated on the basis of performance to date.
9. The year end budget figures.
10. Last year end actual figures.

31. Reading your budget report

Recommended steps are:

(a) Look at the bottom line and any total figures of grouped items to see if they match the budget.

(b) Look at the variances to see if they are favourable or unfavourable.

(c) Examine the items with the biggest variances and find out the causes.

Table 14B *Revenue Budget Report for April 1993 (£ 000)*

	Last year Actual	April Budget	%	April Actual	%	Variance	Budget	%	Year to date Actual	%	Variance	Forecast May/July	%	Year end Budget	%
Sales Revenue	1200	80	100	85	100	+5	480	100	490	100	+10	250	100	1300	100
Cost of product	600	40	50	44	52	-4	240	50	250	51	-10	130	52	650	50
Gross Margin	600	40	50	41	48	+1	240	50	240	49	—	120	48	650	50
Promotion etc	200	14	17	18	21	-4	81	17	98	20	-17	44	18	220	17

Cost Centre Budget Report for April 1993 (£ 000)

	Last year Actual	April Budget	April Actual	Variance (i)	Variance (ii)	Year to date Budget	Actual	Variance	Year end Budget
Wages basic	1000	120	125	-5	-4%	80	500	-20	1100
Overtime	200	20	30	-10	-50%	80	100	-20	200
Travel	400	22	20	+2	+9%	90	85	+5	410

Possible variances are:
(i) Expressed as the monetary difference between Budget and Actual.
(ii) Expressed as the variance as % of Budget. (Note that favourable variances are positive, unfavourable are negative.)

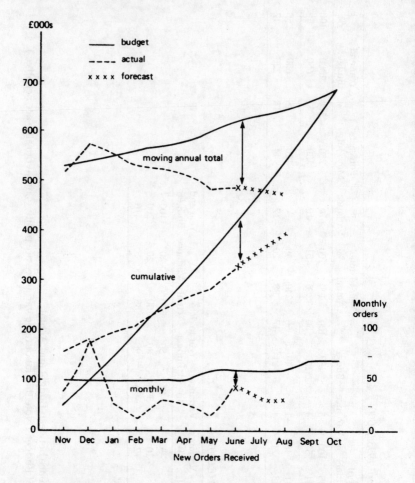

Figure 14.11 *New orders of refrigeration equipment: Z chart*

(d) Repeat this with the next biggest variance and so on.
(e) Remember that cost comparisons as percentages of revenue can be misleading when the cost contains fixed elements.
(f) If the mix of activities has changed, find out why.

32. Actions

(a) Prepare a Z chart (see page 305) or graph to show the trends in the key areas of the budget. A visual representation clarifies relationships and provides a record of actual and budget performance over the year if the graph is updated monthly.

(b) Take the necessary action to bring performance back to budget.

The Z chart

33. Description of the Z chart
There are three curves on this graph forming the letter Z, hence its name. The component curves are:

(a) the individual monthly figures;
(b) the cumulative figures to date;
(c) the moving annual total figures.

The value of the chart. The merit of this chart is that it presents in a visual form the three sets of data and their relationship over a period of time. It has a wide range of application, particularly in the general areas of production, sales and profits which may be expressed in terms of actual, budgeted or forecast performance. At a glance the manager can see how current performance compares against previous periods, against the year's trend or against budget or forecast and whether corrective action is required.

34. Example of the use of the chart
Watford Refrigeration Ltd budgeted for new sales orders for their equipment as shown in column (*i*) below:

Column (*ii*) is the cumulative budget figure from the start of their financial year, 1 November. Column (*iii*) is the moving annual total (MAT) and is the total of new orders budgeted for in the twelve months to date. Thus, for the year ended 30 November this was planned to be £530 000 and for the year ended 31 December, £540 000, and is calculated by subtracting the November figure for the previous year (£40 000) and substituting December for the current year (£50 000). Obviously, the cumulative curve and the moving annual total curve will meet at the year-end point (£680 000).

This information is illustrated in Fig. 14.10, with the actual performance between November and June. In November and December actual orders received exceed budget but thereafter fail to match budget. Performance is disappointing overall: monthly orders are below budget, cumulative are falling behind the planned figures and the moving annual total is falling, indicating that current orders are in fact down on last year. At June a future forecast of orders is made for July and August and indicates to management that immediate action is required if they are to get back to budget. However, the original objectives may now be unobtainable, in which case a 'now-expected forecast' could be made, action taken and monthly performance compared with the new forecast to keep the company on track towards its new objectives.

New Orders of Refrigeration Equipment

| | Budget £000 | | | | Actual and forecast £000 | |
| | (i) | (ii) | | (iii) | (i) | (ii) | (iii) |
	Monthly orders current year	Cumulative	Monthly orders previous year	MAT			
Nov.	50	50	40	530	79	79	520
Dec.	50	100	40	540	92	171	572
Jan.	50	150	40	550	27	198	559
Feb.	50	200	40	560	12	210	531
Mar.	50	250	40	570	31	241	522
Apr.	50	300	40	580	27	268	509
May	60	360	40	600	15	283	484
June	60	420	40	620	45 Forecast	328 Forecast	489 Forecast
July	60	480	50	630	32	360	481
Aug.	60	540	50	640	34	394	475
Sept.	70	610	50	660			
Oct.	70	680	50	680			

Commercial calculations

35. Introduction
Financial decision-making is based on calculations. Sometimes these calculations are based on profit margins and profit mark-ups on costs either in money or percentage terms, and sometimes the calculations are concerned with discounts. This area can cause confusion and the following examples are included to improve understanding.

36. Mark-ups and margins
The mark-up and margins refer to the same money profit figure but:
   Mark-up is based on COST
   Margin is based on SELLING PRICE
   Mark-up and margin percentages are different

(a) To convert mark-up % to margin %
   The margin on Product X is 40%

$$\text{Formula} = \frac{(\text{Margin} \times 100)}{(100 - \text{Margin})} = \frac{(40 \times 100)}{(100 - 40)} = \frac{4000}{60}$$

$$40\% \text{ margin} = 66.7\% \text{ mark up}$$

(b) To convert mark-up % to margin %

The mark-up on Product X is 30%

$$\text{Formula} = \frac{(\text{Mark-up} \times 100)}{(100 + \text{Mark-up})} = \frac{(40 \times 100)}{(100 - 40)} = \frac{4000}{60}$$

$$30\% \text{ mark-up} = 23.1\% \text{ margin}$$

37. Using mark-ups

(a) To calculate the money mark-up

Product X costs £60 and the mark-up is 40%

Mark-up is 40% of cost

$$= 0.40 \times £60$$
$$= £24$$

(b) To calculate the money margin

Product X costs £60 and the mark-up is 40%

The money margin = money mark-up
$$= £24$$

(c) To calculate the selling price

Product X costs £60 and the mark-up is 40%

Selling price is 140% of cost

$$= 1.40 \times £60$$
$$= £84$$

(d) To calculate cost

If the mark-up is 30% and the selling price is £60

The selling price is 130% (1.3) of cost

$$\text{Cost} = \frac{£60}{1.30}$$
$$= £46.15$$

38. Using margins

(a) To calculate the money margin

Product X's selling price is £60 and the margin is 50%

Margin = 50% (0.5) of £60

$$= 0.5 \times £60$$
$$= £30$$

(b) To calculate the cost

Product X's selling price is £80 and the margin is 20%

Cost = Selling price − margin
   = £80 − (0.2 × £80)
   = £80 − £16
   = £64

(c) To calculate the selling price
   Product X costs £30 and the margin is 20%
   Cost = Selling price (100%) − margin (20%)
        = 80% or 0.8 of the Selling price
   Selling price = £30/0.8
                = £37.50

39. Discounts

Some companies offer discounts for prompt payment and it is worth calculating whether to accept the discount or even to offer a discount to debtors. An answer to the problem is to look at the matrix below. If you know your cost of borrowing and how many days early payment need be made to qualify for a discount, then you can read off the percentage discount to accept/reject. For example, if money costs you 12 per cent and you are offered 1 per cent discount if you pay twenty days early, then take it!

| | | | | *Your annual cost of money* | | | | |
No of days earlier	6%	8%	10%	12%	14%	16%	18%	20%
5	0.1	0.1	0.1	0.1	0.2	0.2	0.2	0.3
7	0.1	0.2	0.2	0.2	0.3	0.3	0.3	0.4
10	0.2	0.2	0.3	0.3	0.4	0.4	0.5	0.5
20	0.3	0.4	0.6	0.7	0.8	0.9	1.0	1.1
30	0.5	0.7	0.8	1.0	1.1	1.3	1.5	1.6
60	1.0	1.3	1.6	2.0	2.3	2.6	3.0	3.3
90	1.5	2.0	2.5	3.0	3.4	3.9	4.4	4.9

For sellers: These are the **maximum discounts** you should offer for quick payment or the **minimum premium** you should charge for deferred payment.

For buyers: These are the **minimum discounts** you should demand for quick payment or the **maximum premiums** you should accept for deferred payment.

40. Sales discounts

Often a discount is offered to a customer. However, the salesperson must realise that extra sales volume is needed to cover the discount.

For example, if your current profit margin is 20 per cent and you offer a 10 per cent discount, the sales volume has to increase by 100 per cent in order to generate the same level of profit. Discounts can be dangerous.

Discount/volume relationship

Discount offered	*Current Profit Margin*								
	10%	15%	20%	25%	30%	40%	50%	75%	90%
5%	100	50	33	25	20	14	11	7	6
10%	—	200	100	67	50	33	25	15	13
15%	—	—	300	150	100	60	43	25	20
20%	—	—	—	400	200	100	66	36	29
25%	—	—	—	—	500	166	100	50	39

Progress test 14

1. Compare and contrast the accountant's and economist's approach to break-even curves. **(1–3)**

2. 'Break-even analysis may be usefully employed in the areas of contribution and cash forecasting.' Discuss. **(6–9)**

3. Define marginal pricing and compare with the cost-plus method. **(10–12)**

4. 'Marginal analysis provides a flexible approach to the problem of securing optimum resource allocation but not without dangers.' Comment. **(13–22)**

5. What is the meaning of profit/volume ratio? **(21–22)**

6. Explain what is meant by budgetary control. **(23)**

7. Explain the methods which can help a budget-holder in the preparation of accurate budgets. **(24–30)**

8. What are the three curves which make up the shape of the Z chart? **(33)**

9. Explain how a Z chart can be used to improve the efficiency of an organisation. **(33–34)**

10. Hans Basin is considering the purchase of a guest house. He has details of one which is on the market for £200 000. It has 15 double rooms which are occupied by guests on average 35 weeks a year. Guests pay £25 each per day, and the estimated food cost per person per day is £15. Heat and light cost around £2 per person per day and guests supply £1 per person per day. Overheads are £25 000 p.a. Hans requires a return on investment of 10 per cent before tax.

(a) Prepare a Dupont chart from this information and consider the options.
(b) Suggest some suitable KPIs. **(26–29)**

11. (a) What is the margin percentage if the mark-up is 54 per cent?
(b) What is the mark-up percentage if the margin is 75 per cent? **(36)**

Appendix 1

Examination technique

Examination questions may be classified as follows:

(a) Textbook questions which test your memory of your textbooks and your ability to marshal and organize information. For example, 'Explain the following terms in relation to investment: (*i*) P/E ratio; (*ii*) earnings yield, etc.'

(b) Applied questions which test your knowledge and your ability to apply it to the facts in the question or which test your appreciation of current financial problems and policies. For example, 'Compare and contrast factoring and invoice discounting and their relevance to a firm with a turnover of, say, £75 000 p.a., with average sales values of £500.'

Procedure at the examination

(a) Read all the questions to get the 'feel' of the examination paper and to establish precisely what is required.

(b) Select the questions which you feel you can answer best, bearing in mind your knowledge and ability. Your choice may be limited, as when questions have to be selected from sections within the paper, e.g. 'Answer five questions only: one question must be taken from each part and the fifth question may be taken from any part.' Any such instructions must be followed.

(c) Allocate equal time to each question or apportion time according to the marks carried by each question where indicated. Remember that 'diminishing returns' apply to examination answers; it is comparatively easy to get pass marks but a disproportionate amount of time has to be put in to get very high marks.

(d) Think about each question, jot down the relevant points as they come to mind and shuffle them into a tidy legible plan on the answer paper. Delete it only when you have completed the answer.

(e) Write legibly.

(f) Write your answers in essay form unless you are asked to list points or write a report or letter. Write your answer in short concise sentences without slang or unacceptable abbreviations and try to start paragraphs with 'key sentences'. Finally, check your answer through for inaccuracies.

(g) Do not be politically biased in your answer, and do not waste time attempting to sway the examiner by humour or appeals.

(h) Do not give cross-references between questions; e.g. 'I have already explained this in my answer to question 3'.

(i) You are attempting to impress the examiner and should appear widely read, so give frequent examples. Also, answers may be improved by the use of economic concepts, e.g. elasticity and long- and short-run comparisons.

(j) Do not panic.

Appendix 2

Present value of £1

No. of years
before   Discount rate
receipt

receipt	1%	2%	4%	6%	8%	10%	12%	14%	15%	16%	18%
1	0.990	0.980	0.962	0.943	0.926	0.909	0.893	0.877	0.870	0.862	0.847
2	0.980	0.961	0.925	0.890	0.857	0.826	0.797	0.769	0.756	0.743	0.718
3	0.971	0.942	0.889	0.840	0.794	0.751	0.712	0.675	0.658	0.641	0.609
4	0.961	0.924	0.855	0.792	0.735	0.683	0.636	0.592	0.572	0.552	0.516
5	0.951	0.906	0.822	0.747	0.681	0.621	0.567	0.519	0.497	0.476	0.437
6	0.942	0.888	0.790	0.705	0.630	0.564	0.507	0.456	0.432	0.410	0.370
7	0.933	0.871	0.760	0.665	0.583	0.513	0.452	0.400	0.376	0.354	0.314
8	0.923	0.853	0.731	0.627	0.540	0.467	0.404	0.351	0.327	0.305	0.266
9	0.914	0.837	0.703	0.592	0.500	0.424	0.361	0.308	0.284	0.263	0.225
10	0.905	0.820	0.676	0.588	0.463	0.386	0.322	0.270	0.247	0.227	0.191
11	0.896	0.804	0.650	0.527	0.429	0.350	0.287	0.237	0.215	0.195	0.162
12	0.887	0.788	0.625	0.497	0.397	0.319	0.257	0.208	0.187	0.168	0.137
13	0.879	0.773	0.601	0.469	0.368	0.290	0.229	0.182	0.163	0.145	0.116
14	0.870	0.758	0.577	0.442	0.340	0.263	0.205	0.160	0.141	0.125	0.099
15	0.861	0.743	0.555	0.417	0.315	0.239	0.183	0.140	0.123	0.108	0.084

No. of years
before   Discount rate
receipt

receipt	20%	22%	24%	25%	26%	28%	30%	35%	40%	45%	50%
1	0.833	0.820	0.806	0.800	0.794	0.781	0.769	0.741	0.714	0.690	0.667
2	0.694	0.672	0.650	0.640	0.630	0.610	0.592	0.549	0.510	0.476	0.444
3	0.579	0.551	0.524	0.512	0.500	0.477	0.455	0.406	0.364	0.328	0.296
4	0.482	0.451	0.423	0.410	0.397	0.373	0.350	0.301	0.260	0.226	0.198
5	0.402	0.370	0.341	0.328	0.315	0.291	0.269	0.223	0.186	0.156	0.132
6	0.335	0.303	0.275	0.262	0.250	0.227	0.207	0.165	0.133	0.108	0.088
7	0.279	0.249	0.222	0.210	0.198	0.178	0.159	0.122	0.095	0.074	0.059
8	0.233	0.204	0.179	0.168	0.157	0.139	0.123	0.091	0.068	0.051	0.039
9	0.194	0.167	0.144	0.134	0.125	0.108	0.094	0.067	0.048	0.035	0.026
10	0.162	0.137	0.116	0.107	0.099	0.085	0.073	0.050	0.035	0.024	0.017
11	0.135	0.112	0.094	0.086	0.079	0.066	0.056	0.037	0.025	0.017	0.012
12	0.112	0.092	0.076	0.069	0.062	0.052	0.043	0.027	0.018	0.012	0.008
13	0.093	0.075	0.061	0.055	0.050	0.040	0.033	0.020	0.013	0.008	0.005
14	0.078	0.062	0.049	0.044	0.039	0.032	0.025	0.015	0.009	0.006	0.003
15	0.065	0.051	0.040	0.035	0.031	0.025	0.020	0.011	0.006	0.004	0.002

Glossary of financial terms

absorption costing the system whereby fixed costs as well as variable costs are absorbed into the cost of the goods or service.

accounts payable company creditors.

accounts receivable company debtors.

acid test see *quick ratio*.

ACT. Advance Corporation Tax that part of a company's tax that is paid early, i.e. when it pays a dividend.

activity the sales produced by a given amount of assets (Capital Turnover Ratio). A measurement of efficiency of asset utilisation in a company.

allocation of overheads the charging of the whole overhead to the appropriate cost centre or unit incurring the expense.

apportioning of overheads where overheads cannot be allocated they are apportioned or shared by cost centres or units on an equitable basis.

Articles of Association the internal rules and regulations of a company that stipulate the rights and duties of shareholders and directors and procedures for meetings.

assets expenditure to acquire a long- or short-term item of value as opposed to expenditure incurred in the process of earning income; anything of value held by a business.

asset turnover the ratio of sales to assets, i.e. the number of times that assets are utilized in a year.

associated company a company that has more than 20 per cent (and less than 50 per cent) of its shares owned by another company.

bear an investor who believes that prices of securities will fall.

blue chip an ordinary share of highest investment status.

bonus issue the free issue of shares to existing ordinary shareholders on a proportionate basis, paid for out of the built-up undistributed profits of the business.

book value the value of an asset as shown in the Balance Sheet; usually cost less total depreciation to date.

break-up value/ordinary share the residual value of net assets accruing to each ordinary share if the company went into liquidation.

bull   an investor who believes that the price of securities will rise.

capital employed   the total of the shareholders' funds, loan capital and any other long-term sources of funds; generally, intangible and fictitious assets, are excluded.

capital reserve   a reserve that does not arise from retention of trading profits, e.g. share premium, capital redemption reserve fund. Since the Companies Act 1967, Balance Sheets need not distinguish between capital and revenue reserves.

cash flow   the amount of cash generated in a financial period. The difference between total cash receipts from all sources and total cash payments.

circulating assets   'current assets,' the most liquid of assets that will be converted into cash within the short term, e.g. stocks, debtors.

close company   a company controlled by five or fewer shareholders.

collateral security   any security offered in support of a debt.

Consolidated Balance Sheet   the Balance Sheet showing the financial state of affairs of a group of companies.

contingent liabilities   a possible liability rather than one of a definite nature, shown as a note to the Balance Sheet, e.g. the contingent liability arising from a contract agreed but not yet executed.

contribution   the difference between sales value and variable costs expressed in absolute terms or as a contribution per unit.

convertible loan stock   loan stock that may be converted into ordinary shares at predetermined time and price.

cost centre   a location, function or item of equipment in respect of which costs may be ascertained and related to cost units for control purposes.

cost unit   a cost unit of quantity of output or service.

coupon   the stated rate of interest on a loan security.

cumulative preference shares   preference shares where any arrears of dividend are paid prior to other shareholders.

current assets   assets of a short-term nature that change from day to day, being part of the cycle leading to cash, e.g. stock, debtors, cash.

current liabilities   the claims that must be paid within the short term, e.g. dividends and tax payable and creditors.

current ratio   a measure of solvency, i.e. current assets to current liabilities. A test of liquidity: 2 is the norm.

current taxation   company corporation tax that is to be paid within the year.

current yield   the dividend expressed as a percentage of the current price of the security.

debenture a certificate issued under seal by a company acknowledging a debt.

deferred liabilities a subdivision of long-term liabilities, e.g. tax payable next year and not of a fund-raising nature such as debentures.

deferred taxation corporation tax payable by a company in the longer term, i.e. not within one year.

depreciation the reduction in value of an asset due to obsolescence, wear and tear or the passing of time.

directors' emoluments payments to directors for services in this capacity.

discounted cash flow the present value of future cash inflows and outflows.

dividend profits paid to shareholders expressed as a percentage of the nominal value of their shares.

dividend cover earnings per share divided by dividend per share, i.e. the number of times that earnings cover the declared dividend.

dividend yield see *current yield*.

earnings per share the post-tax profits figures available for the ordinary shareholders divided by the number of shares.

earnings yield this measure how much investors could get at current earnings if they invested £100 in the company's shares at their current price, i.e. earnings per share divided by current market price.

EBIT. Earnings before interest charges and taxation used as a measure of managers' performance when financing arrangements and tax are beyond their control.

equity owners' funds made up of share capital and retained profits.

fictitious assets these items appear on the Balance Sheet because they have not been written off against the profits of the business, e.g. long-term advertising expenditures, which is written off over the expected period of benefit from the expenditure.

first in first out (FIFO) a basis for costing the material content of a job on the basis that the oldest stocks are used first.

fixed assets assets of a long-term nature held for the purpose of earning profits, e.g. machinery, land and buildings. The nature of the business determines whether an asset in a particular case is fixed or current, e.g. normally a motor vehicle would be a fixed asset, whereas in a vehicle-selling firm, the vehicles held at any one time would be more of the nature of stock and are, therefore, current assets.

fixed overheads expenses that do not vary with output.

free depreciation whereby a company can write off the cost of fixed assets how it wishes.

funds statement 'flow of funds statement' or 'sources and uses of funds statement' that shows the sources of new funds and the uses to which they are put.

gearing the relationship between the loan capital, preference capital and ordinary capital of a business. A high-geared company is one where the prior charges, i.e. loan and preference capital are high in relation to the ordinary capital. The reverse is described as low-geared.

goodwill the net value of a business after the deduction of tangible assets; also the excess of the purchase price over the value of the net assets of a purchased company. (An intangible asset.)

historical cost the original cost of assets.

holding company a company that owns the share capital of other companies.

insolvency inability to meet debts.

intangible assets an intangible asset is not physical, yet has long-term value to the business, e.g. goodwill, patent, trademarks.

introduction a method of issuing shares onto the stock exchange.

inventory stocks in hand.

job cost a cost unit consisting of a single job or contract.

k = kilo = 1000.

last in first out (LIFO) a basis for costing the material content of a job on the basis that the newest stocks are used first.

leverage see *gearing*.

liabilities amounts that a business owes to shareholders and outsiders. These may include debts of either a short-term or long-term nature.

limited liability company a company limited by shares or guarantee is one where members are responsible only to the extent of their share capital or guarantee in the event of liquidation.

liquid assets current assets minus stocks, stocks being the least-liquid current asset.

long-term liabilities long-term debts as opposed to capital, e.g. debenture or loan stock.

margin gross margin is the gross profit expressed as a percentage of sales revenue; similarly, the net margin is net profit as a percentage of sales revenue.

marginal cost the cost of producing one extra unit = variable cost.

marginal revenue the revenue from one extra sale.

margin of safety the excess of sales over the break-even volume.

market capitalisation the total value of a quoted company's shares, i.e. the number of shares multiplied by the market price of a share.

market value of a share the market value has no meaning in Balance Sheet terms, merely representing the price which a share will realize if sold at any particular point in time.

Memorandum of Association the constitution of the company, enabling outsiders to assess its structure and powers.

minority interests these represent the capital and build-up reserves of a group of companies owned by shareholders outside the group.

net assets the total of the fixed and current assets less the current liabilities of the business.

net current assets see *working capital*.

net worth the 'equity' of a business representing the total ordinary share capital made up of paid-up ordinary share capital and reserves owned by the ordinary shareholders.

opportunity cost the cost of a lost opportunity, e.g. the cost of running a car should include the interest that could be earned if the capital is invested instead of being locked up in the car.

ordinary shareholders' funds the total of issued ordinary share capital plus the total of the revenue and capital reserves.

ordinary shares the part of the share capital subscribed for by shareholders not entitled to a fixed rate of dividend and not entitled to any preference for repayment of capital in the event of the winding up of the company.

overtrading this is the situation where a firm is operating at a level of activity that cannot be financed by its available funds and may lead to insolvency unless more capital is introduced.

paid-up capital a 'fully-paid' share is one where the nominal value has been fully subscribed; whereas a share of, say, nominal value of £1, if only 50p has been subscribed per share, is described as 'partly paid'.

par value when issued 'at par' the issue price is equal to the nominal value. When issued at a 'premium' the issue price is in excess of the nominal value, and when at a 'discount', below the nominal value.

ploughed-back profits profits retained in the business.

preference shares that part of the share capital preferred to the remainder of the ordinary share capital for the payment of dividend and/or for the repayment of capital on a winding up.

price earnings (P/E) current market price of the share divided by the last reported earnings attributable to the share.

prime costs the total of direct materials, labour and expenses.

private company a company whose Articles of Association restrict the transfer of its shares, limit its members to fifty and prohibit public advertisements for capital.

profit/volume ratio (P/V) the rate at which profits change with a change in output.

provision a charge against profit that provides for the reduction in value of an asset or a liability whose value is uncertain, e.g. provision for depreciation, provision for doubtful debt.

public company a company that is not a private company.

quick assets see *liquid assets*.

quick ratio the ratio of liquid assets to current liabilities. A test of liquidity: 1 is the norm.

reserves these represent the build-up of undistributed profits and consist either of revenue or of capital reserves.

retained profits see *ploughed-back profits*.

revenue reserves these trading profits are distributable as dividend to the shareholders whereas capital reserves may only be distributed to shareholders in a restricted manner, i.e. basically by the issue of fully-paid bonus shares.

rights issue an issue of shares for cash to existing holders of share capital in the company. Normally the issue is at a price lower than the current market price, acting as an inducement to existing holders to take up the shares.

ROCE return on capital employed.

RONTA return on net trading assets.

share capital the amount raised from the shareholders of the business.

shareholders' funds the total of ordinary and preference issued capital plus the total of the revenue and capital reserves.

share premium a capital reserve owned by the shareholders arising when a company issues shares at a price in excess of the nominal value.

source and uses of funds see *funds statement*.

standard cost a predetermined cost, i.e. what it ought to cost to produce something.

standard hour a hypothetical hour that measures the amount of work that ought to be carried out in the hour.

stock turnover ratio of cost of sales to stocks. This measures the number of times stocks are turned over in the course of a year.

tangible asset a physical asset.

times interest earned the number of times that loan interest is covered by profits, i.e. earnings (profits) before tax and interest divided by the interest charge. It indicates how safe creditors' interest charges are.

trading on the equity whereby a company takes advantage of high gearing, paying a modest fixed interest charge for funds that are employed to earn a higher return for the ordinary shareholders.

turnover (assets) the number of times that total assets are turned over to generate sales revenue, i.e. the ratio of sales to assets.

turnover (sales) the total value of sales.

variable overheads indirect expenses that vary directly with output, e.g. power.

variances the difference between a budgeted performance and the actual performance achieved.

wasting assets assets of a fixed nature, but as they are being used by the business are physically diminishing in size, e.g. a mine.

working capital the total of the current assets less the current liabilities.

work in progress semi-finished goods.

yield the rate of return on an investment.

Index